Volume 2:
FOREST of DEAN LINES
and the
SEVERN BRIDGE

G.W. AND L.M.S RLY C.OS
SEVERN AND WYE JOINT RAILWAY

On 11th October 1965, ex-GWR '57XX' Class 0-6-0PT No. 3675 trundles along the Whimsey Branch as it makes its way to Bilson Junction, with a train comprised of a single Berry Wiggins tank and a single South Eastern Gas Board tank, both of which will have delivered bitumen to the Berry Wiggins depot at Whimsey. Behind the brake van is Broadmoor Brickworks, established in 1922 on the site of Duck Colliery by the Lydney & Crump Meadow Collieries Company. Although Crump Meadow Colliery ceased production in 1929, the brickworks continued and, indeed, were extended and modernised with the provision of new plant. After 1929, coal was delivered by rail from the company's other colliery, Arthur & Edward at Lydbrook. However, the rail service to the brickworks had ceased by the date of this picture. The train is just passing over a gated crossing, where the old route from the town to Cinderford's first station had crossed over the line. This utilised 'The Dam', an embankment constructed to hold back water used by the King's Furnace at Soudley, on which were later laid the rails of the Forest of Dean Tramroad, on its way up to Churchway. The mounds seen in the centre of the picture, to the left of the brickworks, are waste from Duck Colliery, which closed circa 1920; some of its buildings were reused by the brickworks. Amongst the trees in the left centre background is Hawkwell Row, a terrace of cottages built for workers at Hawkwell Colliery; the colliery closed in around 1893 – its shafts were later reopened to ventilate Northern United and to provide a second way out from that pit – but the cottages still survive today. Bill Potter/KRM

Previous Page: A view north along the Severn & Wye main line towards Tufts Junction on 24th June 1961. The bracket signal in the foreground has two goods only arms for the Oakwood Branch to Princess Royal Colliery, whilst the larger arm on the right is for the main line. Tufts Junction Signal Box can be seen in the centre distance, whilst the bracket signal just beyond it has a small arm on the right for the junction for the remaining stub of the S&W Mineral Loop, which ran as far as Pillowell Drift mine. Under the terms of the 1894 Joint Line agreement, the Midland Railway had responsibility for signalling between Lydney Junction and Coleford Junction; the signals seen here were all provided by the MR but were controlled from a GWR box built in 1897. Derek Chaplin

Volume 2:
FOREST of DEAN LINES
and the
SEVERN BRIDGE

NEIL PARKHOUSE

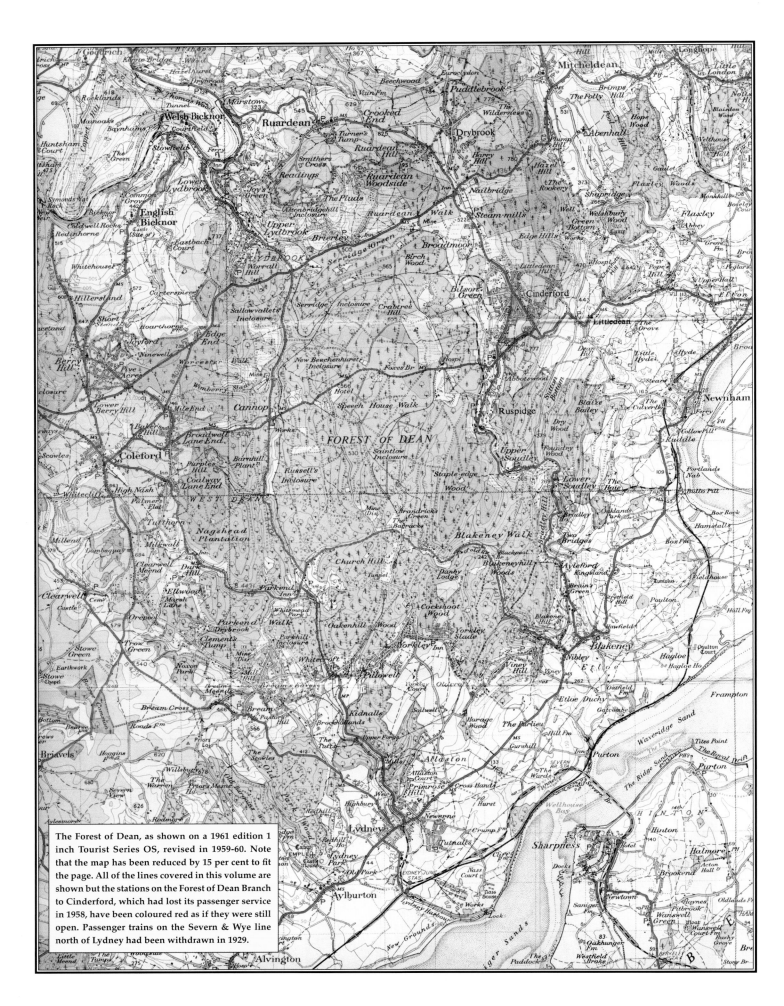

The Forest of Dean, as shown on a 1961 edition 1 inch Tourist Series OS, revised in 1959-60. Note that the map has been reduced by 15 per cent to fit the page. All of the lines covered in this volume are shown but the stations on the Forest of Dean Branch to Cinderford, which had lost its passenger service in 1958, have been coloured red as if they were still open. Passenger trains on the Severn & Wye line north of Lydney had been withdrawn in 1929.

CONTENTS

Published by LIGHTMOOR PRESS

© Lightmoor Press & Neil Parkhouse 2015
Designed by Neil Parkhouse

British Library Cataloguing-in-Publication Data. A catalogue record for this book is available from the British Library

ISBN 13: 9781899889 98 3

BLACK DWARF LIGHTMOOR PUBLICATIONS LTD
Unit 144B, Lydney Trading Estate, Harbour Road, Lydney, Gloucestershire GL15 5EJ
www.lightmoor.co.uk
info@lightmoor.co.uk

Lightmoor Press is an imprint of Black Dwarf Lightmoor Publications Ltd

Printed in Poland
www.lfbookservices.co.uk

The Forest of Dean has a long industrial past and it was this industry, principally coal and iron, which stimulated the construction of, first, tramroads and then railways in the area. By the early 1960s, however, the writing was on the wall for the last vestiges of Dean's deep mined coal industry, as the economics of keeping the mines pumped dry to win the coal finally brought about their closure. New Fancy Colliery, near Parkend, had closed in 1944; these are the tips at New Fancy, as seen from Staple Edge in 1962. ANNE BEAUFOY

With all regular passenger services in the Forest having ceased by late 1958, the occasional rail tours traversing the remaining lines were well supported and well photographed. This is the Stephenson Locomotive Society's (Midland Area) Severn & Wye District Tour of 13th May 1961, passing Fetterhill and the George Inn on its way back down the Coleford Branch, which had lost its passenger trains in 1929. Sandwiched between the auto trailers is auto-fitted '64XX' Class No. 6437, whilst on the Coleford end of the train is '57XX' Class 0-6-0PT No. 8701. The scene is classic Forest of Dean, from the scrub on the hillside to the trees above, with the scattered housing, grazing pigs in the foreground, the ramshackle buildings of Fetterhill Stoneworks at bottom right and the general evidence all round of industrial enterprise – an abandoned head frame, a wooden derrick for lifting stone and several semi-derelict lorries. The stoneworks had once been rail connected, with the formation of the line which served it running down from right to left. ALAN JARVIS

LEFT: No. 1642 edges its way along the Down platform as it hauls the empty coaching stock over the crossover just past the signal box and back into the station. These excursions normally used pre-Nationalisation stock and this is the only special from Parkend that the photographer is aware of that used BR Mk 1 coaches. On one occasion, the train sent was made up to ten coaches and had to be hauled all the way to Travellers Rest for the locomotive to run round using the crossover there. The whole operation had to be repeated when the train returned in fading light at around 8.45pm. COLEFORD GWR MUSEUM (MIKE REES)

BELOW: To enable the tail end of the train to clear the level crossing whilst everyone clambered aboard, the first four coaches were beyond the end of the platform, so passengers had to walk through the corridor connections. The engine, meanwhile, was well in advance of the Up Starter signal, which is already in the 'off' position. No. 1642 took the train as far as Lydney Town, where it was taken over by a Class '43XX' 2-6-0 off Lydney shed, which engines were not permitted north of Town station. COLEFORD GWR MUSEUM (MIKE REES)

BELOW: Driver Vic Rees slows the excursion at Tufts Junction, in order that his fireman can take the Lydney Town token from the signalman. At Lydney, having changed engine, the train ran non-stop through the platforms at Lydney Junction (S&W) and up on to the Severn Bridge line. As a result, it was destined to become the last excursion over the bridge, which was damaged in an accident just a few weeks later and never reopened. After passing Sharpness, the train ran via Berkeley South Junction and then probably followed the old Midland route all the way to Mangotsfield, where it would have turned west to head through Bristol Temple Meads and on to Weston-super-Mare. COLEFORD GWR MUSEUM (MIKE REES)

The Dilke Memorial Hospital was opened in 1923, in memory of the popular local MP Sir Charles Dilke. It was paid for by donations from local businesses and individuals, and by Forest of Dean coal miners donating a penny a week from their wages. Situated a little way up the Speech House Road from Ruspidge Halt, it was bordered on its western side (to the left here) by the Severn & Wye Mineral Loop line and faced Lightmoor Colliery. The original part of the hospital is pictured here on 2nd June 1962, in the sylvan surroundings which it still enjoys to this day. The closure of its maternity unit in 1988 caused much controversy locally, as it affected the law pertaining to free mining rights. ANNE BEAUFOY

The Forest of Dean of the 21st century is a very different region to that shown in these pictures, although, in a few places, there remain landscapes and communities that some of those who documented its social history and customs over the years, such as Winifred Foley in the 1920s and '30s and Dennis Potter in the 1950s and '60s, would still recognise. In many respects too, it is still a land apart, the secret bit of Gloucestershire, bordered as it as by the River Severn to the east and the River Wye to the north and west. This almost makes it an island and that is very much how the area still feels at times. The Forest accent and dialect still survives, as does the inherent reticence with outsiders. This is not unfriendliness. This is their place and Foresters expect you to get to know them and their ways, not the other way around. But make a friend of a Forester and you will have made a friend for life.

This sense of the Forest as a separate place, on and of its own, comes through in these pictures. The scenery is stunning and the railways traversed much of it, which made it quite difficult not to take a good picture. The heavy industry – quarries, deep coal mines and ironworks – were largely hidden in the trees and in the various valleys, so whilst it has marked and shaped the landscape in places, it never dominated it. Now, the few remains provide little in the way of clues as to what took place here in decades past. The industry also shaped the communities that grew around it, where they were established and how. In the 19th century, much of the Forest of Dean was settled by encroachment by 'squatters', a term which has far worse connotations now than it did back then. It is also a term in which many old Foresters take a certain obtuse pride, because it implies a thumbed nose to authority and convention. And it makes them smile when newcomers wonder out loud why it is that they cannot trace their house deeds back beyond the first couple of decades of the 19th century.

Briefly, during the first decades of the 19th century, as the Forest became more industrialised, the colliery owners and ironmasters needed ever more workers. With nowhere available for them to line, most simply encroached on or took over small piece of land – legend has it that if a chimney was erected and smoke rising from the hearth beneath it by nightfall, then that piece of property was theirs. The Forest of Dean is Crown land, so it might be supposed that this would not just have been heavily frowned upon but completely discouraged. However, the Crown benefitted greatly from the exploitation of the 'gales', the mineral rights beneath their land, so they effectively turned a blind eye until the situation was regularised in the 1830s, whilst it was only towards the end of the 19th century that many owners legalised their properties by having proper deeds drawn up. Unsurprisingly, the communities which grew up in this manner tended to be haphazard and scattered, and despite more modern infill building, this is still a feature of the Forest landscape today.

As are the 'ships'. Foresters hold two fiercely and jealously guarded

rights: the right to free mine coal, of which more shortly, and the right to common pasture. In times past, most Foresters kept a pig at the bottom of the garden, to fatten up and butcher when ready. Many also kept sheep or 'ships' in Forest dialect, which were allowed to roam and graze. Referred to as 'commoners', their right to keep sheep and allow them to graze at will in the Forest have become law almost by default and is still a point of argument today, as originally sheep were considered 'uncommonable' because they affected the habitat of the King's deer. It is the reason why 'ships' feature in many of these pictures and despite the loss of the entire Forest of Dean sheep population in the Foot & Mouth outbreak of 2001, it is a tradition that is still enthusiastically carried on today, with new flocks having been brought in.

Free miners' rights are also enshrined in law. Completing a year and a day underground in a Forest coal mine allowed a miner to claim free mining rights. Traditionally, such a person had to be born within the Forest boundaries – the Hundred of St. Briavels – as well. However, the closure of the maternity unit at the Dilke Hospital, near Cinderford, has meant that this aspect is today generally ignored, whilst a recent court ruling now allows females to claim the same rights. So what can a free miner do? Essentially, it allows that person to mine for coal within the Forest of Dean for their own benefit and only a free miner can claim a 'gale' – a defined area underground which can be rented from the Crown. Additionally, the 1904 Dean Forest Mines Act provided for the formation of the deep gales, which were leased to the larger colliery concerns through the Committee of Free Miners. They paid an annual royalty based on the amount of coal raised, which was divided amongst the free miners every year at the Gale Dinner at the Speech House. The deep mined coal pits gradually closed, victims of poor seams and heavy water incursion (necessitating constant costly pumping), the last few going in the late 1950s and early 1960s. Vast reserves of coal still lie beneath the Forest and open cast mining was carried out in a couple of places but the damage caused to the landscape means that this method is unlikely to be permitted again. So a handful of hardy and obstinate souls carry on the tradition of free mining, against a backdrop of falling coal use and ever heavier Government legislation.

Through the medium of colour photography, still something of a novelty and a relatively expensive hobby in the late 1950s/early 1960s, we can give a flavour of the old industrial Forest of Dean as it existed for well over a hundred years. As with everywhere else in the world, the spread of the internet, mobile phones and social media, coupled with the invasion by multi-national corporations which would like us all to dress the same, eat the same food and drink the same drinks, drive the same cars and watch the same films and television programmes, has anodised the Forest to a certain extent. As newcomers arrive – and yes I am one too! – the dilution continues further. But I like to think that the process will never quite be completed. That the certain something that is the essential Forest of Dean will always survive.

And yes, I do love it here.   *Neil Parkhouse, Lydney, 2015*

A HISTORY of RAILTOURS in the FOREST of DEAN

For many enthusiasts, whilst railtours were (and still are) a golden opportunity to ride along obscure lines, they are not considered as 'proper' trains and many railway books try to avoid them, to concentrate on service or working trains, which is what the railway was all about on a day to day basis. Railtour pictures also tend to show enthusiasts swarming over everything, which is a much less satisfactory state of affairs than being able to record the scene with nobody else around. However, this situation is now changing, the history of railtours becoming an important area of study. A major factor in this has been the establishment of the extremely detailed Six Bells Junction website, which is attempting to compile a complete record of railtours; the earliest trip listed took place in 1841 and the site comes right up to date. Much that was photographed on these tours was not otherwise recorded and some did take care to exclude as many of their fellow tour participants from the picture as possible. When dealing with an area like the Forest of Dean, in which the passenger services on the two principle lines ceased in 1929 and 1958 respectively, the opportunity to photograph a locomotive and carriages anywhere in colour was thus limited almost entirely to tours. Indeed, some of the locations and sites featured within these pages would not otherwise have been photographed in colour.

We are fortunate that the Forest proved a popular destination for enthusiasts' railtours and as they feature so heavily within these pages, it would perhaps be pertinent here to provide an historical overview of those that were run. The first known took place on 22nd July 1950, organised by the Birmingham Locomotive Club and ran from Birmingham Moor Street to Coleford, via Stratford, Gloucester, Sharpness and Parkend, using an ex-GWR railcar. The return journey was made via Cinderford, Lydbrook Junction, Ross on Wye, Hereford, Worcester and Cradley, so the route took in the whole of the S&W system. It was clearly a popular tour because it was re-run on 23rd September 1950, following the exact same route apart from at the very end, where instead of heading back to Moor Street, the trip returned to Snow Hill via Cradley Junction. The railcar used on this occasion is known to have been No. W7W. A colour *ciné* film was made of the

trip and a still from this, showing the railcar at Coleford S&W station, has been produced as a slide by Colour-Rail (see page 256).

Less than a year later, on 2nd June 1951, by which date it had been repainted in BR carmine and cream livery, No. W7W made another visit to Coleford. The Wye Valley Railtour was organised by Gloucestershire Railway Society (GRS) and is believed to have travelled via Lydbrook Junction, Serridge Junction and Coleford Junction to reach Coleford; the rest of its route is not known. The journey back out of the Forest is recorded in a painting by the artist Rob Rowland, showing the railcar crossing Lydbrook Viaduct, which resides in the Dean Forest Railway's museum at Norchard.

On 17th May 1952, a further GRS tour traversed the Severn Bridge, on its way from Gloucester Eastgate to Gloucester Central via the Stroud area, Berkeley Road and Lydney. However, the next tour to actually penetrate the Forest was not until 15th April 1956, when the Railway Enthusiasts Club (REC) ran the Severn Venturer, hauled by Class '16XX' 0-6-0PT No. 1625. This operated from Swindon to Serridge Junction, running via Yate (for the Thornbury Branch), Berkeley Road, Lydney and Parkend. At Serridge, it actually reversed up onto the start of the Lydbrook Branch, the last passenger train to venture onto any part of that line. The return crossed back over the Severn Bridge and then ran north from Berkeley Road to visit the Dursley, Stroud (Wallbridge) and Nailsworth branches. This trip was run in connection with a Paddington to Swindon tour, in order that enthusiasts from the London area could travel on it as well.

On 20th April 1958, the REC-organised Severn Rambler tour, from Windsor & Eton Central to Cheltenham St. James, ran in to the Forest at Bullo Junction, having first called at several locations in Gloucester. The tour reached Northern United Colliery at the end of the Churchway Branch but did not call at Cinderford. Having retraced its steps, the Severn & Wye line was then accessed at Otterspool Junction, Lydney, the trip then running all the way up to Coleford. Finally, Sudbrook was visited before the journey back to Windsor was made via Severn Tunnel Junction and the tunnel itself. Motive power on the Forest lines was provided by auto-fitted 0-6-0PT No. 5417, hauling two auto trailers.

A lovely panorama of Bilson Junction, with the SLS tour of 13th May 1961 in the yard. DEREK CHAPLIN

There was then a three year hiatus on tours into the Forest, although mention should first be made of the Ian Allan organised Severn & Wessex Express of 14th May 1960. This travelled from Paddington to Severn Tunnel Junction, where No. 6000 *King George V* was replaced by 'Mogul' No. 6384 for the next leg to Bath Green Park, which ran via Lydney Junction, the Severn Bridge and Berkeley South Junction. The Severn & Wye District tour, organised by the Midland Area Branch of the Stephenson Locomotive Society (SLS), ran on 13th May 1961. This heavily photographed afternoon trip benefitted from glorious weather, auto-fitted pannier tank locomotive No. 6437 in BR lined green passenger livery and three auto trailers. Starting from Gloucester Central, Northern United, Whimsey and Cinderford were visited, before the train made its way from Bullo to Lydney to travel the S&W line. Here, the ensemble then ran first to Coleford Junction, where '57XX' Class No. 8701 was attached to provide additional power on the climb up to Coleford. On returning to Coleford Junction, both locomotives then took the train to the limit of track at Serridge Junction, becoming the last train to reach here. No. 8701, which was presumably sub-shedded at Lydney at this period, was detached at Coleford Junction on the way back down.

The GRS ran another trip on 23rd June 1962, simply called the Forest of Dean Railtour and comprised of No. 6424 with two auto trailers. This is the trip seen in the first volume at Newent and Dymock, this line being the first port of call out from Gloucester. The Forest of Dean Branch was visited next but to Cinderford station only, followed by the S&W lines to Coleford and Speech House Road, which was by then the northern limit of track. This was another afternoon tour.

We now come to the two trips the full details of which have proved the most difficult to unearth, the Severn Bore/Boar railtours of 6th and 20th June 1964, organised by the REC. Firstly, the name – was it Bore or Boar? The clipping advertising the trip, ABOVE RIGHT, is from the May 1964 issue of *Railway World* and it clearly states that it was called 'The Severn Bore'. This makes sense, as it reflected the name of the twice daily tidal wave or 'bore' which sweeps up the River Severn from its mouth near Chepstow to Gloucester and beyond. In the event, the tickets carried the name of the trip as the Severn Boar but it is my belief that this was simply an error on the part of the printer of the tickets. However, as the cover of the tour brochure, RIGHT, indicates, the REC decided to 'go with the flow' so to speak and stuck with the re-spelt name. We do have wild boar in the Forest of Dean now but we didn't back in 1964, so that name makes no

THE SEVERN BOAR RAILTOUR 6TH JUNE 1964		
LOCATION	BOOKED ARR.	TIMINGS DEP.
Gloucester Central		09.55am
Cinderford Town	11.00am	11.10am
Bilson	11.15am	11.25am
Northern United Sidings	11.35am	11.45am
Bilson	12.00am	12.10am
Cinderford Whimsey	12.15am	12.25am
Bullo Pill	12.55am	1.10pm
Lydney Junction	1.25pm	1.40pm
Coleford Junction	2.10pm	2.20pm
Milkwall Station	2.37pm	2.42pm
Coleford GW Station	2.52pm	2.57pm
Whitecliff Quarry	3.02pm	3.15pm
Coleford S&W Station	3.25pm	3.30pm
Speech House Road	4.15pm	4.25pm
Princes Royal Sidings	5.15pm	5.25pm
Severn Bridge Station	5.50pm	6.00pm
Lydney Yard	6.10pm	6.15pm
Lydney Junction	6.20pm	6.30pm
Gloucester Central	7.00pm	

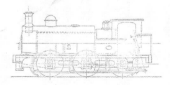

The Severn Boar
Rail Tour
6th June 1964

The Railway Enthusiasts' Club of
Farnborough Hampshire.

The brochure cover for the first tour. IAN POPE COLLECTION

sense really other than as an error. The trip was so popular that, before it even ran, plans had been made to run it for a second time, a fortnight later. This trip was not advertised in the railway press but apparently a flyer for it was handed out on the first trip and the tickets termed it the the Severn Boar II. I have thus used the Severn Boar and the Severn Boar II to describe the respective tours in the captions within these pages.

The other important issue to get to the bottom of has been the motive power that was used. The Six Bells Junction website identifies No. 1664 and another Class '16XX' for 6th June, with No's 1664 and 1658 supplied for the second run on 20th June. In addition, there is a note from a correspondent that the unidentified engine 'ran hot' at some stage during the day, so No. 1664 carried on on its own. The weather also differed markedly for the two trips, 6th June being wet, chilly and overcast, whilst 20th June was warm and sunny.

I then realised that one of the slides I had acquired of the tour double-headed at Coleford Junction was different from the others. The weather appears damp and overcast and the locomotives are identified on the mount as No's 1664 and 1639. This appeared to fill in the missing piece of the jigsaw as to the identity of the other engine but I still needed confirmation. This finally arrived in the form of a description of the tour by a Mr R.W. Mason that appeared in the REC's newsletter shortly after the running of both trips, which clearly identifies No. 1639 as the missing engine and also as having failed at Coleford Junction with a 'hot box'. This description, the booked timings for which are reproduced LEFT, contains much useful additional information and comment, so it is presented here in full:

'*Saturday 6th June dawned very wet and miserable but nevertheless it was not enough to dampen the spirits of 75 REC and other Society members who were to travel on the REC rail tour in the Forest of Dean.*

The train consisting of 6 brake vans hauled by a 16xx tank loco duly departed from the main line platform at Gloucester Central to the astonishment of a number of passengers waiting for Cardiff who must have thought that Dr Beeching was trying another economy measure and using vans as a substitute for coaching stock. The departure was about 10 minutes late due to difficulties at the Motive Power Dept (The loco had not been coaled due to no coal being available in the coaling tower which was due to no wagons of coal being on the ramp which leads to the coaling tower which was due to the loco concerned not being able to get a grip on the wet rails which was due to no sand being available in the sandboxes etc or in other words certain BR personnel needed to get their fingers out!)

After about a 20 minute run on the main line the train arrived at Bullo Pill which is

RIGHT: On 20th June 1964, the Severn Boar II tour heads out from Gloucester. This view on the main line was not used in the first volume because I could not identify the exact location. I now believe it to be just west of Over Junction, although the curvature in the track does not quite correlate with this. There is a colour light signal glowing red in the left background, which is presumably controlling the approach to Over Junction and a tall building visible on the skyline behind the last brake van, which can only be in Gloucester. Further confusing matters is that Trevor Owen also photographed this train from the A48 bridge, which is less than half a mile behind (see Vol. 1, page 72). Perhaps he had a friend or relation stationed with another camera. T.B. OWEN

BELOW: Around an hour later, the tour steams in to Cinderford. As for the first run, a reception party of local residents was waiting on the platform to greet its arrival. T.B. OWEN

(7585)
2nd - DAY EXCURSION
THE RAILWAY ENTHUSIASTS' CLUB
**"THE SEVERN BOAR II"
SATURDAY, 20th JUNE 1964**
Gloucester Central Cinderford Town,
Whimsey, Northern Utd. Colliery, Lydney,
Coleford, Whitecliff, Speech House Road,
Princess Royal Colliery, Severn Bridge Stn.
Gloucester Central.
(W)   For conditions see over
0072

the junction for the first main branch in the Forest area. After some shunting to the branch line we set off on a very severe gradient to climb to Bilson Junction. By this time the weather outside the vans was grim but inside everything was very cosy as most people had lit fires and so the six vans crept along smoking merrily.

At Bilson we diverted to the right to arrive at the old GW station of Cinderford Town to be greeted by a reception party from the local residents. We returned to Bilson and after reversal we took the left hand branch this time, which leads to Northern United Colliery. This is now almost derelict and the track disappears off into a wood with a large tree growing up in the centre of the permanent way not far from where we stopped to reverse. We returned again to Bilson and this time propelled after reversal to Cinderford Whimsey. At this point most people adjoined to the 'snack bar' which was really the third brake van converted by the REC catering dept. to serve everything from tea to peanuts.

After making an additional stop for photographs at Eastern United Colliery we returned through three tunnels to Bullo Pill. Here we had to await a clear path on the main line and should have been preceded by our relief loco which was booked to take over our train at Lydney Junction. We waited for a while and then discovered that through further difficulties at the Motive Power Depot (presumably no one had yet found a shovel to shift sand into the sand boxes) our loco had left Gloucester rather late.

We thus set off along the main line for Lydney passing the Severn Bridge which looked extremely odd after having been cut in two when a barge crashed into one of the huge girders supporting the bridge. At last No. 1639 arrived at Lydney, backed on to our train and we set off on the second stage of the tour with a loco on each end as the Inspector on the train had decided that a second loco would certainly be necessary to climb the line to Coleford. This part of the route is about the most beautiful as it passes right through the centre of the forest area.

However our luck was against us and on arrival at Coleford Junction the second loco had smoke pouring from a 'hot box'. After a hasty discussion it was agreed that the only way of possibly climbing the two miles of 1 in 30 to Coleford was to leave one brake van behind and so with five vans all loaded to capacity we tackled the bank. This was by far the finest part of the tour and almost reminded one of a trip on the Vale of Rheidol but in standard gauge style. The tape recording fans were highly delighted and if the weather had improved no doubt some of the cine photographers would have run along in front of the pannier as it braked away in a really frantic effort.

After a very tense half hour we arrived at the top of the bank at Coleford to be met by a further reception party and after a brief stop we carried on to Whitecliff Quarry which is now the terminus of the old line to Monmouth. We stopped on the return to run into the old S&W station at Coleford and then eventually reached Coleford Junction after what was a rather more leisurely run then we had had on the forward journey.

At the junction our relief loco was still not fit to travel and so having recoupled our other van we set off again for Speech House Road. This particular section had officially closed some months previously and so it was not at all surprising to find sheep completely blocking the line every few yards.

But fate was against us and we now realised that we would have insufficient coal left in the bunker of the loco to make the return trip to Gloucester. Any hope of obtaining a substitute at this stage was discarded and so we pressed on thinking that we should have to return in a DMU.

On the way back we ran to Princess Royal Colliery where we examined some of the very old mining equipment. This is about the only remaining colliery which has kept open but even this has stopped mining coal and now only washes it.

By the time we reached Lydney our coal supply was exhausted and with the shed closed things looked desperate. At the last moment our Inspector remembered seeing one surviving wagon

with some coal situated outside the shed. We shunted around and then drew the train up alongside this wagon outside the shed. There then followed what can only be described as a typical REC type of escapade in which a large squad descended on the shed area in a search for shovels and after the production of 2 the mammoth task was started coaling the tank by hand.

Had it not been for these efforts the tour would certainly not have had a very successful ending and I should like to thank those members who I did not thank on the day for helping with this task. In spite of all the delays the train was only 15 minutes late back into Gloucester after a wonderful high speed run from Lydney.

Our thanks should go to the Western Region who had been very helpful despite all the trials and tribulations, and with the experience gained on this first tour the repeat trip ran even better. On the second occasion the weather was perfect and with no loco failure we kept to the scheduled time throughout the complete tour. My thanks go to the many club members who helped in any way with the heavy and complex arrangements for the two tours.'

On the back cover of the tour brochure illustrated, the names of the railwaymen involved on 6th June are recorded in biro: Inspector G.M.P. Taylor, Driver Fowler, Guard A. Legge, Inspector K.J. Taylor (operating), Fireman Graham Hawkins, Fireman John David, Driver Harry Trigg. A selection of sandwiches were available in the one van at 4d each, with drinks including tea and coffee (6d), lemonade (9d) and various beers (1s 2d to 1s 9d) including 'Larger'! I have also been informed that the three '16XX' Class engines involved over the two tours were not Gloucester-based engines but supplied by Swindon. Both tours were hauled to and from Gloucester by No. 1658, with No. 1639 and No. 1664 respectively being sent down to Lydney to assist with the Coleford Branch leg.

We now move forward to April 1967, for a photographers' charter which does not feature on the Six Bells Junction site. By this date, the Parkend/Coleford/Whitecliff Quarry goods ran on Mondays and Wednesdays only, whilst the Cinderford goods ran Tuesdays and Thursdays. Consequently, this tour took place over two days, Wednesday 26th and Thursday 27th April and was accommodated by the simple expedient of adding three extra brake vans to these trains. The relaxed schedule then in operation on both lines allowed for plenty of photographic stops and both trips are well covered in these pages. However, I have not found any advertisements for this trip, nor reports of it anywhere, so exactly who organised it is currently not known.

Despite the loss of much of the surviving Forest railway system in

1967, the line to Parkend and Marsh Sidings remained in use, so the occasional railtour still called. The next official trip was the Branch Line Society's Gloucestershire Railtour on 22nd March 1969, which covered all of the remaining branch lines in the county, including Lydney to Parkend, Llanthony Docks, High Orchard Docks, Hempstead Docks, Coaley to Dursley and Sharpness Docks. The tour, which started and finished at Bristol Temple Meads, began by running through the Severn Tunnel to access the east Monmouthshire branches to Sudbrook, Caerwent and Tintern Quarry. The day long tour utilised an unidentified DMU. On 15th May 1971, the Great Western Society (Bristol Branch) in conjunction with the Wirral Railway Circle ran the Tintern Rambler railtour, which also visited Parkend during its itinerary but started and finished from Cardiff General station. The short Sudbrook Branch, serving the Severn Tunnel pumping station, was also becoming a popular destination and this tour called there too.

Over two years then passed until two railtours ran within a couple of months of each other in 1973. First, on 23rd September, the Dean Forest Railway Society ran a special from Bristol Temple Meads, via Parkway to Gloucester and then Lydney, for a journey up to Parkend and back. Then, on 24th November, the Railway Correspondence & Travel Society's (RCTS) Bristol Avon railtour made the trip from Lydney to Parkend and back (the tickets were actually missprinted 'British Avon'). This tour started from Birmingham New Street and after leaving the Forest ran through the Severn Tunnel to traverse various branch lines in the Bristol area, with a detour then from Berkeley Road to Sharpness as the special headed back north to the Midlands.

British Railways finally closed the branch to Parkend in 1976 but one further tour traversed the line before the Dean Forest Railway began operating along it. This was the joint Monmouthshire Railway Society/RCTS Caerwent Cannonball tour, which ran on 15th March 1980. Starting and finishing at Cardiff Central (by now renamed from General), visits were made to Blaenavon, the Caerwent MoD Branch, Netherhope (the tour was booked to go to Tintern Quarry but traffic had ceased and passage through Tidenham Tunnel was not permitted) and finally to Parkend. Two DMUs were used, making a six-car train, a Class '118' (No's 51304+59477+51319) and a Class '101' (No's 51522+59546+51450).

This very last railtour over the old S&W is, somewhat ironically, the only one into the Forest on which I was a passenger. Even more ironically, I had black and white film in my camera on that day!

On the occasion of the 26th April 1967 photographers' charter, No. D9555 is seen at the old Severn & Wye station at Coleford, getting ready to head back down the branch to Coleford Junction. The following day, brake vans were attached to the Forest of Dean Branch goods for a similar trip up to Cinderford. BILL POTTER/KRM

BULLO PILL

Up Goods Loop (West Box)

Trains must stand clear of the foot crossing leading from the West Box to the Cinderford Branch Line.

Shunting in Sidings which have Connections at both ends

Before shunting a train or wagons into the Down Siding, Dock Line Siding, or Siding adjoining the Up Goods Loop, the person in charge of the shunting must communicate with the Signalman at Bullo Pill East or West as the case may be and obtain his permission.

In no case must one end of the Sidings be fouled by a train or wagons being pushed Up or Down the Sidings until permission has been obtained from the Signalman at the other end.

Wagon Repairs Ltd. Siding

This Siding is a trailing connection off the Up Goods Loop, and, together with a protecting catch point, is worked from a Ground Frame, the key of which is held by the West Box Signalman.

ABOVE: The combined Cinderford goods/photographers' special of 27th April 1967, back at Bullo Junction having completed its tour of the Forest of Dean Branch. I have not been able to find out who organised the trip but it was run over two days, this being the second day; on 26th April, brake vans were attached to the Coleford goods and we shall meet up with this train later on in these pages. Amongst those on board were Pershore-based businessman and film enthusiast Jim Clemens, who captured both trips on *ciné*. This has been made available commercially on video and DVD but his son Michael has also recently loaded it up on to the internet; it includes *ciné* of other trips in the Forest too. BILL POTTER/KRM

INSET ABOVE: Instructions for shunting Bullo yard from the *Appendix to the Working Time Table*, October 1960. NPC

TOP RIGHT: Engine restrictions for the Forest of Dean Branch, from the *Working Time Table of Freight Trains (Gloucester and Worcester Districts)*, September 1958. NPC

CENTRE RIGHT: Permitted speeds of trains through junctions on the Forest of Dean Branch, from the *Working Time Table of Freight Trains*, September 1958. NPC

BOTTOM RIGHT: Opening hours of signal boxes on the Forest of Dean Branch, from the *Working Time Table of Passenger Trains (Gloucester and Worcester Districts)*, September 1955. NPC

FOREST OF DEAN BRANCHES

Route Colour, Dotted Blue

Types of Engines authorised:—Blue, Yellow and uncoloured Groups. Blue Group Engines are subject to a speed restriction of 25 miles per hour.

0-6-0T 57XX and 2-8-0 " Austerity type." These engines may work over the undermentioned Sections of Line, subject to the observance of service restrictions and the following prohibitions:—

Routes:
(1) Bullo Pill to Whimsey.
(2) Bilson Junction Loop to Cinderford Station.
(3) Bullo Pill to termination of the Dock Branch.
(4) Churchway Branch. To the Stop Board at termination of Branch.

Prohibitions.
Route: (1).   Eastern United Colliery.
Sidings.   Under Screens.

K190   Speed of Trains Through Junctions—continued

BRANCH LINES—continued

Name of Place	Direction of Train		Miles per Hour
	From	To	
FOREST OF DEAN BRANCH			
The speed of trains between Bullo Pill and Bilson Junction must not exceed 30 miles per hour and must be further restricted to lower speeds as shewn:.			
Bullo Pill (Goods Trains only 330 yards outside Up Distant Signal for Bullo Pill West Box at spot where restrictions commence)	Forest of Dean Branch	Main Line	5*
Bullo Pill West Box	Main Line	Forest of Dean Branch	15
Bullo Pill West Box	Forest of Dean Branch	Main Line	10
Bullo Pill West Box	Yard	Forest of Dean Branch	10
	Forest of Dean Branch	Yard	10
2¼ m.p. (at Upper Soudley Halt)	Newnham	Cinderford	25
2¼ m.p. (at Upper Soudley Halt)	Cinderford	Newnham	25
At Staple Edge 3m. 24ch. and 3m. 30ch.	All Up and Down Trains...		20
At Ruspidge Halt 3m. 78ch. and 4m. 9ch.	All Up and Down Trains...		20
Bilson Junction and Whimsey, 5m. 5ch and 7m. 24ch.	All Up and Down Trains...		25
Bilson Junction	Newnham	Whimsey	10
Bilson Junction	Whimsey	Newnham	10
Bilson Junction	Newnham	Cinderford	15
Bilson Junction	Cinderford	Newnham	15
Cinderford Junction	Bilson Junction	Cinderford Station	15
Cinderford Junction	Cinderford Station	Bilson Junction	15

FOREST OF DEAN BRANCH									
—	—	Newnham			8. 0 a.m.	8. 0 a.m.	3.20 p.m.	—	—	Yes.
—	74	Bullo Pill East			5. 0 a.m.	—	—	—	8. 0 a.m. †	Yes.
—	26	Bullo Pill West			5. 0 a.m.	—	—	—	2. 0 p.m. †	Yes.
3	47	Cinderford (Eastern United)			8. 0 a.m.	8. 0 a.m.	A M D	—	—	Yes.
1	38	Cinderford (Bilson Junction)			6.45 a.m.	6.45 a.m.		—	—	No.

†—Unless otherwise ordered by Control.   A—Until last Freight train has cleared.   D—Until last train has cleared.
M—Saturdays until 11.25 a.m. Freight ex Bilson Junction has cleared.

LEFT: The two water tanks and the bottom of the Forest of Dean Branch as seen from a train passing by on the Down Main line in 1962; the picture lacks sharpness but shows much of interest. The number of wooden bodied wagons in the rake in the siding is remarkable – the one visible through the legs of the nearer tank shows signs of an old private owner livery coming through its worn paintwork. BILL POTTER/KRM

BELOW LEFT: The point to point time allowances for freight trains traversing the branch, from the *Working Time Table of Freight Trains*, September 1958. NPC

BELOW: Again taken on 27th April 1967, the Bullo Pill West Box signalman makes his way across the tracks to hand the token for the branch to the driver of No. D9502. The steep ascent at the start of the branch is accentuated by the fact that the main lines are also dropping away slightly. A frontal view of the signal box appears in Volume 1; it was provided in 1898, as a replacement for two earlier boxes, Bullo Pill West, situated about 400 yards further along in the Lydney direction, and Bullo Pill Centre, which had stood just to the left of the brick huts seen here on the left. The yard was well supplied with water tanks and cranes, and the water supply here appears to have been maintained up until the last vestiges of the yard were removed in 1967-68. BILL POTTER/KRM

Time Allowances for Freight Trains—continued

FOREST OF DEAN BRANCH

DOWN				Point-to-Point Times Mins.	UP				Point-to-Point Times Mins.
NEWNHAM	...	...	...	...	Cinderford (Whimsey)	...	...	...	
Bullo Pill	...	...	...						
Bullo Cross Halt	...	...	...		Northern United Colliery	...			
Soudley Sidings	...	...	...	13	Brick Works Siding	...	...		
Upper Soudley Halt...	...	...		Stop Board...	...	...	...		
Staple Edge Halt	...	...							
Eastern United Colliery	...	...	9	Bilson Goods Yard	...	...		3
Ruspidge Halt	...	...	...	2	Bilson Junction	...	...	...	
Bilson Junction	...	...	...		CINDERFORD	...	...		
CINDERFORD	...	...			Stop Board...	...	...	...	
Bilson Junction	...	...	...		Bilson Junction	...	...	...	
Bilson Goods Yard	...	...	3	Stop Board	...	...	...	4
					Ruspidge Halt	...	...	...	
Northern United Colliery	...	...		Eastern United Colliery	...	...	4
					Staple Edge Halt	...	...	...	
Cinderford (Whimsey)	...	...	4	Stop Board	...	...	...	6
					Upper Soudley Halt...	...	...		
					Soudley Sidings	...	...	...	
					Bullo Cross Halt	...	...		
					Bullo Pill	...	...	...	16⅝
					NEWNHAM	...	...	...	16⅝

ABOVE: Looking west towards Haie Hill from the site of Bullo Cross Halt platform on 3rd June 1966. Through the trees on the skyline, above the eastern portal of Haie Hill Tunnel, the manor house known as 'The Haie' can just be made out. The original house, then referred to as 'Ruddle Manor', was constructed by Roynon Jones circa 1770 but only a part of this now remains. The main section was rebuilt in the 1850s and renamed 'Newnham Park' by William Willetts. Sold to the Kerr family in 1857, they added substantial extensions to it in the early 1880s and renamed it 'The Haie'. Sold again shortly after World War Two, it has since been converted into apartments. Roynon Jones was one of the four promoters behind the Bullo Pill Railway Company, builders of the Forest of Dean Tramroad. His son, the Rev'd Edward Jones, who inherited his tramroad and colliery interests, was later to complain of the tunnel drawing off all the water from the springs which served the house. These views, incidentally, are all from colour prints, not slides. ROBIN BARNES

ABOVE: Having walked up the track, our intrepid photographer captured this glimpse of the eastern portal of Haie Hill Tunnel and the Down Distant signal for Soudley No. 1 Crossing. This was a late BR(WR) tubular post replacement for a signal on a very short wooden post positioned on top of the stone retaining wall. Allowing for the slow speed of colour film at this time, Robin had wisely aimed his camera lens skywards to allow in as much light as he could whilst still just keeping the rails in view, otherwise, the picture would have come out excessively dark. ROBIN BARNES

RIGHT: Standing in the shadow of the western portal of the tunnel, looking towards Soudley No. 1 Crossing Ground Frame. Again the signal seen here, the Down Distant for Soudley No. 2 Crossing, on the other side of Bradley Hill Tunnel, was a 1960s WR tubular post replacement for an earlier wooden-posted signal. ROBIN BARNES

We shall follow the progress of the SLS Special of 13th May 1961 around the Forest, as several of our favourite photographers dashed from point to point to capture it. Here it is seen exiting Haie Hill Tunnel and passing over Soudley No. 1 Crossing. Having been built originally for a horse operated tramroad, the narrow bore of the 1,064 yards long tunnel lacked any internal ventilation and proved a trial for crews heading up the branch to Cinderford – which in railway terms is actually the Down direction! The lack of exhaust from No. 6437 suggests that perhaps a photographic stop had been made. On the right are some of the remains of Soudley Ironworks, which were erected in 1836-37. Iron production was a notoriously fickle industry and the works spent many years idle, whilst also changing hands on several occasions. Iron was last produced here in 1877 but it was not until the late 1890s that demolition of the furnaces commenced and it was to be nearly another decade before the site was cleared. The ruins seen here have now also mostly disappeared. B.J. ASHWORTH

Looking in the opposite direction and giving some idea of how deep was the tree cover into which Ben Ashworth had ventured for his picture, the SLS Special is seen heading away from Soudley No. 1 Crossing towards Bradley Hill Tunnel. The tramroad route here turns right, through the gate and along the lane. This was a delightful spot, enhanced by the railway and the accoutrements of the crossing; the ground frame hut survived for many years in a nearby garden, whilst the house on the right was originally provided for the crossing keeper. In the early part of the 20th century, a short wooden platform with a corrugated iron goods lock up had stood opposite the hut; a rare instance of trains being able to load goods (other than at a station) whilst stopped on the main running line. The facility had been provided for the Dulcote Leather Board Co. Ltd, who had taken over the leather board works at Camp Mill, Soudley in 1901. Camp Mill, situated around half a mile up the lane to the right, is today better known as the home of the Dean Heritage Centre. Note that the Soudley No. 2 Crossing Down Distant signal is a wooden posted version of much older vintage than that shown a couple of pages earlier. This indicates that BR renewed much of the signalling on the branch some time after 1961, a hugely unnecessary expense given that the passenger service had ceased but probably carried out to make the line uneconomic – a familiar BR trick of the time to justify closure. BILL POTTER/KRM

The neat southern portal of Bradley Hill Tunnel, with No. D9502 emerging into the daylight on 27th April 1967. The tramroad, with its tighter curvature, avoided Bradley Hill but the railway was forced to burrow through as it curved round from Soudley towards the entrance to Haie Hill Tunnel. This was a much shorter bore, however, just 299 yards in length, so provided much less of a test for steam era footplate crews. The 'D95XX' Series Type 1 diesel-hydraulics were universally nicknamed 'Teddy Bears' – except in the Forest where they were generally referred to as 'Yogi Bears'. The nickname apparently came about because of a witty remark made by Swindon Works' foreman George Cole in 1963 – "*We've built the Great Bear, now we're going to build a Teddy Bear!*". The series of fifty-six engines were built between July 1964 and October 1965. No. D9502 being the third of them completed in that first month of construction. Built for trip working, shunting and branch line duties, as replacements for the Western Region's legions of pannier tanks, the general run down of the railways at this period saw the work for which they were intended rapidly disappearing, whilst they had also proved rather unreliable in service. BR had withdrawn the entire '95XX' Series by early 1969, negating the need for most of the planned improvements to the design but many of them subsequently went on to have far longer careers in industrial use with British Steel and the National Coal Board. No. D9502 went to first Burradon and then Ashington collieries in the north east. Finally ceasing work in the late 1980s, it is now preserved by the Heritage Shunters Trust at Peak Rail in Derbyshire. COLOUR-RAIL

RIGHT: The northern portal of Bradley Hill Tunnel seen from the verandah of the lead brake van as the photographers' charter clattered back down the branch to Bullo. The line curved round to the south east through the tunnel, only straightening out and then turning round to head in an easterly direction at the far end, so it was impossible to see right through. Both portals of the tunnel are accessible today. NPC

ABOVE AND LEFT: Soudley No. 2 Crossing was situated approximately 100 yards north of the tunnel. The crossing keeper's cottage here was provided by the GWR in 1894, so was not a requirement of the passenger service. This picturesque spot was a favourite of postcard and railway photographers over the years, so was well documented. Here, '57XX' Class 0-6-0PT No. 3675 heads past on 11th October 1965, with a train of coal empties bound for Northern United Colliery. Notice how the low roofed tunnel has caused the smoke and steam from the engine to pool in the wagons. There was a very short siding here, as indicated by the buffer stops just visible on the left, which could hold only three wagons. It was used mostly for loading timber but also for the occasional delivery of coal. BOTH BILL POTTER/KRM

BELOW: The instructions for working Soudley Siding, from the *Appendix to the Working Time Table,* October 1960. NPC

SOUDLEY

The Siding points are worked from a Ground Frame released by the Electric Token.
The gate across the Siding is secured by padlock and the key kept by the Crossing Keeper when not in use.
The Guard in charge of the train is responsible for seeing that the gate is properly set and locked after the Siding has been used.

RIGHT: With No. 1658 at the head, the Railway Enthusiast Club's Severn Boar II railtour of 20th June 1964 exits Bradley Hill Tunnel and passes over Soudley No. 2 Crossing. TREVOR OWEN

LEFT: A Down train of empties bursts out of the gloom of the tunnel and the trees enveloping Bradley Hill, into bright autumn sunshine at Soudley on 12th October 1960. No. 8701 is working hard up the gradient, whilst the photographer's preferred method of transport can be seen propped against the fence. The signal prominent in all of these pictures was the Up Distant for Soudley No. 1 Crossing and again had, seemingly completely unnecessarily, been replaced by BR in the early 1960s. B.J. ASHWORTH

OPPOSITE PAGE TOP: The first of two very similar views of Soudley No. 2 Crossing, this shows the line curving round to the north portal of the tunnel on 22nd September 1965. This was just over three months before steam finished on the branch and on the Western Region of British Railways as a whole. JOHN PHILLIPS/NPC

OPPOSITE PAGE BOTTOM: This second picture dates from the summer of 1968, after the branch had closed to all traffic but with the rusting rails still *in situ*. Lifting of the whole of the line was completed by the end of 1969. Note the Up Distant, which in later years seems to have been kept permanently at 'clear', had finally been returned to the 'caution' position; this signal was operated from Soudley No. 2 Crossing Ground Frame. The crossing gate had also now been secured in the open position for traffic using Tramway Road. Happily, the cottage has survived closure of the line and the trackbed alongside now forms part of its garden. NPC

RIGHT: A rare colour glimpse of the Forest of Dean Branch passenger service, as No. 3740 calls at Upper Soudley Halt with a Down train in October 1958, a few days before it ceased running. DAVID BICK/NPC

BELOW: On 22nd September 1965, '57XX' Class No. 4689 coasts downhill past the remains of Upper Soudley Halt with a mixed goods from Cinderford, which includes vans loaded with assembled products from the Rosedale Plastics factory and Meredith & Drew's biscuits factory. Just above the cab of the locomotive is the roof of the White Horse Inn; still open today, the trackbed here now forms part of the inn car park. The underbridge that the rear end of the train is passing over, which was very low and had a span of just 12ft, remained in place for many years after the line closed but was eventually demolished. The south abutment remains but the north side and the embankment beyond was levelled, and a small housing estate built on the site. BILL POTTER/KRM

With its smokebox numberplate gone and the number chalked on the door instead, No. 3675 heads up the branch with coal empties for Northern United Colliery and some vans at the rear for Cinderford. The remains of the platform are hidden behind the train, whilst St. Michael & All Angels Church can be seen in the background. When Upper Soudley Halt first opened in 1907, locals were not amused by the GWR's spelling, as they had commonly written it as 'Sewdley'. Note that the fireman is leaning out of the cab and appears to be using a piece of chalk to pick out the numbers on the numberplate! BILL POTTER/KRM

A most unusual view of the branch as it snaked through the village of Soudley, taken from the SLS special of 13th May 1961 and looking back towards the halt. This is the section of embankment which has now gone, bulldozed for a new housing estate. The row of grey council houses in the right background still remain today, whilst the building directly behind the telegraph pole is the White Horse Inn again. The Blakeney to Cinderford road runs in front of the bay-windowed house on the far left, whilst the railway now executed a sweeping turn to the north, to cross over the road on a low narrow bridge, which again no longer exists. NPC

It was apparently not unusual for the crews of Down trains heading up the branch to stop at Soudley to 'get up steam' – a euphemism for a quick visit to the White Horse Inn! This may have just happened on this occasion, as photographer Ben Ashworth had had time to get on his bike and ride a further half a mile up the road from Soudley No. 2 Crossing and position himself in the trees before capturing No. 8701 again. Beautifully lit by a fortuitous shaft of late autumn sunlight, the train has just crossed over the Blakeney to Cinderford road and is heading towards Blue Rock Tunnel. B.J. ASHWORTH

By 1967, the goods service on the branch was reduced to just two trains a week, on Tuesdays and Thursdays, hence the rusty sheen to the rails. However, this also allowed plenty of scope for stops on the photographers' charter of 27th April that year, in order that those riding on it could also photograph it. Here, No. D9502 and its short train have come to a halt just south of Blue Rock Tunnel, alongside a permanent way hut and with the Soudley sewage works on the left. These were part of an underground drainage and sewage treatment system, built here on the Soudley Brook by the Westbury Guardians in 1876-78, to serve Ruspidge and Cinderford. Enlarged over the years since, the plant seen here dated from a complete rebuild carried out in 1936 but has since closed, replaced by a large new sewage treatment facility constructed at Crump Meadow, Cinderford by Severn Trent Water. Note the check rail on the sharply curving line and the small castellations decorating the tunnel portal. BILL POTTER/KRM

LEFT: The SLS Special exits Blue Rock Tunnel as it drifts back down the Soudley Valley on its return to Bullo. In the left foreground is one of the sewage plant filter beds. This view is taken from the Soudley to Cinderford road and the remains of a couple of these concrete constructions are still just visible today but the tunnel mouth is now hidden by trees. B.J. ASHWORTH

ABOVE: The north end of Blue Rock Tunnel on 11th May 1967. This end was in plain stone, without the castellations which embellish the south portal. The tunnel was quite short, just 109 yards long and was cut through a rocky outcrop which the tramroad had skirted around; the route of this can just be made out at a slightly lower level on the right and a section of the Soudley Brook can also be seen at the bottom right of the picture. BILL POTTER/KRM

RIGHT: In drizzle and low lying mist, '57XX' Class 0-6-0PT No. 3775 works an afternoon mixed goods up to Bilson Junction on 11th October 1965. The train is passing Shakemantle, just north of Blue Rock Tunnel. BILL POTTER/KRM

Type 1 diesel-hydraulic No. D9555 passing Shakemantle Quarry on the approach to Blue Rock Tunnel with a short Up goods train on 11th May 1967. The final locomotive in the class, they have since become somewhat notorious for their short life on the main line. No. D9555 was built in November 1965 and withdrawn in April 1969. British Railways redesignated them as Class '14' under TOPS but none lasted long enough to be renumbered. As well being as the final '95XX' Class constructed, the engine also had the distinction of being the very last locomotive to be built by Swindon Works. After withdrawal by BR, No. D9555 was sold into industrial use, ending up far from home in the north east of England at NCB Ashington Colliery. Happily, it not only survived to be preserved in September 1987 but is today back at home on the Dean Forest Railway, working trains between Lydney and Parkend. BILL POTTER/KRM

RIGHT: On 29th October 1965, No. 3675 heads through autumn colours at Shakemantle, as it approaches the site of the closed quarry with a load of empty mineral wagons for Northern United. Shakemantle Quarry had ceased operations around 1948, the north and south connections to the loop siding serving it being taken out of use in June 1950. However, they were not removed straight away, the north connection surviving until 1962. Locomotives were not permitted through the gate into the quarry, so wagons were gravity worked through it, empties being dropped off by Down trains, with the loadeds being collected by Up workings. Note that locomotives on the branch always worked smokebox first up to Cinderford, in order to keep water over the firebox on the steep gradients. BILL POTTER/KRM

Signal Box	Signals affected	Dates (inclusive) between which Signal Lamps will not be lighted
Eastern United Colliery ..	All signals	Until further notice.

Notice regarding signal lamps, from the *Appendix to the Working Time Table,* October 1960. NPC

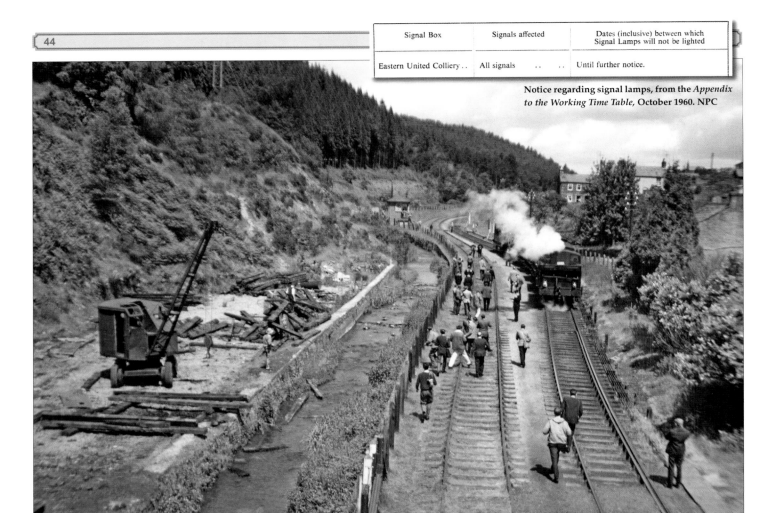

The Severn Boar II tour alongside the site of Staple Edge Halt on 20th June 1964. In the distance is Eastern United Colliery Signal Box, brought in to use by the GWR in 1913. A standard GWR design in red brick, this was its last day, the box being closed after the tour departed. The Cinderford Brook, which runs down the centre of the scene, becomes the Soudley Brook further down the valley. COLEFORD GWR MUSEUM (MIKE REES)

The bracket signal in the foreground controlled the exit for Up trains from the goods loop and entry to the colliery sidings; it also provided the vantage point for the picture above. On the left in both views, the mobile crane is engaged in dismantling the redundant sidings at the closed colliery. JOHN RYAN

LEFT: The 27th April 1967 photographers charter rattles past the remains of Eastern United Colliery, which had ceased coal production suddenly in January 1959. Sunk in 1909, coal production at Eastern United had commenced the following year and at its height the colliery employed 900 men. However, once the main seams had been won, the costs of pumping out water to keep the mine dry (an issue which bedevilled all Forest pits), coupled with geological problems encountered in the remaining coal seams after 1945, were to lead to its closure, although it came as something of a shock as a new good seam had just been discovered and developed at great expense. Some of the buildings seen here still remain today, in light industrial use. NPC

ABOVE AND ABOVE RIGHT: The Severn Boar II brake van trip of 20th June 1964 between Ruspidge and Staple Edge. The train is close to Cullamore Bridge, which carried the early 19th century tramroad branch to Lightmoor Colliery from the Bullo Pill Tramroad. A chimney and the roof of the engine house of Lightmoor Colliery can be glimpsed in the distance behind the trees top right. The route of the tramroad, which can just be discerned on the extreme right edge of the picture ABOVE, remained in use as a cart track and the bridge, partially rebuilt in 1923 by Crawshays, the owners of Eastern United Colliery, survived into the 1960s. The meadow in the foreground was used by the Eastern United pit ponies. The train is seen first heading north, ABOVE RIGHT, and then on the way back down the branch behind No. 1658. BOTH T.B. OWEN

Looking north from Cullamore Bridge towards Ruspidge and Cinderford Bridge on 29th October 1965, with St. John's Church on the skyline in the left distance and the Cinderford Brook running parallel to the railway in the foreground. Ex-GWR '57XX' Class 0-6-0PT No. 3675 makes its way down the valley with a train loaded with coal from Northern United Colliery. BILL POTTER/KRM

RIGHT: In frosty morning conditions, another '57XX', No 4698, threads its way up the Ruspidge Valley with empty mineral wagons for Northern United on 30th March 1965. JOHN DAGLEY-MORRIS

BELOW: We are fortunate that some railway photographers saw something more than the trains when out taking pictures and Bill Potter clearly recognised this as a scene worth recording. Looking north towards Ruspidge Halt, with the Ruspidge Crossing Distant signal, permanently fixed at caution, prominent on the left, the railway has gone from here today but Railway Road still winds its way along the valley floor on its way from Ruspidge Road to meet the Speech House Road at Cinderford Bridge. It follows the route of the tramroad, which was maintained here for some years after the railway was built. Today it is lined with recently constructed houses, whilst the trackbed has also been partially built on. BILL POTTER/KRM

No. 3675 approaching the level crossing just before Ruspidge Halt, on its way up the valley to Bilson Junction. A wartime build, being new in to service on 6th June 1940, the pannier tank finished its career at Gloucester Horton Road shed just two months after this photograph was taken – hence its careworn state – in December 1965. The village of Ruspidge is spread across the hillside in the background. Today, this section of the trackbed has been tarmaced and now leads into a small private housing estate. BILL POTTER/KRM

The Gloucester-Cinderford passenger service ceased four years before the Beeching cuts, finishing with a whimper rather than the sad public farewells which were to be afforded to more popular services elsewhere upon their withdrawal in the early 1960s. In truth, Forest folk had long preferred the bus services so its loss was hardly noticed. Here, on a damp and dismal day in late October 1958, albeit with a little more light than he had encountered at Soudley, photographer David Bick captured No. 3740 with its two-coach train paused at Ruspidge Halt. The maroon and cream livery ('blood & custard') introduced by British Railways was attractive but was found to fade quickly in use, so was being phased out by the end of the 1950s. As can be seen from its weed grown state, the siding on the left was falling out of use by this date and it is rare to see it occupied. The two mineral wagons seen here were probably delivering house coal for a local merchant. No. 3740 was another Gloucester-based engine and had only three months of service left itself, being withdrawn in late January 1959. DAVID BICK

TABLE P LEVEL CROSSING GATES—OPENING AND CLOSING BY TRAINMEN

The following is a list of Level Crossings where, in the absence of a Crossing Keeper, the gates must be opened and closed by the Trainmen.

Trains must be brought to a stand well clear of the gates, after which the gates must be unlocked and opened by the Fireman for the passage of the train over the Crossing. When the train has passed over the Crossing, the Guard (or Fireman in the case of a Light engine) must close the gates across the railway and re-lock them, the Driver taking care not to again proceed on his journey until he has received an " All Right " Signal from the Guard. Enginemen and Guards concerned must see that they are supplied with keys of the gates.

Any defects in the gates or the locks securing them or in the lamps, must be reported immediately by the Guard or in the case of a Light engine by the Fireman, to the Station Master concerned.

Name of Crossing	Situated at or between	Remarks
BULLO PILL WEST TO CINDERFORD		
Ruspidge	Between Bullo Pill West and Bilson	See page 143
BILSON TO WHIMSEY		
Cinderford	Bilson & Whimsey ..	The gates are bolt locked by a lever in the Ground Frame which is released by a key attached to the Wooden Train Staff

In Indian Summer sunshine on 22nd September 1965, No. 4689 slows as it approaches the crossing at Ruspidge, working a freight bunker first from Bilson Junction. In February 1960, the three-lever ground frame situated at the Bullo end of the station building, from which were operated the Up and Down Distant signals protecting the crossing and the gate bolts, had been removed, the signals themselves being replaced by stop boards. The responsibility of opening and closing the gates had then been transferred from the station staff to the train crew, so the train had to come to a halt for the guard to climb down from his brake van and open them. As the train slows to a halt here, the guard can just be seen on the running board of the brake van, holding on to the hand rail as he prepares to jump down. The posts which formerly held the nameboard on the platform are still in place and the photographer's wife sits in the sun, blissfully reading her book and completely ignoring the train. BILL POTTER/KRM

INSET ABOVE: Notes regarding the level crossing gates at Ruspidge and Whimsey, from the *Appendix to the Working Time Table*, October 1960. NPC

A couple of minutes after the previous picture was taken and under the watchful eye of the guard standing on the platform, No. 4689 picks its way carefully over the crossing. Ruspidge was originally established as a goods station in 1866, being provided with a crane as well as the building seen here. The GWR referred to it as Cinderford station, although locally it tended to be known as Cinderford Bridge station, after the nearby hamlet where it was situated. It became Ruspidge after the opening of a new goods station at Whimsey in 1884, which was named Cinderford in its place. For the opening of the new passenger service in 1907, the main building, which was used as the goods office, was converted and equipped inside with a waiting room and booking office, and the platform adapted for public use. No. 4689's train comprises eight loaded mineral wagons of what looks to be power station grade coal from Northern United, three Berry Wiggins bitumen tanks working back down from Whimsey and the brake van. BILL POTTER/KRM

INSET RIGHT: Instructions for the operation of the crossing gates at Ruspidge. *Appendix to the Working Time Table*, October 1960. NPC

BELOW: A general view of the halt on 3rd April 1966; the siding had been taken out on 25th February 1962 but the small stone-built goods shed remained. The date when this shed was provided is not known but it is possible that all of the buildings seen here were contemporary with each other. The fencing and gates seem to have been especially erected for the start of the passenger service in 1907. Note the gas lamps still in position and the blue enamelled Great Western Railway notice on the end of the station building. A circa 1908 postcard view of Ruspidge Halt shows a second stone building attached to the rear of the goods shed; its purpose is unknown but from its appearance it may have been a stables and hay loft. The purpose of the stone-built hut at the end of the platform is also unknown. NPC

RUSPIDGE CROSSING

The normal position of the gates is across the railway and they are padlocked in that position. All Up trains, including light engines and engines and vans, must stop at the incline stop board and to assist the Driver of a train to stop his train, the Guard must, if requested by the Driver, pin down wagon brakes before leaving Bilson. The gates must be unlocked and opened by the Fireman and incline instructions, where applicable, carried out. When the train has passed over the crossing, it must again come to a stand at the marker post, which is 40 wagons' length from the crossing, to enable the Guard (or Fireman in the case of a light engine) to close the gates across the railway and re-lock them. The Guard must re-adjust the wagon brakes before the train proceeds and the Fireman must exchange hand-signals with the Guard at the first opportunity.

Down trains must stop at the marker post provided 10 yards on the approach side of the crossing, the gates then being unlocked and opened by the Fireman. When the train has passed over the crossing and the brake van is opposite the incline stop board for Up trains, the Guard must exhibit a " stop " hand-signal to the Driver. The Guard must then close the gates across the railway and re-lock them, the Fireman to undertake this duty in the case of a light engine.

Enginemen and Guards concerned must see that they are supplied with keys of the gates, the keys being kept in Bullo Pill West Signal Box, to which point they must be returned. Any defects in the gates or locks securing them or in the lamps must be reported immediately by the Guard or Fireman to the Station Master concerned.

A very useful study of the station building from a modeller's perspective, albeit semi derelict, with plants growing through the roof and awaiting its ultimate fate. Solidly built of local stone, the decision to demolish it looks short sighted now given that the station site forms the southern end of the linear park that was formed along the line of the railway but such random acts of vandalism were commonplace and vast swathes of our historic railway architecture were swept away after closure with little thought to their potential future use. The three-lever ground frame which had operated the Up and Down Distant signals and the gate bolts had been positioned on the platform adjacent to the end window and the operating wires had come out through the aperture visible in the platform face. There was another window in the wall at the far end of the station building but views of the rear of it are inevitably obscured by the trees. However, it is not thought that there were any windows or doors in the rear wall. NPC

RIGHT: A final view of the halt, taken in July 1967. Official closure was still a month away but the lack of polish to the tops of the rails shows that traffic was by now virtually non-existent. The sleepers just beyond the gates had become quite oily, from the Series 'D95XX' diesels as they paused here waiting for the gates to open and then accelerating as they started away again. Note that the GWR enamelled notice had disappeared by this date (it had been purchased by a local enthusiast) and the stone hut at the end of the platform had also been demolished. Colour pictures like this are useful for all sorts of modellers' detail, such as the random patterned brickwork on the station building's chimney. IAN POPE COLLECTION

3rd-SINGLE   SINGLE-3rd
Ruspidge Halt
Ruspidge Ht.   Ruspidge Ht.
Upper Soudley Ht.   Upper Soudley Ht.
UPPER SOUDLEY HALT
(W)   4d.   FARE   4d.   (W)
For Conditions see over For Conditions see over

BELOW: A view from just north of the halt, looking back towards it, with a car on Valley Road in the left background keeping pace with the train. No. 6424 heads towards Cinderford with the Gloucestershire Railway Society's Forest of Dean railtour of 23rd June 1962. As detailed in the introduction, this trip had already traversed the branch to Newent and Dymock. Take away the nameboard mounted on the front bufferbeam and this could be a regular Forest of Dean Branch passenger train of the previous decade. JOHN STRANGE/NPC

RIGHT: Moments after the previous picture, the photographer had turned to capture this view of No. 6424 with the town of Cinderford spread out in the background. The large factory buildings belong to R.A. Lister & Co., manufacturers of various types of engines for agricultural, marine and industrial use. The signal just ahead of the train is the Ruspidge Up Distant, whilst further round and nearly hidden in the trees is the Bilson Down Distant. JOHN STRANGE/NPC

LEFT: Two years later, the Severn Boar II railtour is seen in almost exactly the same spot as the GRS train above but photographed from the north west side of the line, looking towards Lightmoor. T.B. OWEN

RIGHT: The remains of Cinderford Ironworks, photographed circa 1965 shortly before their final demolition. Also derelict behind and soon to be demolished as well is Whitechapel Row, with the roof of the end house on the left having already collapsed. The Forest iron producing industry suffered many vicissitudes, despite the availability locally of both coal and iron ore, and plentiful supplies of water. Although the first furnace here was erected in 1795, successful iron production at Cinderford really only began in 1829-30, under Moses Teague and partners, who had managed to solve the problems of making iron with the poorer quality Forest ore and coal which was not suitable for coking. William Crawshay, a successful South Wales coal and iron master, became a partner and later sent his son Henry up to the Forest to manage his interests. The ups and downs of the iron industry, with continually rising and falling demand and thus prices, affected the small Forest iron producing industry more than other areas and its death knell was to be sounded by the growth of much bigger iron producing areas, such as in the North East of England, which were working on a far grander scale. Cinderford Ironworks closed for good in 1894 but a siding ran to here from Ruspidge for a number of years, for the removal of slag. IAN POPE COLLECTION

I shall henceforth dispense with the superlatives as regards Bill Potter's photographs, because so many of them are of this standard; I shall instead simply remark that we are indeed fortunate that he enjoyed visiting the Forest and took so many pictures, both in black & white and colour. Here, in a very similar spot to the photographs on the previous page, with the Bilson Down Distant in the right centre background, No. 9672 trundles back down the branch towards Bullo with a single Berry Wiggins tar tank and an ex-GWR 'Toad' brake van, on a bright autumn day on 6th November 1965. Talking to Bill many years later, one of his regrets was that he left photographing the Forest lines until late, only making a concerted effort to visit on numerous occasions in 1965, the last year of steam for the Western Region. In point of fact, he had first ventured here to photograph an Excursion train at Parkend in 1957 and then the SLS railtour in 1961 but these seem to have been his only previous forays into the Forest of Dean. BILL POTTER/KRM

LEFT: A portrait study of Class '57XX' No. 9672 of Gloucester shed after arrival at Bilson Yard with a Down train for Whimsey on 6th November 1965. The picture also provides useful detail of the Berry Wiggins logo on the tank wagon behind, the tar it carried being marketed by the company as 'Liquaphalt'. BILL POTTER/KRM

RIGHT: A '57XX' tank engine in the process of positioning an ex-GWR 'Toad' brake van at the far end of a rake of empty mineral wagons at Bilson, prior to propelling them up to Northern United Colliery. This viewpoint, off the Crump Meadow Tramroad embankment, again provides additional useful detail, this time of the rear of the pw motor trolley sheds. Note that the one trolley could be railed either directly on to the running line or on to the stub siding. IAN POPE COLLECTION

BELOW: The north end of Bilson Yard on 11th October 1965, looking south from the embankment which carried the S&W line across Bilson Green to Cinderford station. No. 3675 is about to run round the rake of empties that it has just brought up the branch. BILL POTTER/KRM

ABOVE: A short while after the previous picture, No. 3675 starts propelling the empties through the old S&W line abutments and up the Churchway Branch to Northern United Colliery. However, the train will shortly halt in order for the locomotive to take on water from the water tank positioned here. The embankment had been built in 1899 to carry the Severn & Wye Joint line to Cinderford station across the GW lines at Bilson. The line had seen ever decreasing use after the cessation of the S&W passenger service in 1929 but had still carried a goods service and the very occasional special passenger train up until 1950. The track between Serridge Junction and Cinderford was finally severed on 31st December 1951. Today, the heavily overgrown embankment has been chopped back for a short way on both sides and the trackbed here is now a cycle and footpath. BILL POTTER/KRM

LEFT: This view was taken from the left-hand abutment in the picture above, on 7th April 1965. The train of empties on the left are about to join with the brake van to be shunted up to Northern United. The yard looks quite crowded with wagons, with more visible in the distance. HOWARD BURCHELL

BELOW: Instructions for working the Whimsey and Churchway branches, from the *Appendix to the Working Time Table (Gloucester Traffic District),* October 1960. NPC

BILSON TO WHIMSEY

The points leading to Whimsey Yard are worked from two Ground Frames which are released by a key on the Staff.
All Freight trains on the Whimsey Branch must be worked by two Guards.

BILSON TO NORTHERN UNITED COLLIERY SIDINGS

All up trains must come to a stand at the Bilson Severn & Wye Ground Frame Home Signal; the Porter may then lower that Signal, and the train can then draw into Bilson Yard.
Two Guards must travel with each train when working over this portion of the Line.

BRICK WORKS SIDING

The points connecting the Siding with the Main line are worked from a Ground Frame which is released by a key on the Staff.

NORTHERN UNITED COLLIERY SIDINGS

Ground Frames working connections to and from the Sidings and released by a key on the Train Staff are provided as follows:—
South Ground Frame—fixed on Down side of Line at 5 m. 69 chs.
North Ground Frame—fixed on Down side of Line at 6 m. 3 chs.
On arrival at the Sidings, the Brake van must be placed on the end of Branch clear of the Colliery connection from which point the empty wagons will be propelled without a brake van up the rising gradient to the " Empty " Sidings ; a man must walk in front during this operation.
Only opens and mineral wagons are permitted in the Colliery Sidings.
After the empties have been placed in the " Empty " Sidings, the engine will return, pick up the brake van and draw it to the " Loaded " Sidings, after which the brake van will be secured and left on the Main Line whilst loaded wagons are picked up.   When this has been done, the brake van can be gravitated on to the rear of the loaded trucks, and the train will then be ready to leave.
The empty wagons will be gravitated by the Colliery Company's Staff from the " Empty " Sidings via the Screens to the " Loaded " Sidings.
Owing to the gradient of 1 in 41 falling to Bilson Junction, great care must be exercised by all concerned in securing wagons or brake vans left on the Main Line, and sprags must be used if necessary. Before loaded wagons are drawn out from the " Loaded " road, sufficient brakes must be applied to ensure the engine bringing the wagons to a stand immediately over the points for the brake van to be attached.
Guards, Shunters and other B.R. employees must not proceed beyond the Overbridge on the " Loaded " road as there is insufficient clearance.   Loaded wagons will be coupled up and gravitated on the " Loaded " road by the Colliery employees to a point the Bilson side of the Overbridge.
No marshalling must be performed at the Colliery; this must be done at either Bilson or Bullo Pill.

No. 3675 heads a train of vans up the long curving embankment which led from Bilson to Cinderford station on 11th October 1965. Bilson Yard and signal box can be seen in the right background and the Whimsey Branch Up fixed Distant signal is prominent in the right foreground. The various workings around the Cinderford area provided a busy schedule for No. 3675 and its crew, as the various photographs of it on this particular day indicate. This was the second trip of the day, working the vans from Bullo Yard up to Cinderford, to be loaded with products from either Rosedale's plastics factory or Meredith & Drew's biscuit factory. Previously, as we have already seen, No. 3675 had brought coal empties up from Bullo, which we shall see being propelled up to Northern United a few pages further on. After that, we shall encounter the locomotive again working up to Whimsey with coal for the tar depot. After a hard working shift, No. 3675 will then head back to Gloucester (Lydney shed having closed the previous year) with any loaded wagons gathered during the day. BILL POTTER/KRM

ABOVE: Taken a few moments after the previous shot, No. 3675 climbs away towards Cinderford. Bill was standing part way down the side of the redundant S&W embankment, with the town of Cinderford spread across the hillside in the right background. BILL POTTER/KRM

BELOW: Two days earlier, on 9th October, No. 4698 was captured passing the site of Cinderford Junction Signal Box, where the S&W and GWR lines met, heading away from the station. In the left foreground is a glimpse of the arch which had carried the S&W line over the Forest of Dean Tramroad. BILL POTTER/KRM

ABOVE: No. 4698 a few moments later, trundling down the embankment towards Bilson with its train of loaded vans and empty mineral wagons. BILL POTTER/KRM

BELOW: No. 3675 again but this time on 29th October 1965, leaving Cinderford with seven empty mineral wagons and a brake van. Bill was taking black & white shots as well as colour and the fact he returned here several times indicates how fascinated he was with the various workings and the photographic opportunities that the branch offered. BILL POTTER/KRM

The Up and Down time tables for the Forest of Dean Branch, from the September
1958 *Working Time Table*. NPC

WEEKDAYS   FOREST OF DEAN BRANCH

SINGLE LINE, worked by Electric Train Token between Bullo Pill West Box, Eastern United and Bilson Junction, and by Train Staff only (one engine in steam or two or more coupled at a time) between Bilson Junction and Churchway, Bilson Junction and Whimsey, and between Bilson Junction and Cinderford. The only intermediate crossing place is Eastern United Colliery. Worked by Electric Train Token between Bullo Pill West and Bilson Junction when Eastern United Box is closed. Trains may be booked to pass at Bilson Junction via Bilson Goods Yard.
The length of the Loop at Eastern United Colliery is 380 yards, capable of holding engine, 50 wagons, and van.

Mileage		Mile Post Mileage from Forest of Dean Branch Junction		DOWN	Ruling Gradient 1 in	K	K	K		K	K		K			
M	C	M	C			am	am	SX am		SX am	SX PM		SX PM			
—	76	—	—	NEWNHAM .... arr ... dep	—	..	7 5	..	..	8 40	1 15		1 50			
3	12	2	7	Bullo Pill......... dep Soudley Sidings...	48 R	..	..	..	..	..	..		..			
4	36	3	31	Eastern United Colliery	71 R	..	..	..	..	9X 4	..		2 10			
5	79	4	74	Bilson Junction ... ... arr ... dep	99 R	..	7 34 7 49	..	..	N	..		..			
6	62	5	57	CINDERFORD		..	7 54	..	..		..		..			
—	—	—	—	Bilson Junction		..	..	..	..		..		1 44			
—	—	—	—	Bilson Goods Yard ... arr .... dep		..	..	8X35 9 5	..		10 20		2 0			
7	22	6	17	Northern United Colly. arr	41 R	..	..	..	..		10 30		2 10			
6	65	5	60	Cinderford (Whimsey) ... arr	82 R	..	..	9 10	..		..		..			

N—Extended to Bilson Jn. with Colliery Empties by arrangement: Bilson Jn. arr. 9.12 am

---

WEEKDAYS   FOREST OF DEAN BRANCH

Mileage		UP	Ruling Gradient 1 in	K	K	K	G EBV	K	K	K	K		K					
M.	C.			am	am		SX N am	MO am	SX am	SO am	SX am		SX PM	SX PM				
1	44	Cinderford (Whimsey) ... dep	—	..	9 30													
—	—	Northern United Colly.	41 F	..	..			10†45	11 0	..	..		..	2 40 R P				
—	—	Brick Works Siding............		..	..				P									
—	—	Stop Board................		..	..													
—	—	Bilson Goods Yard .... arr .... dep	52 F	..	9 35			10 50	11 15	10 45	11 25		..	2 55 3240				
2	30	Bilson Junction	76 F	..	..													
—	—	CINDERFORD	—	8 30 P	..													
—	—	Stop Board............... arr	51 F	..	..													
2	30	Bilson Junction	76 F	8X35	..													
3	18	Stop Board... ... ... dep	178 F	..	..					10P51 10 55	11P31 11 35		..	3P44 3 49				
3	73	Eastern United Colliery	58 F	..	..			10 0		11P10	11P50	3X15		4N20				
5	5	Stop Board............... arr	49 F	..	..			10P 8		11 14	11 54	3P23 3 27		4P28 4 32				
5	17	Soudley Sidings..............	48 F	..	..			10 12										
7	33	Bullo Pill ... ... arr	54 F	..	..			10 34		11 36	12 16	3 49		4 54				
8	29	NEWNHAM .... arr ... dep		..	..													

N—Starts from Bilson Jn. at 9†33 am E. & B.V. when 8.40 am Bullo Pill runs to Bilson Jn.

Train worked by one Guard— load not to exceed 25 loaded wagons

SUSPENDED

N—Arrive 3X53 pm may perform second trip to Northern United Colliery when required

NOTE.—Up Freight Trains which, upon arrival at Eastern United, will consist of more than equal to 30 wagons of Class I traffic when worked by a Class " A " Engine, or more than equal to 35 wagons of Class I traffic when worked by a Class " C " Engine, to carry " H " Headcode.

LEFT: The approach to Cinderford station from the bridge carrying Valley Road over the line, with the SLS tour climbing up through the shallow cutting. On the right is Meredith & Drew's biscuit factory, built in 1950-1, which was later taken over by Engelhard Metals Ltd. Now part of the BASF Metals Recycling Ltd group, the company still occupies the factory, whilst the house on the left also still remains but the cutting has largely been landscaped out of existence. COLEFORD GWR MUSEUM (MIKE REES)

RIGHT: Having photographed No. 4698 from Letcher's Bridge, arriving at Bilson Junction on 30th March 1965, photographer John Dagley-Morris had time to scoot along Valley Road to capture the train again on the approach to Cinderford, where he climbed down to track level to take this picture. The signal just visible through the trees, immediately above the locomotive's chimney, marks the site of Cinderford Junction. There had been a signal box here, opened with the connecting line from Bilson to Cinderford station in 1908; it was closed at the end of December 1950, traffic along the S&W route having effectively ceased, although the line was not officially closed for another year. JOHN DAGLEY-MORRIS

LEFT: The Severn Boar II tour pulls in to Cinderford station, beneath Valley Road Bridge. The bright concrete beam and clean brickwork indicate that the bridge had relatively recently been rebuilt, although exactly when has not been ascertained. The new span replaced a pair of wrought iron bridge girders and was placed on the original abutments. The double track clearance alludes to the fact a headshunt had run back through the bridge in earlier years. The bridge survived for many years after closure but was eventually demolished as the road here was levelled and straightened. T.B. OWEN

The view from Valley Road Bridge towards the station, with No. 4698 engaged in shunting operations on 9th October 1965. The two wagons loaded with coal will eventually be deposited in one of the sidings on the left but will apparently be used first to drag the empties out. These will be placed on the run round loop (the second line from the right) and then the two full wagons will be shunted along in their place, next to the red liveried coal merchant's lorry waiting in the background. As already indicated, there were two businesses at Cinderford sending traffic out by rail in vans at this time, so it is likely that some of those seen here in and around the goods shed will be loaded with small plastic products, whilst others will be filled with boxes of biscuits. To the left of the wagons in the yard is the 5-ton crane installed when the station opened in 1900, whilst the small mound of earth between the lines near the end of the row of vans marks the site of Cinderford Signal Box, which was closed in 1927 as an economy measure. BILL POTTER/KRM

No. 3675 again, seen from the top of the embankment alongside the station throat, shunting a mixture of loaded, partially loaded and empty mineral wagons on 29th October 1965. Presumably, a bout of complicated shunting was about to ensue, to sort the empties from the rest prior to taking them back down to Bullo. On the goods shed road, smoke can be seen rising from the stove chimney of the brake van, which is coupled to three loaded coal wagons which have just arrived here. Note the rake of vans parked alongside the station platform; after removal of the passenger service, this platform was also used for goods loading. In the right background is, firstly, R.A. Lister & Co. Ltd's Cinderford Division factory and, on the far right, the gas holders of Cinderford Gasworks, which had ceased production by this date. Listers' main factory was (and still is) in Dursley, alongside the terminus of the Dursley Branch and will feature in the next volume in this series. The Cinderford factory was acquired in 1944 but has closed since this picture was taken. BILL POTTER/KRM

Another aspect of No. 4698 as it carries out shunting operations in Cinderford goods yard on 9th October 1965. BILL POTTER/KRM

One of the '16XX' Class of small pannier tanks, No. 1627, at Cinderford with a passenger service from Gloucester in 1958. A BR build, No. 1627 was new into service on 31st August 1950 at Gloucester Horton Road, where it spent much of its time sub-shedded at Lydney. Repainted into green livery, it had migrated to Oxford by June 1963, from where it was withdrawn in June 1964. The left-hand cabside numberplate survives in a private collection today COLOUR-RAIL

The '16XX' Class were a lightweight design for branch line work, that were seen as the successors to the '2021' Class, which had begun life as saddle tanks in the late 19th century but the majority of which had been converted to pannier tanks by the end of the 1920s. The '2021' Class had become synonymous with Forest passenger and goods services in both their saddle and pannier tank guises, so it was natural that the Hawksworth-designed small-wheeled '16XX's would take over from them. With the closure of the bay platform at Newnham and the extension of all Forest of Dean Branch passenger trains to run to and from Gloucester, services tended to be placed instead into the hands of the larger wheeled and auto-fitted '54xx' and '64XX' classes, and the '16XX's migrated elsewhere as a result. No. 1617 was new on 31st December 1949, going first to Oxford. After leaving Gloucester, the engine finished its career at Hereford, in November 1963. Note the canopy valance on the left, which had been trimmed at some stage to provide clearance for the local parcels delivery lorry. I love the character talking to the footplate crew; I'm guessing his rounded back and stooped posture mark him out as an old Forest miner, the coal seams in the Dean being notoriously thin. COLOUR-RAIL

THIS PAGE: The SLS Special at Cinderford in May 1961. The goods shed doors were home-made replacements, the original wooden doors having been damaged at some stage. ALL NPC

BOTTOM RIGHT: An excursion notice from August 1958, for a day trip from Cinderford to Weston-super-Mare. The train made its way out from Gloucester at 9.30am, picking up from Cinderford first where it arrived at 10.15 and departed at 10.55am. Stops were made on the way back down the branch at all of the halts and then at Newnham, Grange Court Junction and Gloucester on the main line. Heading south, the train travelled via Standish Junction and Yate South Junction, passing through Bristol and heading to Locking Road (the terminus station at Weston-super-Mare closed on 6th September 1964), where arrival was timed for 1.35pm. Departure that evening was at 7.35pm, with Cinderford being reached again at 10.27pm, ending a twelve hour trip that constituted a half day excursion! NPC

10

THURSDAY, 28th AUGUST—contd.

HALF-DAY EXCURSION—CINDERFORD TO WESTON-SUPER-MARE.

"A" Headcode.   Train No. 01.

Forward.	Arr. A.M.	Dep. A.M.	Return.	Arr. P.M.	Dep. P.M.
Gloucester Central	—	9†30	Weston-super-Mare (Locking Road)	—	7 35
Bullo Pill	9†50 **W**	9†55			
Cinderford	10†15	**N** 10 55	Yate South Jct.	8/47	
Ruspidge Halt	11 0	11 2	Standish Jct.	9/13	
Staple Edge Halt	11 5	11 6	Gloucester Central	9 28 **K**	9 35
Upper Soudley Halt	11 10	11 12	Grange Court	9 48	9 49
Bullo Pill	11/18		Newnham	9 55	9 56
Newnham	11 21	11 23	Bullo Pill	9 59 **W**	10 3
Grange Court	11 29	11 30	Upper Soudley Halt ..	10 9	10 11
Gloucester Central	11 43 **A**	11 54	Staple Edge Halt ..	10 15	10 16
	P.M.	P.M.	Ruspidge Halt	10 20	10 22
Standish Jct.	12/ 7		Cinderford	10 27 **N**	10†45
Yate South Jct.	12/32		Bullo Pill	11† 7 **W**	11†12
			Gloucester Central	11†33	—
Weston-super-Mare (Locking Road)	1 35				

Formation of Empty Stock leaving Gloucester for Cinderford : Brake Second X, 3 Seconds X.

Formation leaving Gloucester for Weston-super-Mare : Brake Second X, 5 Seconds X (Gloucester portion), 3 Seconds X, Brake Second X (Cinderford portion). **Load : 10.** Rolling Stock Control to arrange.

Notes—**A.**   Attach Gloucester portion front.
    K.   Detach Gloucester portion rear.
    N.   Reverse.

Cinderford to advise this office **immediately** train leaves, details of loading and timekeeping.

ABOVE AND BELOW: No. 6424 poses with the Gloucestershire Railway Society's Forest of Dean rail tour of 23rd June 1962. A selection of British Railways parcels lorries and trailers are on show, giving a good indication of the amount of traffic that was still flowing through the station at this date. BOTH NPC

Cinderford from the buffer stops circa 1962. The pine trees on the left are all that remains as a physical reminder of the station today. The crossover between the platform loop line and the goods shed road was not inter-connected, so the points could be set either way independently. IAN POPE COLLECTION

With a brown-liveried 'Toad' brake van in tow, No. 8701 arrives to shunt the yard and collect any loaded wagons one day in late summer 1962. DEREK CHAPLIN

A short while after the previous picture, No. 8701 prepares to shunt the yard. The locomotive has first deposited the 'Toad' brake van on the goods shed crossover and is now seen back along the goods loop. If the rake of box vans on the goods shed road are all ready to go, No. 8701 will couple up and then gently shunt them through the building in order that the brake van can be reattached. The station platform was also used for goods loading after passenger services finished in 1958, hence the rake of vans parked on that line. Two small boys watch operations with some fascination from the platform. Built for the GWR by Beyer, Peacock Ltd of Manchester in 1931, No. 8701 was a Gloucester-based engine for much of its life (although often sub-shedded at Lydney) and was withdrawn from there in March 1963. DEREK CHAPLIN

This was the classic view of Cinderford station, from the buffer stops end, with the photographer's back to Station Road. There had been a second crossover connecting the platform line and goods loop, permitting running round between these two lines but this had been removed in March 1961. Sited parallel to the loop to goods shed road crossover, its removal had further complicated the shunting manoeuvres required here; it meant that the only way of a locomotive running round its train was by dint of running through the goods shed, a practice normally frowned upon. Presumably a certain amount of gravity shunting was also used. IAN POPE COLLECTION

An unidentified '95XX' Series Type 1 diesel shunts the yard at 8am on 2nd March 1966. General goods and parcels traffic had been withdrawn from the beginning of the year and there was now only the coal merchants' traffic on offer here. There is a glimpse of the Station Hotel at the far end. ROBIN BARNES

A couple of spectators watch as the Cinderford goods prepares to leave on 27th April 1967, behind No. D9502 and with the additional brake vans for photographers attached. I have not been able to find a date for the last goods train; a note on the mount of this slide states that this was it but the Bill Potter view taken on the same day, overleaf, would suggest otherwise, with full coal wagons having just been deposited in the yard. The last train from Whimsey ran on 1st May, so perhaps the empties were also collected from here on that day, making this the last trainload of coal delivered here. At least one more train reached here before official closure of the branch on 14th August 1967, however, when BR ran up the line with No. D9517 and the District Engineer's Inspection Saloon on 18th July. NPC

No. D9501 shunts the yard having arrived with the 6.15am freight from Gloucester on 30th March 1967. Note the line of local coal merchants lorries on the left, waiting to load up and begin their daily deliveries. The second of the 'D95XX' Series, No. D9501 was stored at Worcester a year later. John Tolson/Trevor Davis collection

An overall view of Cinderford station and goods yard on 27th April 1967, with lorries again to be seen loading coal directly from the wagons on the left. No. D9502 stands alongside the platform with the branch goods and the brake vans added for the photographers charter. As mentioned on the previous page, at least one more visit must have been made to the yard to collect the wagons on the left once they had been emptied of coal. Bill Potter/KRM

LEFT: We finish our study of Cinderford station with three detail shots of some of the buildings, for the benefit of modellers. In point of fact, Cinderford already exists as a 4mm or 00 gauge model, albeit as a mirror image and with the inclusion of an additional siding for an engine shed, behind the platform at the road bridge end. Here, the Severn Boar II tour arrives alongside the platform, with the photographer having pressed the shutter a second or two before the detail of the station building beneath the canopy could be obscured by the train. T.B. OWEN

RIGHT: The station building and the end of the goods shed, looking south in 1967, after all services had ceased. This view also provides a glimpse of the brick-built hut situated just back from the main building at this end, which was a carpenters' shop provided in 1907-8. The goods shed extension was authorised in 1900 and was built originally for the Nailsworth Brewery Company. It later came under the ownership of the Cheltenham Original Brewery Company, from whom the GWR and LM&SR Joint Committee purchased it in 1930. At this date it was in use as a garage and stables but was later used to store sugar and latterly for cement. IAN POPE COLLECTION

LEFT: Both the station and goods shed were built of local Pennant sandstone which, as the splashes of red oxide here indicate, has a strong iron ore content in places. This view shows the road loading side and note the steps up to the goods office situated at this end, which was raised so as to be level with the internal goods platform. The sliding doors were probably original and note the small canopy, provided to protect against the worst of the elements. This view was taken in spring 1967, before the coal traffic finally ceased. IAN POPE COLLECTION

No. D9501 trundles through a deserted Bilson yard with a short Cinderford to Gloucester freight on 30th March 1967. The locomotive had a very brief life indeed. New in July 1964, it was withdrawn in March 1968 and scrapped three months later by C.F. Booth of Rotherham – not four years old! JOHN TOLSON/TREVOR DAVIS COLLECTION

Four weeks later, on the occasion of the 27th April photographers' charter, No. D9502 heads back down the branch, passing the immaculately painted and maintained Bilson Junction Signal Box but with nothing to be seen in the by now little used sidings. BILL POTTER/KRM

SECTION 1A
The CHURCHWAY BRANCH

The Churchway Branch served the Coleford Brick & Tile Company's brickworks at Hawkwell and Northern United Colliery, and was a little under one mile in length. Departing northwards from the top end of Bilson Yard, it also made a triangular junction with the Severn & Wye line via the South Loop, the connection for which was still *in situ* beneath the wheels of the locomotive, and the North Loop, which joined further on up. These two views show No. 3675 taking water on 11th October 1965. As can be deduced from the limited height clearance available, the abutments for both the Churchway and Whimsey branches had supported shallow wrought iron girder spans, whilst the abutments themselves were constructed of locally quarried stone. BOTH BILL POTTER/KRM

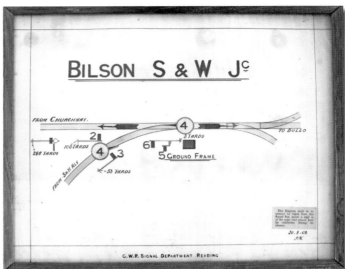

ABOVE: The GWR signalling diagram from Bilson S&W Junction Ground Frame. Note the disc & crossbar signal on the left; originally provided in 1878 to protect Brain's Tramway Crossing, it survived until circa 1958, when the track was lifted from the loops and the site of Cinderford 'old' station. IAN POPE COLLECTION

LEFT: The start of the Churchway Branch as seen from the S&W embankment on 7th April 1965. On the left is the short remnant of the South Loop, which had curved round and up to join with the Severn & Wye line. The North Loop, which can be seen in the distance, provided a northwards connection to the Churchway Branch that, in reality, was little used. The course of Brain's Tramway can just be discerned beyond the trackway also crossing over the Churchway Branch and leading to Cinderford 'old' station. Large stacks of timber sleepers grew on either side of the South Loop during the Second World War, although, perhaps surprisingly in such an afforested region, they were imported from Canada. HOWARD BURCHELL

BELOW: A '57XX' 0-6-0PT propels empty mineral wagons away from Bilson Yard and up the Churchway Branch on 7th April 1965. HOWARD BURCHELL

Having replenished its tanks, No. 3675 accelerates up the gradient to Northern United, which grew steeper as the line neared the colliery. To the left of the train is almost the full expanse of the triangular junction between the GWR and S&W lines, with the South Loop junction, which had been under the control of Bilson S&W Junction Ground Frame when it was still in operation, just off picture on the left; the hut housing the ground frame had stood just the other side of the bridge, opposite the water tank. The site of Cinderford 'old' station was hard against the trees in the background above the wagons, whilst Bilson North Junction, where the North Loop joined the Churchway Branch, can just be glimpsed ahead of the train. The dark ground in the right background was the site of a short lived coal washery, established in the early 1960s, details for which are contained in the caption for the picture on page 95. The brake van is just about to pass over the track leading to Cinderford 'old' station; just beyond this, the shallow embankment marking the course of Brain's Tramway can be seen more clearly in this view. This 2ft 7¹/₂ins gauge line ran from Brain's Trafalgar Colliery to an interchange with the GWR's sidings at Bilson. In 1869, a second line was opened to the Golden Valley Iron Mine at Drybrook, which also served a coal landsales wharf at Nailbridge, where the tramway terminated in its later years. It was this line which crossed the Churchway Branch on the level, albeit the tramway was there first. It was locomotive worked up until circa 1905, when the section to Bilson was closed. Thereafter and up until final closure in 1925, when the colliery shut, it was horse worked. It. BILL POTTER/KRM

A rare colour view of the remains of Cinderford 'old' station, with a section of the platform wall evident on the left. This was not Cinderford's first station, however, that honour being claimed by Bilson Platform, opened in 1876 and situated on the S&W line, about a half mile east of Drybrook Road and close to the junction where the North and South Loops bifurcated. This was only ever intended as a temporary solution but its replacement, the station seen here, was only marginally closer to Cinderford, the S&W seemingly being reluctant to incur the cost of bridging the GWR lines to reach the town. The station opened on 5th August 1878, the new platform being built alongside the existing north curve but having a new connection put in to make a run round loop. Accommodation was provided in the form of one of the familiar Eassie wooden buildings (replicas of which can be seen on the Dean Forest Railway today). A horse bus service

which met every train was provided from 1880, to anywhere in the town but at a cost of 6d per passenger. A goods platform complete with a small shed and crane were later added alongside the south curve. The old station closed in 1900 when the new station in Cinderford was opened but the sidings remained in use for wagon storage for many years and were extensively used for the storage of various materials during the Second World War, particularly in the build up to D-Day; around twenty-five American bogie tank wagons were stored here, built from kits of parts whch had been imported through Newport Docks. Ironically, whilst there is little left on the site of Cinderford 'new' (1900) station, the remains of this platform wall can still just be made out today, hidden in the trees. MICHAEL HALE

Again taken on 11th October 1965, No. 3675 arrives back at Bilson with a loaded train from Northern United Colliery. The locomotive is just passing the point and short remaining stub of the north curve, whilst in the left foreground is the remains of the buffer stop which formed the terminus of the S&W line alongside the platform of Cinderford 'old' station. The empties from the previous picture have been exchanged for this rake of loadeds at the colliery. Note the two Berry Wiggins tanks tacked on the end of the train; these have made the journey up to the colliery and back, the train crew apparently deciding this was easier than leaving them in Bilson Yard and then collecting them on the return, prior to heading back down to Bullo. BILL POTTER/KRM

No. 6437 with the SLS Tour of 13th May 1961 at the head of the Churchway Branch. NPC

Our first sighting of the Railway Enthusiast Club's Severn Rambler railtour of 20th April 1958. Calling at several locations in the Gloucester area first, this was the tour's only stop in the Forest, having come up the branch from Bullo. Loaded wagons were gravity worked away from the colliery, as locomotives were not permitted beneath the very low bridge in the foreground. In the left distance, just on the bend in the line, is a glimpse of Hawkwell Brickworks. T.B. Owen

ABOVE: Two views of No. 1658 propelling the Severn Boar II railtour up the empty wagons line to Northern United on 20th June 1964; note the rake of loadeds part way down the road on the left; these were gravity worked away from the colliery and are waiting here to be collected by the next train. T.B. OWEN

BELOW: The Churchway Branch officially ended in the trees just off to the left, the terminus including a short loop. The line down to the colliery empties sidings branched off beneath the end of the train. T.B. OWEN

LEFT: The loading screens at Northern United Colliery, with enthusiasts from the Severn Boar II tour in the left foreground. Whilst they were allowed to wander all over BR property, the colliery itself was strictly 'off limits'. Northern United was the newest and most modern of Dean's deep mines, the site having been acquired by Crawshays from the Crown in 1931 and the colliery sunk from May 1933 to February 1934. Coal production began in earnest in 1935, so the colliery had a working life of just over thirty years, closing at Christmas 1965. At its peak, Northern United had employed a workforce of some 700 men but this figure had dropped to 215 by the time of closure. JOHN RYAN

ABOVE: The loading screens from the empties road, with the sidings for empty wagons just visible in the left background. Locomotives could shunt the wagons into these sidings but then had to return via this road, as they were not permitted to travel through the screens or beneath the bridge seen previously. Empty wagons were run through the screens for loading by gravity. The brake van was also gravity worked back down the empty wagons road on to the end of the loaded train, which it joined adjacent to Hawkwell Brickworks. The covered tub route from the shaft can be seen coming in on the right. DAVID BICK

RIGHT: Looking north from near the screens in June 1964, with the steel headframe marking the site of the main shaft in the left background and the coal washery on the right. JOHN RYAN

ABOVE LEFT: Looking towards the end of the Churchway Branch in May 1961. Latterly, only a short portion of this had been used, to stable the brake van whilst the empty wagons were shunted into the colliery sidings, the section including the run round loop having fallen out of use to the extent that bushes had grown up through the track. The notice board on the right read 'ENGINES MUST NOT PASS THIS BOARD'. DAVID BICK

ABOVE RIGHT: Taken from a position just behind the bushes seen in the previous picture, this is looking back along the track to the SLS train. DAVID BICK

LEFT: A sylvan study of Northern United's spoil tip looking across Meadowcliffe Pond circa 1964. The tip was reworked for a couple of years in the 1980s, for coal waste that could be burnt in power stations but the venture was not very successful and most of it still remains today, now overgrown with trees. ANNE BEAUFOY

RIGHT: The Coleford Brick & Tile Co's Hawkwell Brickworks in 1987. The main building had been extended since the closure of the railway and there had been four brick chimneys here but otherwise the works looks much the same as it had done in 1960. The route of the Churchway Branch is just behind the stacks of bricks on the right, whilst the flat ground to the left of these marks the site of the siding serving the works. The Private Siding Agreement (PSA) was terminated in June 1965, when the siding was also removed but it is likely to have been out of use for some time prior to that. The Coleford Brick & Tile Co. was established in 1925, first acquiring the Marions Brickworks near Coleford. Looking to expand, the company purchased the old Hawkwell Brickworks site in 1936, which had ceased production by 1925 and subsequently been demolished. The new brickworks was in production by 1938 and the PSA was signed in the same year. The works is still in operation today, the company specialising in hand made bricks. DAVID BICK

SECTION 1B
The WHIMSEY BRANCH

The Whimsey Branch was originally the northernmost section of the Forest of Dean Branch, prior to the opening of Cinderford 'new' station. The line north from Whimsey was built by the Mitcheldean Road & Forest of Dean Junction Railway, to provide a northern outlet for Forest iron ore and coal, but it proved an expensive white elephant, running over budget and taking years to complete. By the time it was finished, it had been superceded by the opening of the S&W's Lydbrook line. Absorbed by the GWR, the branch made only an indirect connection with the Hereford, Ross and Gloucester line at Mitcheldean Road (*see Volume 1*) and was never brought in to operation north of Drybrook. The Drybrook to Mitcheldean Road section was lifted during the First World War but was partially relaid north from Drybrook Halt to serve Drybrook Quarry in the late 1920s. The section north of Whimsey was finally closed in the early 1950s when the quarry ceased rail operations. The Whimsey Branch thus only became such for the last decade and a half of its existence; just less than half a mile in length, it served a tar distribution depot established in the old Cinderford Goods station by Berry Wiggins & Co. Ltd. These two views show 0-6-0PT No. 9672 on 6th November 1965, passing the Bilson Up Distant signal and then heading through the remains of the arch which carried the S&W line over the branch. Its short train comprises three tank wagons – one Berry Wiggins and two South Eastern Gas Board tanks in red oxide livery – with an ex-GWR 'Toad' brake van bringing up the rear. BOTH BILL POTTER/KRM

Photographed from the embankment of the S&W line, No. 4698 heads away from Bilson Junction with three South Eastern Gas Board tank wagons bound for the Berry Wiggins depot at Whimsey on 9th October 1965. The locomotive is just passing the fixed Up Distant signal for Bilson Junction, which provided a permanent cautionary aspect for trains approaching the yard in the background from off the Whimsey Branch. The SEGB covered Kent, along with parts of south London, Middlesex, Surrey and Sussex, and the wagons may have originated from the large Thames-side gas works at Greenwich, the site of which now houses the O2 Arena, previously known as the Millenium Dome. On the left is the curved embankment which carried the Cinderford Branch up from the junction to Cinderford station. Note the makeshift animal pen between the two lines and the cast iron milepost in the left foreground. BILL POTTER/KRM

LEFT: A slightly different aspect of the start of the Whimsey Branch and the fixed Distant signal, taken from the bridge abutment on the Cinderford side of the line. On 29th October 1965, No. 3675 works a single wagon load of coal up the branch to Whimsey. The coal was destined for the boilers of the steam heating plant at Berry Wiggins depot, which was used to liquify the bitumen. BILL POTTER/KRM

RIGHT: Looking in the opposite direction north towards Whimsey, as No. 4698 heads back to Bilson Junction with an empty Berry Wiggins tank and an empty SEGB tank, on 9th October 1965. The branch was on a gradient heading down the valley to Bilson, although not as steep as that from Churchway. The lower part of Cinderford is hidden by the trees, whilst today, industrial premises now cover much of this landscape, including the marshy area on the right. BILL POTTER/KRM

LEFT: Viewed from the verandah of the brake van, the 27th April 1967 charter with No. D9502 at the head clatters back down the branch. The train is about to pass through the remains of the arch which carried the S&W line across the branch. The span was removed in the 1950s and the two abutments have in recent years been demolished, as the aperture was opened up to allow Forest Vale Road, which serves the new industrial estate here, to be built through it. The road is on a different alignment to the railway, which is why the gap had to be opened out but this has also served to make it quite difficult to work out exactly where the railway ran from ground level. However, from the air, as a study of the area on Google Earth shows, the route of the branch is still clearly defined. NPC

The Severn Boar II tour, looking in opposite directions from the S&W embankment. The first view, ABOVE, shows the branch curving round from the north, with Broadmoor Brickworks in the background and then, BELOW, heading south towards Bilson. BOTH T.B. OWEN

This view is a companion to that which forms the title page double spread and shows No. 3675 a little further along on its way back down the branch to Bilson, on 11th October 1965. Hawkwell Row features again in the trees in the right background, whilst above the wagons there is evidence of some of the extensive workings to which this area had been subjected throughout the 19th century. The route from the town to Cinderford 'old' station also passes from right to left behind the train, along the old dam, later used by the tramroad; passage along it could not have been an attractive prospect in the dark or during inclement weather, which was why townsfolk pressed hard for a more advantageously sited new station. The Churchway Branch climbs up the valley in the left background, passing just to the other side of the white-washed cottage, before turning to head through the trees just by the brick hut. The dark patch of ground between the two buildings marks the site of a washery, set up in 1962 by Beaver Transport Ltd, to wash spoil from various of the local tips and extract small coal, which was sold to the Central Electricity Authority. An application was made for a private siding, with an anticipated two trains per day emanating from the site but, in the event, it was not proceeded with due to the cost and the recovered coal was despatched by road instead. The washery seems only to have been in operation for a couple of years at most, although this was long enough to seriously contaminate the ground, a legacy still causing problems fifty years later. Today, much of this area is now covered with industrial premises and new roads but the washery site remains undeveloped. Bill Potter/KRM

ABOVE: On the occasion of the visit by the Severn Boar II railtour to Berry Wiggins' Whimsey depot, established in what had been Cinderford Goods station, this view is looking north from the site of Regulator Colliery, a 19th century enterprise which ceased operation around 1865. The level crossing was situated at the southern end of the station and carried the minor Whimsey Road across the railway. To the left, where the train is standing and on the same side of the line as the photographer, was the site of Whimsey Halt, closed with the withdrawal of the passenger service north of Cinderford in 1930. JOHN RYAN

INSET FAR LEFT: Wagon label for the delivery of the Severn Tunnel Junction Signal & Telegraph Department mess van to Whimsey, for attention to Whimsey Ground Frame in January 1964. NPC

ABOVE: Good detail of some Berry Wiggins tank wagons, with No. 1658 having shunted the brake vans to what was now the limit of the line. T.B. OWEN

RIGHT: No. D9502 scurries back down the Whimsey Branch on 27th April 1967. Berry Wiggins depot had closed by this date so this part of the trip up the Cinderford Branch was purely for the benefit of the photographers in the brake vans. The train is passing Broadmoor Brickworks, which had retained one of Duck Colliery's sidings when it was established in 1922. The siding seems to have been used mainly for deliveries, of coal for the brickwork's boilers and shale from local tips for brick making. It was extended in 1945 but taken out in 1951. One of the Broadmoor Brick Company Ltd's lorries is visible on the left. In the left background, Cinderford Goods depot can just be made out, with the stone-built goods shed just glimpsed beyond the brickworks building. BILL POTTER/KRM

An overall view of Berry Wiggins Whimsey depot, looking north from the Whimsey Road level crossing and taken on 31st May 1966. A selection of tar tank wagons can be seen along with several mineral wagons delivering coal for the boilers. In the right foreground is Cinderford Crossing Ground Frame. Cinderford Goods opened as a broad gauge depot and tramroad interchange in 1854 and was one of the two northernmost terminal points of the branch, along with the depot at Churchway. On the left are the remains of Whimsey Colliery, which was no doubt intended to provide traffic but which closed soon after the line opened. The Mitcheldean Road & Forest of Dean Junction Railway was built northwards from here, from where the line curves away to the left at the far end. Berry Wiggins took over Cinderford Goods station in 1949, whilst J. Joiner & Sons Ltd of Cinderford moved into the saw mills site to the north east of the depot in 1952, with the intention of sending their output by rail but whether this traffic actually began and, if so, when it ceased is unknown. In spring 1967, Berry Wiggins transferred their operations to a new depot at Lydney, which spelt the end for this site and proved the death blow for the Forest of Dean Branch. BILL POTTER/KRM

K148

WEEKDAYS BERKELEY ROAD AND MIERY STOCK SIDINGS

Double Line From	Double Line To	Single Line From	Single Line To	Worked by	Crossing Stations	Staff Stations
Berkeley Rd. Sth Jn.	Berkeley Loop Jn.	Berkeley Road	Otters Pool Jn.	Electric Train Tablet or Token	Sharpness South	Berkeley Rd. and Berkeley Loop Jn.
—	—	—	—		Severn Bridge	Sharpness South, Severn Bridge.
Otters Pool Jn.	Lydney Town	Lydney Town	Parkend		—	Otters Pool Jn., Lydney Town, Tufts Jn. & Parkend
Parkend	Coleford Jn.	Coleford Jn.	Speech House Rd.			
—	—	—	—			
—	—	Tufts Jn. (Oakwood Branch)	Princess Royal Sdgs.	Train Staff (one engine only or two coupled together).	—	Coleford Jn., Speech House Road.
—	—	Speech House Rd. (Wimberry Branch)	Cannop Sdgs.		—	—

Mile Post Mileage from Berkeley Road M	C	Mileage from Coleford Junction M	C	DOWN		Ruling Gradient 1 in	F		F		K	K		K		K
							3.5 pm Newton Abbot to Rogerstone		2.55 am Stoke Gifford to Cardiff		4.35 am Gloucester	5.0 am Gloucester				
							6590		6643							
							MX		MX		MX	MO				
							am		am		am	am		am		am
—	—	—	—	BERKELEY ROAD ... dep	1	—					6 15	6 50				
—	—	—	—	Berkeley Road South Jn.	2	150 F	12 43		3 50							
1	26	—	—	Berkeley Loop Junction	3	200 F	12*53		3 54							
2	24	—	—	Berkeley	4	200 F										
3	44	—	—	Sharpness South ... arr	5	132 R					6 30	7 5				
				... dep	6											
4	15	—	—	Sharpness	7	132 R	1W11		4W 9							
5	40	—	—	Severn Bridge ... arr	8	132 R										
				... dep	9											
7	71	—		Otters Pool Junction	10	132 F										
N	—	—		Lydney (Main Line)	11	—	1*30		4*28							
8	15	—	—	Lydney Junction ... arr	12	132 F	Sharpness arr. 1W6 am		Sharpness arr. 4W4 am					M		
				... dep	13									7 30		8 0
8	32	—	—	Engine Shed	14	160 R								M—Assisted		
8	73	—	—	Lydney Town	15	160 R										8 5
—	—	—	—	Norchard Siding	16	—										
10	60	—	—	Tufts Junction ... arr	17	117 R										
				... dep	18	—										
—	—	—	—	Princess Royal Siding arr	19	—										
11	32	—	—	Whitecroft	20	173 R										
12	25	—	—	Parkend	21	173 R										
12	71	—	—	Coleford Junction ... arr	22	106 R								7 55		
				... dep	23									8 25		
15	47	2	56	Milkwall ... arr	24	31 R										
				... dep	25											
—	—	—	—	Sling	26	—										
15	79	3	8	Stop Board ... arr	27	31 R								8P42		
				... dep	28									8 47		
16	49	3	58	Coleford ... arr	29	47 F								8 53		
				... dep	30									9N30		
—	—	—	—	Whitecliff Sidings ... arr	31	—								9N35		
13	62	—	—	Bicslade Siding	32	96 R								N—Q Coleford to Whitecliff Sidings		
14	67	—	—	Speech House Road ... arr	33	132 R										
				... dep	34											
—	—	—	—	Cannop Siding ... arr	35	—										
16	33	—	—	Serridge ... arr	36	40 R										
				... dep	37											
17	37	—	—	Miery Stock Sidings ... arr	38	507 R										

N—Distance Otters Road Jn. to Lydney Jn. (ML) Signal Box 8 chains.

K149

WEEKDAYS BERKELEY ROAD AND MIERY STOCK SIDINGS

SINGLE LINE worked by Train Staff (one engine in steam) between Coleford Junction and Coleford and between Coleford and Whitecliff. No intermediate crossing place.

	K			K		K	K		K	K		K		K	F	SUNDAYS F	F		
						10.0 am Gloucester			2.45 pm Miery Stock Sidings to Lydney Jn.			To Lydney			7.35 pm Bristol (East Depot) to Rogerstone	11.40 pm (Sats.) Stoke Gifford to Cardiff	3.5 pm (Sats.) Newton Abbot to Rogerstone		
															6530		6590		
	SX						SX		SX	SX									
	am			am		am	am		PM	PM		PM		PM	PM	am	am		
1						11 30													
2															10 33	12 28	12 43		
3															10 36	12 32	12*53		
4																			
5						11 45													
6														6 15					
7												1 35			10NW51	12W47	1W11		
8																			
9																			
10																			
11															11*10	1*44	1*30		
12												1 56		6 37	For continuation see page 27		Sharpness arr. 1W6 am		
13	9 25						11 20			12 15									
14																			
15																			
16																			
17	9 39									12 29									
18	9 50									12 34									
19	10 5									12Z49									
20							11N48			Z—To make additional trip when necessary between Parkhill and Princess Royal Siding, arrive 2.0 pm					N—Sharpness arr. 10W46 pm				
21																			
22							12W 0												
23				11 45			12W 5												
24				12 0			N—Whitecroft arrive 11.38 am									Lydney arr. 1.8 am			
25				12 30															
26																			
27				12P34															
28				12 39															
29				12 45															
30				1N 0															
31				1N 5															
32				N—Q Coleford to Whitecliff Sidings															
33							12 22		3 33							Sharpness arr. 12 W42 am			
34							12 32		3 43										
35							12 37		3 48										
36							1 53												
37							2 8												
38							2 18												

K150

WEEKDAYS MIERY STOCK SIDINGS AND BERKELEY ROAD

Mileage M	C	Mileage from Coleford M	C	UP		Ruling Gradient 1 in	H	H	K	K	K	K	K	G	K	
							11.0 pm Severn Tunnel Jn. to Bristol W.D.	1.0 am Severn Tunnel Jn. to Exeter		To Gloucester				L E	To Gloucester	
							7217	7322								
							MX	MX				SX				
							am	am	am	am	am	am	am	am	PM	
—	—	—	—	Miery Stock Sidings	1	—										
1	4	—	—	Serridge ... arr	2	—							N—Q Whitecliffe Sidings to Coleford			
				... dep	3	—										
—	—	—	—	Cannop Siding ... dep	4	—										
2	50	—	—	Speech House Road ... arr	5	40 F										
				... dep	6											
3	55	—	—	Bicslade Siding	7	132 F							M			
—	—	—	—	Whitecliffe Sidings ...	8	—							10 10N			
—	—	—	—	Coleford ... arr	9	—							10 15N			
				... dep	10								10 50			
—	—	—	49	Stop Board ... arr	11	47 R							10P58			
				... dep	12								11 1			
—	—	—	—	Sling	13	—										
—	—	—	77	Milkwall ... arr	14	31 F	Sharpness arr. 12W33 am	Sharpness arr. 2W13 am								
				... dep	15											
4	46	3	53	Coleford Junction ... arr	16	Z96 F							11 23	11‖54		
				... dep	17											
5	12	—	—	Parkend	18	106 F										
6	16	—	—	Whitecroft	19	173 F										
—	—	—	—	Princess Royal Siding ...	20							10 35				
6	57	—	—	Tufts Junction ... arr	21	173 F		Berkeley Road South Jn. arr. 2*37 am	Assisted to Severn Bridge when necessary			10 40				
				... dep	22							10 50	M—Assisted			
—	—	—	—	Norchard Siding	23	—										
8	44	—	—	Lydney Town	24	117 F					9 5			PM		
9	5	—	—	Engine Shed	25	160 F										
9	22	—	—	Lydney Junction ... arr	26	160 F					9 10	11 5		12‖ 5		
				... dep	27	—			6 45							
—	—	—	—	Lydney (Main Line)	28	—	12*12	1 55								
9	46	—	—	Otters Pool Junction	29	132 R									N—Arr. 12.47 pm	
11	77	—	—	Severn Bridge ... arr	30	132 R										
				... dep	31											
13	22	—	—	Sharpness	32	132 F	12W38	2W18								
13	37	—	—	Sharpness South ... arr	33	132 F			7 3							
				... dep	34					7 55					12 40	
15	13	—	—	Berkeley	35	132 F									12N52	
16	11	—	—	Berkeley Loop Junction	36	200 R	12 51	2 31								
—	—	—	—	Berkeley Road South Jn.	37	150 R	12 55	3*18								
17	37	—	—	BERKELEY ROAD ... arr	38	200 R				8 10					1 2	

K151

WEEKDAYS MIERY STOCK SIDINGS AND BERKELEY ROAD

	K		K	K		K		K	K			H	H	H		SUNDAYS H		H	
			11.20 am Lydney to Miery Stock Sidings									To Stoke Gifford	6.50 pm Sev. Tun. Jn. to Bristol (East Depot)	To Stoke Gifford		11.0 pm (Sats.) Severn Tunnel Jn. to Bristol W.D.		1.0 am Severn Tunnel Jn. to Newton Abbot	
												7251	7277	7251		7217		7322	
			SX	SX		SO		SX	SX			SO		SX					
	PM		PM	PM		PM		PM	PM			PM	PM	PM		am		am	
1								2 45											
2								2 56											
3								3 18											
4			1 30					4 8											
5	N—Q Whitecliffe Sidings to Coleford		1 35					4 13											
6			1 40					4 23											
7								R											
8	1N20																		
9	1 25																		
10	1 45																		
11	1P53																		
12	1 56			N—Norchard Siding arr. 3.17 pm															
13																			
14												Berkeley Road South Jn. arr. 11*23 pm		Berkeley Road South Junction arr. 11*23 pm		Sharpness arr. 12W33 am		Sharpness arr. 2W13 am	
15																			
16	2 18					Assisted to Severn Bridge when necessary			Assisted to Severn Bridge when necessary										
17	2 30																		
18	R																		
19	Z																		
20	Z—Time allowed for Cash Box purposes			2 45															
21				2 55									N—Sharpness arr. 8W37 pm					Berkeley Road South Jn. arr. 2*37 am	
22				3 5															
23				3N25															
24																			
25																			
26	3 6			3 33				5 0											
27						4 25			4 50			9 30		10 30					
28													8 20			12*12		1 55	
29																			
30																			
31																			
32													8NW42			12W38		2W18	
33						4 44			5 8			9 50	8 44	10 50					
34												10 5	9* 1	11 5					
35																			
36												10 16	9 13	11 16		12 51		2 31	
37												10*30	9 35	11*29		12 55		3* 0	
38																			

The Down (Top) and Up (Bottom) Working Time Tables for goods trains on the Severn & Wye line, from Berkeley Road to Mierystock and Coleford for September 1958. Note the various sections of line listed at the top, along with how they were worked; Severn Bridge station was still noted as a place for trains to cross. NPC

RIGHT: Lydney Junction (S&W) station circa 1964, looking south east towards the river. Note the Midland style target nameboards and slanted wooden fencing. IAN POPE COLLECTION

BELOW: Looking in the opposite direction, with the GRS tour at the Up platform, whilst the passengers make their way towards the footbridge and the GWR station. The special had previously visited Dymock and Cinderford, and traversed the S&W line to Speech House Road, prior to being seen here. NPC

BELOW: A similar view to this appeared in the first volume but here the driver of No. 4671 has paused his engine closer to the photographer, no doubt in order that he could take his picture, from the footbridge linking the S&W and GWR junction stations, in September 1964. The '57XX' had arrived here from Severn Tunnel Junction shed, Lydney shed having closed a few months earlier, and was engaged in shunting the old GWR/S&W Joint transfer sidings. In the centre distance is Lydney Junction Signal Box, an ex-GWR timber-built structure which was pictured more closely in Volume One. To the left, Otterspool Junction box can just be seen partially hidden by telegraph poles and with the twin tracks of the passenger lines to Berkeley Road heading towards it. In the centre, rows of empty steel-bodied mineral wagons wait to be taken up to Princess Royal Colliery, to be loaded with coal delivered and screened there from the drift mine at Pillowell. ALAN JARVIS

RIGHT: From the *General Appendix to the Working Time Table (Gloucester District)*, October 1960. NPC

BELOW: Taken a few moments prior to the previous picture and looking in the opposite direction, No. 4671 shunts a condemned wagon into the siding next to the works of Wagon Repairs Ltd. Note the footbridge ramp down to the S&W station on the right. The background is dominated by the spire of St. Mary's Church and just below it can be seen Lydney Engine Shed signal box. To the left of it are the single-storey, stone-built sheds that had housed the West of England Wagon Company's works but operations here had ceased in the late 1950s. The square chimney just glimpsed through the steam on the left marks the site of Lydney engine shed. The SEGB tank wagon on the right was coupled to the van and loaded coal wagon seen in the previous picture, and are likely to have been heading to or from the Forest of Dean Branch, via Bullo Junction. ALAN JARVIS

Working of Freight Trains and Light Engines from Sharpness Direction to Lydney S. & W. Joint Yard during the time Lydney Engine Shed Box is closed

During the time Lydney Engine Shed Signal Box is closed Freight trains and Light engines from the Sharpness direction for Lydney S. & W. Joint may be dealt with as follows :—

Over Down Goods Line Otters Pool Junction to Lydney Junction and thence to Lydney S. & W. Joint via Sidings under the supervision of the Shunters and the Foreman or Pointsman on duty, who will be responsible for the disposal of trains and engines through the Sidings.

Light engines to and from Lydney Running and Maintenance Depot and the W. R. Yard may also pass in accordance with the instructions 'respecting "Shunting in Sidings between Lydney Junction W.R. and Lydney S. & W. Joint Line ", see page 130.

LEFT: No. 6424 waits with the GRS tour. The train was worked in auto mode back to Gloucester. With the closure of the Severn Bridge, the Up line through the station had become little used. The oil lamps here were quite delightful but had mostly assumed rather drunken angles by this date. BILL POTTER/KRM

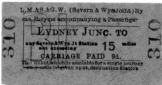

ABOVE: The equivalent of what used to be known as 'Taking coals to Newcastle'! With the Forest's collieries having all by now closed, No. D9555 heads through Lydney Junction (S&W) yard on 26th April 1967 with a mix of empty and loaded steel mineral wagons. The coal was bound for Coleford. The trip included an extra couple of brake vans for photographers and took place on the day prior to the similar trip which traversed the Forest of Dean Branch. Note the Berry Wiggins tank wagons on the left; the company had just transferred their depot to here from Whimsey. BILL POTTER/KRM

RIGHT: The derelict station awaits its ultimate fate on 22nd April 1967, with the passenger lines, no longer required, having been lifted. The station has since been recreated by the Dean Forest Railway, on the same site, with a new island platform on which sits a replica Eassie station building. A run round loop has been laid where the Up line ran but the Up platform has, to date, not been rebuilt. At the far end, a new link road to and from the Lydney by-pass passes over the station throat by means of a level crossing, protected by lifting barriers. BILL POTTER/KRM

Ex-GWR '14XX' Class 0-4-2T No. 1430 propels a two coach auto train from Lydney Town station into Lydney Junction (S&W) bound for Berkeley Road on 7th August 1957. The photographer was standing with his back to Lydney engine shed and on the extreme right is a glimpse of Lydney Yard signal box, a Midland Railway box dating from December 1906. BILL POTTER/KRM

Lydney Engine Shed signal box was another Midland Railway structure, new in March 1918 and seen here circa 1967. It was a busy box as it also controlled the access to Richard Thomas & Co's Lydney Tinplate Works but this had closed in 1957. The box itself was closed on 2nd October 1967. IAN POPE COLLECTION

ABOVE: Having taken the top picture on the previous page, Bill turned round to photograph the shed. On the right is BR-built '16XX' Class 0-6-0PT No. 1630, in the company of a sister engine and a '57XX' Class 0-6-0PT. The shed opened in 1868 and was closed in March 1964. Coded LYD by the GWR, it became a sub shed to Gloucester Horton Road in 1935, which was coded 85B by BR. Lydney's allocation comprised mainly pannier tanks but also included a couple of '14XX' 0-4-2Ts as well up until the Lydney Town-Berkeley Road passenger service ceased in 1960. An engine for the nightly goods train to Stoke Gifford yard via the Severn Bridge was also stabled here, usually a Class '43XX' 2-6-0 but occasionally a Collett 0-6-0 instead, up until the loss of the bridge in 1960. BILL POTTER/KRM

BELOW: A '57XX' Class 0-6-0PT, No. 3737, stands outside the shed alongside the coaling platform in February 1964, just a few weeks before its closure. The building on the right housed the offices, whilst those just glimpsed on the far left were the old S&W workshops. The line just featuring in the bottom right corner ran in to Lydney Tinplate Works, which had been under the ownership of the Steel Company of Wales from 1949 up until its closure in 1957. R.H. MARROWS

Class '16XX' No. 1626, built by BR in August 1950, with an unidentified '57XX' pannier tank on the back road or engineer's siding at Lydney shed probably in 1963. The second engine is likely to be No. 8729, which was also photographed in this position with No. 1626 on 10th March 1963 by Bob Marrows. Both locomotives had been withdrawn in 1962, officially from Gloucester Horton Road shed; their number plates had been removed and the numbers painted on the cab sides in readiness for their final journeys for disposal, which occurred in August 1963. The stone wall on the right borders Station Road; although this has been partially closed, having been superceded by the new link road from the by-pass, the wall can still be seen today. The houses in the left background, which are still in existence, were built in the early 19th century for workers at the tinplate works, the buildings of which are just out of sight to the right. BILL POTTER/KRM

ABOVE: Driver Donald Powell takes a 'fag' break on the footplate of No. 5420 at Lydney Junction on 15th March 1962. This was one of the regular auto-fitted locomotives outstationed at Lydney for the unadvertised afternoon school train to Sharpness that ran between 26th October 1960 and 27th July 1962. The crew were Lydney-based, and worked through to Sharpness. From there, they completed two round trips to Berkeley Road with the two auto trailers, before returning empty to Lydney. The coaching stock was usually stabled near the engine shed, Lydney Grammar School pupils joining the train from the Up platform at Lydney Junction GW station. The morning journey was achieved by using scheduled passenger services, a Bristol-Bradford express making a special stop at Berkeley Road, whilst a school bus provided transport from and to Lydney Junction. Donald Powell, incidentally, had driven the Lydney-Stoke Gifford goods across the Severn Bridge just before the tankers collided with it on 25th October 1960. Note the hosepipe used for cleaning the footplate hooked over the handrail. NPC

ABOVE RIGHT: Class '31' Bo-Bo diesel No. 31244 in the remains of Lydney Yard in May 1974, with ex-GWR 'Manor' Class 4-6-0 No. 7812 Erlestoke Manor. Sold for scrap to Woodham Bros of Barry after withdrawal, the 'Manor' had been purchased for preservation on 28th June 1973. It was delivered to Parkend for an appearance at a Dean Forest Railway open day, after which No. 31244 hauled it to the Dowty Railway Preservation Society's site at Ashchurch. No. 31244 was new into stock on 24th November 1960 and originally numbered D5672. It was reclassified from Class '30' to '31' in early 1968 and withdrawn from traffic in May 1983. It is seen here still fitted with an automatic tablet exchanger which the photographer recalls as being stamped 'M&GNR'. R.H. MARROWS

RIGHT: The instructions for shunting the transfer sidings at Lydney between the Western Region (ex-GWR) and S&W yards, from the *Appendix to the Working Time Table (Gloucester Traffic District)*, October 1960. NPC

LYDNEY

Shunting in Sidings between Lydney Junction, W.R., and Lydney Junction, S. & Wye Joint, which have Connections at either end

There are six Sidings between Lydney Junction, W.R., and Lydney Junction, S. & Wye Joint, with connections at either end. These Sidings are named:—

    Outside
    Middle
    Back Road
    Sharpness New Siding
    Sharpness No. 1
    Sharpness No. 2

Before shunting wagons into any of these Sidings, the person in charge of the shunting must communicate by telephone with the Foreman or Shunter in charge at the other end. In no case must one end of the Sidings be fouled by wagons being pushed up or down as the case may be, until permission to do so has been received from the person in charge at the other end, nor must wagons be propelled from Lydney Junction W.R. beyond the footbridge which crosses the Sidings at the S. & Wye Joint end, without the permission of the Foreman or person in charge.

The hand points at the Lydney Junction W.R. end of the Sidings must be left set as under:—

Sidings					Hand points to be left set for
From			To		
Middle Road	.. .. ..		Outside Road	.. .. ..	Middle Road
Sharpness No. 2	.. ..		Sharpness No. 1	.. ..	Sharpness No. 2

Wagon Repair Sidings

The points leading to both the Railway and the Wagon Repairs Ltd. Repair Sidings are padlocked, the keys being held by the Yard Foreman.

LEFT: In March 1961, No. 1642 is seen at the west end of Lydney Junction (GWR) station, coupled to a shunters truck and with an ex-LM&SR box van which it is in the process of attaching to the rear of a Gloucester Railway Carriage & Wagon Company-built Class '119' DMU. The train is the Saturdays Only 10.15am working from Carmarthen to Cheltenham, which called at Lydney at around 2.50pm and regularly received such attachments. No. 1642 would have waited in Lydney West Loop, on the Up side of the line just beyond the signal in the extreme left background. The loop was added in 1941 and was taken out in December 1968 but the Down line to Up line crossover permitting manoeuvres such as that seen here was removed in July 1963. This view also provides a rare glimpse of the Docks Branch level crossing, which ran between the boarded pedestrian crossing and the road. Note the positioning of the Down Starting signal, 'wrong side', presumably because the three crossings precluded it being placed to the left of the Down line. R.H. MARROWS

RIGHT: Lydney West Box, seen here in Western Region chocolate and cream livery in February 1967 and also illustrated in the first volume, controlled the west end of the station, the road level crossing and traffic passing over the railway level crossing to and from the docks. Due to the S&W Tramroad being on the scene first, for many years docks traffic had precedence over main line trains. This state of affairs was only changed after 1894, when the GW and Midland railways jointly took control of the Severn & Wye. The box dated from 1918 and had a 25 lever frame, removed when it was reduced to first ground frame and latterly gate box status. For the last years of its life, its purpose was to operate the lifting barriers installed at the level crossing and to remotely monitor the lightly used crossings at Nass Lane and Awre. When these functions were taken over by the new signalling centre at Cardiff in 2012, the box was closed and demolished. NPC

LEFT: This view of Lydney Junction (GWR) has been acquired since the publication of the first volume, in which the station was illustrated in more detail. Looking south west towards Chepstow, it was taken from a train paused at the Up platform around 1962. In the right background, a box van and a brake van can be seen at the end of the sidings which paralleled the branch to the docks. The main station building dated from South Wales Railway broad gauge days but the canopy and the flat roofed extension at this end were later post-First World War additions by the GWR. For most of its life, the station was named simply Lydney; it was only renamed Lydney Junction following amalgamation with the S&W station on 21st May 1955. With the severe rationalisation of the railways during the 1960s, it became unstaffed in 1969 and the main buildings were demolished shortly afterwards. However, the shelter on the Down platform remains and still retains much of its original stonework, this being the only station today serving the Forest of Dean area. Four members of the station staff can be seen on the platform, outnumbering the prospective passengers. NPC

The outer basin at Lydney Docks, viewed from the pier in 1959. On the left beyond the entrance gates is No. 9 tip, the last coal tip to remain in use here and from which the final load of coal was tipped into the MV *Yarra*, a de-masted, motorised wooden trow, in October 1960. In the foreground is the beacon lamp, with the harbour master's hut just behind. The houses forming the dock village can be seen in the centre background. DEREK CHAPLIN

SECTION 2A

LYDNEY DOCKS

A second view of the outer basin and No. 9 tip in 1959, with the lock into the inner basin on the right. After being tipped, empty coal wagons were winched back from the tip and then turned on a wagon turntable, to be run down the slope behind the creosoted shed into the empties sidings. Locomotives were not permitted to haul wagons down to the tip, they had to be shunted, with the engine remaining at the Lydney end. The black shed still stands today and is now protected, along with the rest of the harbour, which English Heritage has listed as a Scheduled Ancient Monument. The smaller hut above was for the tip crew. ALAN JARVIS

It is likely that Lydney Pill had been a place of shipment since the time of the Romans, it is only much later that the first documented evidence of its use appears. Court records show a Lydney-based boat trading in stolen timber and venison in 1270, whilst in 1282 another six vessels were reported carrying timber, again stolen. Lydney was also a customs collection point mentioned in a list of 1347. In the 17th century, several large sailing vessels were built here, including two wooden frigates for the Navy. However, around this time Lydney Pill began silting up, to the extent that, by the end of the 18th century it was probably only accessible by quite small vessels, of maybe 20 tons maximum.

It was the building of the Severn & Wye Tramroad which led to the establishment of a new harbour. One of the proposals suggested that it should be at Nass Point and noted that a basin would be required due to the river being silted up and to protect vessels from the tides. The Severn & Wye Railway & Canal Company Act of 1810 included construction of a canal and basin to connect with the River Severn at Nass Point. Thomas Sheasby was appointed as resident engineer in 1811. There was to be an outer harbour with a lock into a length of canal connecting with an upper harbour.

Lock gates were provided at the entrance to the canal but a shortage of funds meant the outer harbour was not proceded with. The new docks, which comprised the upper harbour, were opened on 17th March 1813. There were cranes for loading and unloading, with the whole being overseen from a dock office building, which still survives today. It is estimated that the new harbour and canal cost in the region of £20,000 to construct. Trade was further boosted when the outer harbour was finally built, being completed in 1821. The tramroad was extended down to it along the north bank of the canal, a branch crossing over by means of a swing bridge to serve tips on the south side of the basin. Coal traffic, which from the outset was hampered by a duty imposed on it, was boosted when the Duty Acts were repealed in 1833.

The new harbour quickly established itself, the S&W permitting a gratuity to masters of vessels sailing to Chepstow, Newport and Bristol in order to build the new markets. Within a few years, a pattern of Bristol Channel ports and harbours regularly traded to had built up, which continued well into the 20th century. However, Lydney was always a difficult harbour to navigate into, as there was only a half hour window at the top of the tide for vessels to arrive and leave. The docks enjoyed a busy life throughout the 19th century, both basins regularly being crowded with waiting and loading ships, such that it was often possible to walk from one side to the other across the decks. Unnecessary time spent in harbour was money lost, so vessels were turned around as quickly as possible and the short tidal window meant boats had to leave with the tide whatever time of day or night it was. So the docks worked round the clock and this remained the case up until the end of the coal trade, although cargoes were much more intermittent by then.

By 1867, despite the restrictions on larger vessels, Lydney was handling around 200,000 tons of trade a year, mainly coal, pig iron, bark, timber and paving stone. Major change came when the S&W was finally converted into a railway and new mechanical tips, capable of handling the bigger and heavier railway wagons, replaced the old wooden tramroad tips. There were nine tips, supplemented by three cranes and by the end of the 19th century, Lydney was shipping out around 300,000 tons of coal a year. Over half the tonnage shipped went to Bridgwater, to Sully & Co., shippers and coal merchants based there. Competition for the docks arrived in 1879 with the opening of the Severn Bridge, which provided access for Forest coal to the newly opened dock at Sharpness. Towards the end of the 19th century, sail began to give way to steam in the coasting trade, although Lydney continued to be one of the small harbours still visited by sailing boats right up until the early 1950s.

Trainloads of coal arrived at Lydney Junction, the rows of wagons then being shunted down to the docks and lined up in sidings awaiting

Two extremely rare colour views of coal traffic at the docks in 1957. In the top picture, '16XX' Class 0-6-0PT No. 1627 is seen shunting its train down towards No. 9 tip, with the guard keeping a lookout from his van. The train comprises a motley collection of battered and much repaired wooden bodied wagons, loaded with coal which at this date could have come from Arthur & Edward Colliery at Lydbrook, Cannop Colliery or Princess Royal at Bream. The photographer was standing with his back to No. 6 tip, still extant but out of use. As mentioned on the previous page, wagons were gravity worked to and from the tips and this picture nicely illustrates the different levels involved to achieve this. The lines to the left of the lamp slope down to No's 6 and 7 tips respectively, with that to the right of the lamp being the empties road running away from No. 6 tip. The swing bridge is just off picture to the right. COLEFORD GWR MUSEUM (MIKE REES)

No. 1627 and its train on the top road above No. 9 tip, visible in the background. Regular visitors to the docks today will recognise that the locomotive is standing on the bridge over the overflow outfall into the River Severn, which you can still walk over today. The fence on the left still survives; it here overlooks the empties road from No. 9 tip, which ran at a lower level immediately below. COLEFORD GWR MUSEUM (MIKE REES)

These two views of the docks before the railway infrastructure was removed are taken from colour prints of indifferent quality but again are invaluable. The docks line bifurcated immediately after crossing the main line, with the Upper Docks Branch heading east along the north side of the canal and the Lower Docks Branch along the south bank. This view shows the Upper Docks Branch, with the dock office prominent in the centre. This line originally terminated part way along the canal but, in 1941, was extended down to the Ministry of Supply's Pine End Works, visible in the distance beyond the dock office. The sidings which branched off here had served the Upper Basin tips but these had closed in 1927; the sidings were retained, however, for wagon storage. The Upper Dock Branch was officially closed in August 1963 and the rails lifted from 1st September. This view was probably taken in summer 1963 and clearly shows that the line had not been used for some time prior to closure. The dock office has happily survived and stands in the midst of what is now a modern estate of small industrial units. IAN POPE COLLECTION

The sidings of the Lower Dock Branch, alongside the inner basin, had been laid to serve No's 6, 7 and 8 tips, which had fallen out of use by 1958 although they were not removed until early 1961. The Lower Dock Branch was closed on 18th November 1960 and the rails had been removed by the end of 1963. IAN POPE COLLECTION

tipping into ships, the liveries of the various collieries and merchants painted on the sides of the wagons providing a contrast to their dirty cargo. After 1918, however, the great run down started. Coal production had risen to support the war effort but afterwards dropped substantially. Closures amongst the big Forest collieries began in the 1920s, with Trafalgar going in 1925, Flour Mill in 1928, Crump Meadow in 1929 and Foxes Bridge in 1930. A new power station was opened next to Norchard pit in 1923, the two being connected by conveyor so coal could be fed directly in. In 1927, the two tips at the top of the canal, used by smaller vessels, were closed and dismantled, and thereafter it was mainly the tinplate traffic which kept the upper basin in use and by 1940 that had dwindled away too.

The Second World War brought another resurgence of activity, with the coal trade picking up again and the establishment of Pine End Works, making plywood for use in the manufacture of various types of aircraft. A concrete gantry with crane atop was erected over a new unloading wharf part way up the canal and dumb barges laden with logs were towed by tugs up-river from Avonmouth. This traffic continued into the 1970s, and the dock and canal were often crowded with barges waiting to be unloaded or to be towed back to Bristol. A railway branch had been laid down to the works when it opened, being an extension of one of the sidings by Cookson Terrace; it closed in 1963 but had probably not seen any traffic since the previous year. The Pine End traffic transferred from water to road in 1977 and the works closed in 1986. The coal traffic finished in October 1960, the last load being shipped out aboard the MV *Yarra*.

LYDNEY JUNCTION

Working between Lydney Junction Yard and Lydney Docks or Pine End Works

One shunting truck and one 16-ton Goods Brake Van specially branded are provided at Lydney Junction Yard for the use of trips between that point and Lydney Docks or Pine End Works, and the following instructions must be observed :—

(1) All trips from Lydney Junction Yard to Lydney Docks or Pine End Works must be brought to a stand at the signal controlling the crossing over the Main Line and the Guard and Shunter must proceed over the Main Line and, after satisfying themselves that the points are in the correct position, the Guard must station himself at the end of the wall between the level crossing and the subway and the Shunter on the roadway from the Goods Station and Lydney Docks. It will be their duty to warn all approaching road traffic, each man exhibiting a Red Flag or Lamp, and when they are in position the Guard must verbally advise the Signalman at Lydney West Signal Box that it is all right for the trip to proceed ; the Signalman will then lower the appropriate signal.

(2) In propelling wagons from Lydney Junction Yard to Lydney Basin or Upper Dock to the Sidings leading to Coal Tips Nos. 3 and 4 and also the Sidings as far as the Turntable Road or Long Siding, the man in charge of the shunting operations must walk in advance of the wagons.

(3) In propelling wagons from the Turntable Road or Long Siding to the Lower Docks or Harbour, a shunting truck or goods brake van must be placed in front of the leading wagon for the man in charge of the shunting operations to ride upon, and it must be returned to the Turntable Road Siding or Junction Yard, whichever is the more convenient, formed at the rear of the train from the Lower Dock.

(4) In propelling wagons to Pine End Works, a shunting truck or goods brake van must be placed in front of the leading wagon for the man in charge of the shunting operations to ride upon, and in addition to the instructions contained in clause (1) above, the trip must in all cases be brought to a stand at the intermediate road crossings situated midway between Lydney West Crossing and Pine End Works, and the entrance gates to the Lydney Trading Estate. Before proceeding over the crossings referred to, the Guard and Shunter must warn all approaching road traffic by the exhibition of a Red Flag or Lamp. Similar precautions must be taken in regard to these crossings when returning from Pine End Works, and the shunting truck or goods brake van must be formed at the rear of the train.

(5) All trips from Lydney Docks and Pine End Works to Lydney Junction Yard must be brought to a stand at the signal controlling the crossing over the Main Line, and after the Guard and Shunter have stationed themselves in their appropriate positions, each man exhibiting a Red Flag or Lamp, and have satisfied themselves that the points are in the correct position, the Guard will verbally advise Lydney West Signalman who will lower the necessary signal.

Swing Bridge over Canal, Lydney Basin

The swing bridge is secured in position when closed against the waterway by a lever which also moves the points of the Safety Siding.

The lever for unlocking the bridge is secured by a padlock, the key of which, when not in use, must be kept in Lydney West Box ; and whenever the key is out of the possession of the Signalman he will keep the Signals leading from and to the Dock Lines at " Danger ", and not allow any train or engine to proceed in the direction of the swing bridge until the key has been returned to him.

When it is necessary to open the swing bridge the man appointed for the duty must fetch the key from the Signal Box, unlock the lever and open the bridge for vessels to pass to and from The Steel Company of Wales' Private Wharf, and after the bridge has been closed, and properly secured, at once return the key to the Signalman.

Without special arrangement, the bridge must only be opened when required between the hours of 6.0 a.m. and 6.0 p.m. at such times when it will not interfere with the traffic, and before it is opened, the man appointed for the duty must, in addition to placing at " Danger " the Signal worked from the ground controlling the passage of trains and engines from the Docks on to the swing bridge, go 200 yards in the direction of the Lower Docks and place three detonators ten yards apart on the Running Line, and at the same time satisfy himself that there is no engine in the Sidings between the bridge and where the first detonator is placed on the rails.

ABOVE: **The instructions for both docks branches, from the** *General Appendix to the Working Time Table* **for October 1960. NPC**

LEFT: **A view through the entrance lock gates to the drained outer basin in October 1966. The gates would remain open until the next incoming tide filled the basin again, although this method of filling it was also responsible for the deposits of silt.** JOHN STRANGE, TOWY COLLECTION

BELOW: **A sadly slightly blurred view of a youthful Mike Rees, on the right, posing with his father Vic Rees, driver of No. 1627, on the top road to No. 9 tip in 1957.** COLEFORD GWR MUSEUM (MIKE REES)

The inner basin at 12.15pm on a damp and gloomy 21st January 1964, with a pair of laden log barges tied up to some of the bollards awaiting tug haulage up to Pine End Works. The works was built in 1941 and began production in 1941, initially of plywood for use in the construction of Mosquito fighter-bombers and later the Horsa troop gliders used at Arnhem. After the war, plywoods and veneers were produced by a workforce whch numbered over 500, for use in furniture making, house building, and vehicle and carriage construction. Trade products included 'Hydrobord', used as a shield by the nuclear industry, and 'Par-k-Ply' flooring. The barges had the names of places (and some counties), many of which were associated with the waterway system in southern England; here was see *Froxfield* (on the Kennet & Avon Canal near Hungerford) and, behind, *Ufton* (possibly referring to Ufton Nervet, also adjacent to the K&A, near Reading). Brought over from Avonmouth in pairs, haulage was provided by Ashmeads of Bristol, their tug *Peter Leigh* being a regular visitor to Lydney, certainly during the early 1970s. The harbour village, in the background, comprised the lockkeeper's cottage, facing the inner lock, plus five other residences arranged in two blocks. There was also a storehouse and workshop for the docks in one of the blocks. In the far left distance is a glimpse of the large detached house provided for the harbour master and the Pine End Works crane is just visible above the trees. ANNE BEAUFOY

ABOVE: The inner basin circa 1970, crowded with empty barges waiting to return across the river to Avonmouth; identifiable are *Semington*, with *Essex* and *Seend* by the far bank, possibly *Somerset* behind them and then *Totterdown* moored to the nearer bank inside *Semington*. Behind is a good view of the dock village, with No's 1 and 2 Dock Cottages nearest (the workshop and stores were at the end nearest the dock) and then the lockkeeper's cottage and No's 4, 5 and 6 Dock Cottages beyond. As can be seen from the state of the roofs of No's 1 and 2, the accommodation here had all been abandoned by this date. DEREK KNIGHT

ABOVE: A second view from slightly further back, with *Dursley* in front of *Semington* and *Devizes* moored to the far bank. The barges were owned by Ashmeads and *Dursley*'s ultimate fate was to be hulked on the river bank at Purton, near Sharpness, where her remains are now preserved. Around fourteen barges can be made out here in these two views awaiting return, possibly during a downturn in production at Pine End, as empties would normally be swapped for laden barges on each trip. DEREK KNIGHT

LEFT: The barges *Dursley* and *Tamar*, laden with hardwood logs from Africa, wait in the outer harbour, having been recently locked in, for transport along the canal to the works, probably circa 1976. DENNIS PARKHOUSE

LEFT: The swing bridge in June 1977. With the docks now a tourist amenity that includes viewpoints across and down the Severn, as well as a stone monolith compass for visitors to enjoy, Health & Safety has today seen the railings being encompassed in wire mesh. As can be seen, the bridge was swung simply by means of the handle on the left. DENNIS PARKHOUSE

RIGHT: The entrance gates and outer basin, again in June 1977. The Severn estuary has the second highest tidal range in the world, with a difference between the lowest and highest tides of 28 feet and this view graphically illustrates the size of gates that were required here to deal with that. The scouring effect of the tides has taken away much of the mud protecting the base of the pier walls since this picture was taken and this, coupled with water incursion and frost, has rendered large cracks in the stonework in several places. DENNIS PARKHOUSE

BELOW: A circa 1970 view along the upper level trackbed; this is the point where No. 1627 and its train are standing in the picture on page 112. The beams which carried the track across the outfall had not yet been fenced off. On the left are some of the wooden sailing ships which were hulked here in the late 1950s and early 1960s to try and protect the river bank. BILL POTTER/KRM

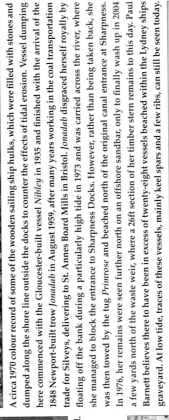

A circa 1970 colour record of some of the wooden sailing ship hulks, which were filled with stones and dumped along the shore line outside the docks to counter the effects of tidal erosion. Vessel dumping here commenced with the Gloucester-built vessel *Nibley* in 1935 and finished with the arrival of the 1848 Newport-built trow *Jonadab* in August 1959, after many years working in the coal transportation trade for Silveys, delivering to St. Annes Board Mills in Bristol. *Jonadab* disgraced herself royally by floating off the bank during a particularly high tide in 1973 and was carried across the river, where she managed to block the entrance to Sharpness Docks. However, rather than being taken back, she was then towed by the tug *Primrose* and beached north of the original canal entrance at Sharpness. In 1976, her remains were seen further north on an offshore sandbar, only to finally wash up in 2004 a few yards north of the waste weir, where a 26ft section of her timber stern remains to this day. Paul Barnett believes there to have been in excess of twenty-eight vessels beached within the Lydney ships graveyard. At low tide, traces of these vessels, mainly keel spars and a few ribs, can still be seen today.

ABOVE: The bows of the Stroudwater barge *Nibley*, with her sister *Llantony* behind and Sharpness Docks in the background. ABOVE RIGHT: The stern of *Jonadab*, looking south towards Oldbury Power Station and the Severn Road Bridge. BELOW: The collapsed remains of the 1892 Saul-built Gloster trow *George*, with *Jonadab* to the rear. BELOW RIGHT: Another study of *Jonadab*, looking across the river towards Berkeley. ALL DEREK KNIGHT

ABOVE: Nass House is believed to date from the first half of the 17th century and is generally considered to be one of the most interesting manor houses in Gloucestershire, not least because of its distinctive cupola lookout tower. It was built by the Jones family – William Jones was a wealthy man, originally from Newland, who founded the Haberdasher's Company – almost certainly as a replacement for an earlier smaller house. The family left the house probably in the second half of the 18th century, in favour of their new home at Ruddle Manor, near Newnham. A later descendant, Roynon Jones, was a promoter of the Forest of Dean Tramroad and his son, the Rev'd Edward Jones, held a large share in it, as well as having interests in several Forest collieries. Nass House was bought circa 1920 by the Biddle family, who owned it until the late 1990s. It is most likely one of the younger Biddles that is seated on the tractor here. The house was Grade II listed in 1954 and is still used as a private residence today. DEREK KNIGHT

BELOW: A postcard view of Newerne Street, Lydney in 1966. The scene is still recognisable today, although the Bridge Inn on the right is no longer operating as a pub and petrol is no longer sold at the garage in the right middle distance. As the colours on the wall indicate, the long building just the other side was the Red & White Services bus garage; it survives today in retail use. NPC

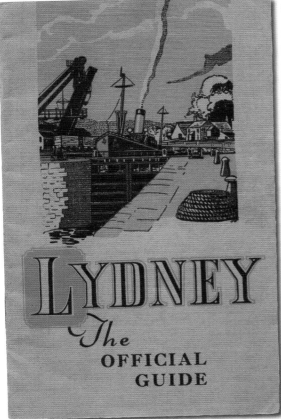

ABOVE: A woodcut image of the docks was used on the front cover of this circa 1946 Lydney guidebook. NPC

ABOVE: A service from Berkeley Road via the Severn Bridge at Lydney Town station on 7th August 1957. Photographer Bill Potter was standing on the steps of the footbridge leading down on to the Up platform for this view. Class '14XX' 0-4-2T No. 1430 was new into stock in July 1934 and was initially shedded at Aylesbury, no doubt for working services on the branch to Princes Risborough. Spending its early years migrating between Aylesbury and Banbury sheds, followed by a couple of years at Leamington Spa, it then spent the second half of the 1940s and the first half of the 1950s at Bristol Bath Road and Yatton. No. 1430 arrived at Lydney shed for the first time in November 1955, from where it worked out its final few years, being withdrawn from there on 18th October 1957, two months after this picture was taken. BILL POTTER/KRM

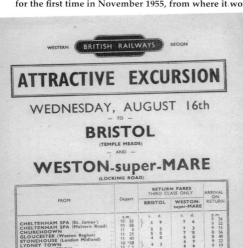

LEFT: A bill for a Cheltenham and Gloucester to Bristol or Weston-super-Mare excursion, which ran via Lydney Town and the Severn Bridge on 16th August 1950. NPC

BELOW: No. 1431 waits to depart for Berkeley Road on 4th June 1960. This engine was also new in July 1934, to Ebbw Junction shed. After a veritable tour of GWR sheds, it arrived at Lydney in February 1960 but its time here was short. Just a month after this photograph, on 7th July, it was put into store at Lydney and it was withdrawn on 27th April 1961. Like sister engine No. 1430, it was cut up at Swindon. The original S&W wooden station buildings can be seen behind No. 1431. BILL POTTER/KRM

Framed by the iron footbridge, No. 1426 sits at Lydney Town after arrival from Berkeley Road on 20th June 1959. Note that the footbridge also acted as a pedestrian crossing for when the gates were closed to the road, so had steps leading off in both directions on either side. A boarded barrow crossing was also provided for station staff, with a typical cast iron sign at the top of the footbridge steps on the left, proclaiming that 'PASSENGERS ARE REQUESTED TO CROSS THE LINE BY THE BRIDGE'. Gas lighting survived here until the end, with the small Lydney Gasworks being situated just to the south west of the station, although it was never directly served by rail. Lydney shed saw its fair share of the '14XX' Class, with another example, No. 1426, being featured here. New into stock in November 1933 and alternating originally between Southall and Staines sheds, it arrived at Lydney in September 1958. It spent much of the next two and a half years working from here before transfer to Gloucester Barnwood shed in April 1961, from where it was withdrawn on 3rd April 1962. The leading coach is Compartment Trailer No. W4350W, built in 1935 to GWR Diagram D117, Lot No. 1525, which is seen here looking reasonably freshly painted in BR Crimson livery. ALAN JARVIS

Having crossed lines to the Up platform, passengers now board the train for the trip across the Severn Bridge to Sharpness, Berkeley or Berkeley Road, which will shortly depart here auto trailer leading. The trailer cannot be positively identified but looks to be one of the four Suburban Brake Thirds built in 1938 to GWR Diagram A34, Lot No. 1600, with the van end as a driver's compartment; they were numbered 1668 to 1671 and at least one of them was lettered for working between Lydney and Berkeley Road. The stone building on the left was the original signal box, which was replaced by the brick-built cabin seen in the previous view in 1897; it was converted for use as offices for the stationmaster and parcels, whilst the superstructure may have gone to Serridge Junction. This was as part of major works carried out at the station, when the new building, to a standard GWR design, was built on the Down platform and the entrance to the goods yard was improved. A glimpse of the small goods yard can just be gained here, with the gable of the creosoted timber goods shed visible above the end of the station building. On the right is the end of the wooden Eassie station building provided by the S&W and the line's later joint status is indicated by the Midland Railway wooden fencing on the right. ALAN JARVIS

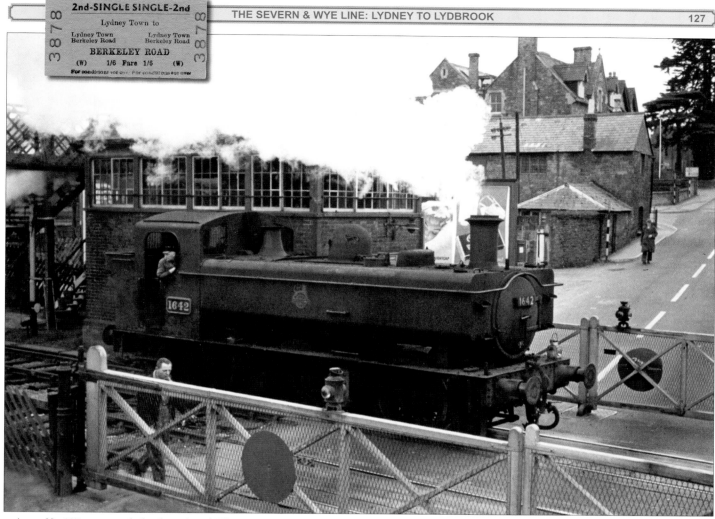

2nd-SINGLE SINGLE-2nd

Lydney Town to

| Lydney Town | Lydney Town |
| Berkeley Road | Berkeley Road |

BERKELEY ROAD

(W)   1/6 Fare 1/6   (W)

For conditions see over   For conditions see over

3878   3878

ABOVE: No. 1642 runs over the level crossing of Hill Street, Lydney, circa 1960. It is not immediately apparent how our unknown photographer obtained his slightly elevated viewpoint – from a double-decker bus perhaps? The crossing was a bone of contention for local people throughout the later years of the 19th century, with both traffic and pedestrians regularly being held up. Eventually, in 1903, the Joint Committee authorised the provision of a footbridge, which was erected by the contractors Cross & Cross in January 1904; kits for such structures could be bought from various manufacturers. No. 1642 was a long standing resident of Gloucester Horton Road shed, from where it was withdrawn in January 1962. Behind the signal box can be seen the road entrance to the goods yard; the site is now a fire station. IAN POPE COLLECTION

RIGHT: A waybill advertising the availability of tickets to visit Lydney Horse Show in 1960. NPC

BELOW: Auto-fitted passenger-liveried Class '54XX' No. 5417 at Lydney Town probably in 1960. Note the footbridge steps, leading to both the street and the platform. No. 5417 was withdrawn from Banbury shed in early 1961. JOHN TARRANT/KRM

WESTERN REGION

LYDNEY HORSE SHOW AND NATIONAL 'DAILY EXPRESS' FOXHUNTER JUMPING COMPETITION

SATURDAY, 9th JULY

Cheap Day Return Tickets
will be issued
— TO —

LYDNEY

FROM ALL STATIONS AND HALTS WITHIN A RAIL DISTANCE
OF

30 MILES

TICKETS WILL BE AVAILABLE FORWARD AND RETURN
BY ANY TRAIN ON DAY OF ISSUE.

A SPECIAL TRAIN WILL DEPART LYDNEY TOWN AT
9.0 p.m.
CALLING AT ALL STATIONS TO BERKELEY ROAD

TICKETS CAN BE OBTAINED IN ADVANCE AT BOOKING STATIONS AND AGENCIES

Further information will be supplied on application to Stations, Agencies, to Mr. J. Powell, District Traffic
Superintendent, Northgate Mansions, Gloucester (Telephone, Gloucester 21121, Extension 61); or to Mr. R. L.
Charlesworth, Commercial Officer, Paddington Station, W.2.

Paddington Station, W.2   J. R. HAMMOND,
June, 1960.   General Manager.

(G 13-4990)   Printed by Joseph Wones Ltd., West Bromwich; also Birmingham and London

ABOVE: An unidentified Series '63XX' Type 2 diesel hydraulic shunts a rake of steel mineral wagons loaded with house coal into the goods yard at Lydney Town in June 1967. The building visible above the first two wagons was used as a stores by the Signal & Telegraph Department in later years but is now believed to have been built circa 1870, soon after the tramroad was converted to a railway, to house the Inspection Saloon built for Severn & Wye General Manager G.W. Keeling. By the end of the 19th century, it is believed to have been in use as stables and a blacksmith's shop, whilst the blue engineering brick water tower alongside, with cast iron tank on top, is thought to have been constructed by the Joint Committee in 1897 to provide water for the horses and the smithy. The building was constructed of stone but when the Midland blocked the rail entrance off, some time after 1906, they built a timber wall across the end, complete with windows and a door, as can be seen. ARTHUR DAY, COURTESY MONMOUTH MUSEUM

LEFT: Lydney Town Signal Box dated from 1904 and was again to another standard GWR design of this period, built of blue brick with timber gables. It housed a 26-lever frame and a wheel to operate the gates. Pedestrians were expected to pass through the wicket gate just visible at the end of the box (which was locked from the box by another lever), rather than walk on the road. On the left is the Down Starter signal which, because it was tucked in between the box and the end of the platform, seemed to get missed out from most pictures of the station. IAN POPE COLLECTION

NBL Type 2 No. D6354 skirts the Norchard Colliery site and passes the fixed Down Lydney Distant signal with another train of loaded ballast hoppers in April 1971. One of the last of the class built, in August 1962, the locomotive's appalling condition is an indicator that its days were numbered; it was to be withdrawn just a month after this picture was taken and cut up by British Rail Engineering Ltd (BREL) at Swindon in February 1972. Although today commonly referred to as Class '22' under their TOPS designation, none of them lasted long enough in service to be allocated their new '22XX' Series numbers. The early demise of the class, with the last two examples succumbing on 1st January 1972, ensured that none survived to be preserved. However, a project has recently been established to build a new one from scratch – see www.class22newbuild.co.uk for more details. In the late 1970s, the colliery site was cleared and taken over by the Dean Forest Railway. R.H. MARROWS

RIGHT: New Mills waterfall on the Cannop Brook or Newerne Stream in August 1976. Just to the north of the site of Norchard Colliery, the remains are of a 19th century tinplate works. New Mills Works was built in 1824 by John James, on land leased from the Bathurst family of Lydney Park. An old furnace is believed to have stood on the site previously. Situated midway between the Upper and Middle Forges, the works comprised a large waterwheel which drove a rolling machine, a blowing machine and a forge hammer and wheel. A 60hp engine was installed to enable the works to operate when there was a shortage of water and there was also a puddling house and three labourers' houses. DAVID BICK

ABOVE: Looking north towards Tufts Junction on 3rd March 1966, with the only arm remaining on the bracket signal in the foreground being that for the 'main line'; this signal is shown complete in the picture on the front title page. The Cannop Brook is hidden in the trees on the right but will cross to pass under the railway just to the north of the junction. ROBIN BARNES

FAR LEFT: A record of the gradient post at Tufts Junction, showing the change from a 1 in 173 drop down towards Lydney to 1 in 240. DEREK CHAPLIN

LEFT: This Severn & Wye 10 mile post was situated between Norchard and Tufts Junction. DEREK CHAPLIN

Hidden away somewhat off the beaten track, surrounded by typical Forest scenery and with only the signalman's house for company, Tufts Junction was as pretty a spot as any in a region abounding with attractive landscapes and vistas. Here, on 31st April 1961, the crew of No. 8729 slow their train to collect the token for the section to Lydney Town from the signalman, who has come away from his box onto the boarded crossing to meet them. The mixed consist behind the pannier tank comprises some steel mineral wagons, probably empties which had delivered coal to Parkend goods yard, six hoppers with ballast stone from Whitecliff Quarry and some vans which have come from either Coleford or Speech House Road. On the left, the Oakwood Branch curves away towards Princess Royal Colliery, whilst the line on the right connected to the Mineral Loop, which in its later years had remained merely to serve a drift mine at Pillowell. The houses in the centre background are part of Pillowell village, whilst the signalman's cottage on the right, provided in 1899, is no longer extant. DEREK CHAPLIN

ABOVE: Tufts Junction Signal Box circa 1962, looking north west. The box dated from 1897 and was a replacement for an earlier box sited on the opposite side of the line, which had been provided in 1875. The box was executed in blue engineering brick to a standard GWR design and was built at the time the line to Parkend was doubled. Virtually identical boxes were provided at Lydney Town, Whitecroft and Travellers Rest, whilst the box at Parkend was of a similar design but built of timber. The siding with wagons standing on it visible at the start of the Oakwood Branch on the far right was a loop provided to serve Tufts loading bank. DEREK CHAPLIN

ABOVE: Another view of the box. It was originally equipped with a 30-lever frame but this was replaced in October 1948. The box closed on 2nd October 1967. Today, the Dean Forest Railway have erected a replacement box at Tufts, although it has not yet been fitted out for use. IAN POPE COLLECTION

LEFT: A glimpse of the other end of the box from the Severn Boar II railtour, which was just completing its return journey down the Oakwood Branch. JOHN RYAN

SECTION 2B
THE OAKWOOD BRANCH

The Oakwood Branch originated as a tramroad, built in the mid 1850s, which the S&WR took over in 1870 and subsequently converted to a railway. The first section, serving Tufts loading bank, the remains of which just feature on the right, was rebuilt immediately with the laying of a broad gauge siding. The loading bank served South Oakwood Level and Tufts Level iron mines, and narrow gauge tramways from both ran onto it but they had fallen out of use by 1920. It was then used by the wood distillation works seen below until 1948. The remains of the loading bank can still be seen today, although much of the surrounding land is now privately owned. This view again features the Severn Boar II railtour, which photographer Trevor Owen chased round the Forest. Also shown is more of the railway paraphernalia to be found at the junction, including the two shunt signals in the centre, the oil lamp and cast iron lamppost just to the left of the brake van and the wooden posted Midland Railway bracket signal with its attendant stay wires. The larger arm was the Tufts Down Starter, the smaller arm applying to the Mineral Loop. T.B. Owen

The railtour poses for the photographer at the bottom end of the Oakwood Branch. This view is interesting because it shows the other end of the loop siding which ran alongside Tufts loading bank and also, behind the locomotive on the right, part of the derelict Morgan's Chemical Works. This had been started in 1887 by one Isaac Jacobs, who distilled tar from poor quality wood. Another loop siding had been provided on the far side of the running line, with a spur leading off into the works but this had been lifted in 1959. The chemical works had closed in 1913 but was reopened in 1917 and continued in production then until 1948. It was also known as Whitecroft Chemical Works. T.B. Owen

INSET LEFT: No. 1664 crosses the Bream to Whitecroft road as it shunts the Severn Boar II railtour into the sidings at Princess Royal. T.B. OWEN

BELOW: A close up of No. 1664, looking east towards Whitecroft; the point in the right foreground suggests that the exact location is at the top end of Park Hill Loop, part way along the Oakwood Branch. Prominent in the left background is the Whitecroft pin factory, originally the Whitecroft Patent Fuel Works. This had commenced operations in 1866-7, producing fuel briquettes from coal mined at Pillowell Level Colliery. The works was taken over by the pin factory in 1910 and has been through several owners since but is still in operation today as Whitecroft Essentials (Lydney) Ltd. NPC

RIGHT: Pannier tank No. 4671 shunts its way up the Oakwood Branch in October 1964, with a train of wooden-bodied empties bound for Princess Royal Colliery. The train is near the top end of the branch, between Park Hill Loop and the colliery. There were level crossing gates across the running line at the loop, which the guard, seen riding on the footboard of the brake van, had to operate. As the operating instructions, below left, indicate, he was then expected to remain at the gates until the train returned. The three-quarter mile branch up to Princess Royal was worked engine propelling from Park Hill Loop, where the locomotive ran round its train. No. 4671 was to finish its career at Severn Tunnel Junction shed just over a year after this picture was taken. R.H. MARROWS

INSET BELOW: The instructions for working the Oakwood Branch, from the *Appendix to the Working Time Table (Gloucester Traffic District),* October 1960.

TUFTS JUNCTION—PRINCESS ROYAL COLLIERY SIDINGS (OAKWOOD BRANCH)

The Line is unfenced between Park Hill Crossing and the Colliery Sidings and Drivers must proceed with care.

Gates are fixed at Park Hill Level Crossing, the normal position of which is across the railway ; on approaching them Drivers must give three whistles, and, in each direction, be prepared to stop before reaching the gates.

A man must be at Tufts Junction on arrival of the trains which go to Princess Royal Colliery, assist at Tufts Junction with the shunting, precede the train to Park Hill Level Crossing, and open the gates to allow the train to pass to the Colliery, remaining at the crossing to protect it until the train returns, and after it has passed over the Level Crossing, secure the gates in their normal position.

The levers working the points at Park Hill Sidings are secured by padlocks, the keys of which are attached to the Staff.

Guards must see that the points in the Branch line leading to the screen lines are locked in position for the screen lines and the points leading to the Loading Siding are locked in position for the Branch line before leaving.

All vehicles must be taken in front of the engine from the Park Hill Sidings to Princess Royal Colliery Sidings.

138

BELOW: Seen a few minutes later, No. 4671 shunts the wagons through the screens at Princess Royal Colliery. A local coal merchant has also backed his lorry up for loading with land sales coal. The colliery had actually been closed for over two years at this date but coal was still being delivered here for screening, by lorry from the reopened Pillowell Drift mine, this operation continuing until 1965 and generating two to three trains a week on the branch. R.H. MARROWS

Princess Royal Colliery from the top of the spoil tip on a damp day circa 1964, with the Oakwood Branch heading off to the right, back down the valley to Tufts Junction. The railway turns sharply to the left just past the white roofed building and Park Hill Loop lay just beyond the bend. The branch was extended from Park Hill up to Princess Royal in 1890-91, upon formation of the Princess Royal Colliery Company Ltd, and extra sidings were subsequently laid at the pit in 1897, with more being added in 1906 and 1918. Most of the surface layout of the colliery can be seen here, with the main headframe, erected in 1914, on the left and, just to the right of it, the red brick building housing the electric winding engine installed in 1938. The screens are largely out of sight behind and below the trees on the left. The other buildings housed workshops and stores, whilst the remains of the original headframe can also be seen, standing in front of what had been the engine house which operated it. In the right foreground, partially hidden by the tip and the conifer trees, are the colliery offices, whilst the steps across the road on the extreme right lead to the pit head baths, provided for the benefit of miners in the 1930s and controversially demolished in 2009 after a long campaign by local historians failed to save the building for posterity. Princess Royal was also known as Park Gutter Colliery and was worked in conjunction with the adjacent Flour Mill Colliery, here situated a few hundred yards off picture to the left. Some of the miners' housing can be seen on the hillside on the left and the pin factory at Whitecroft features again in the left distance. The waste ground to the right was the site of the colliery brickworks. ANNE BEAUFOY

A view down the Bream to Whitecroft road, showing the bridge which carried the spoil tramway from the colliery to the new tipping area to the south of the road. As the picture below shows, this had been lifted by this date, with coal winding operations here having ceased in March 1962. John Ryan

The colliery from the south, with the winding house for the electric winding engine on the left and the head frame beyond. The stone building on the right, beyond No. 1664, had originally housed the colliery offices. John Ryan

ABOVE: Looking south from the very end of the branch which terminated beyond the colliery, with one of the empty wagon roads on the left and scrap narrow gauge tubs abandoned on the right. The derelict siding on which the photographer was standing was one of two added in 1918. JOHN RYAN

BELOW: Looking towards the colliery from the start of the sidings at the top end of the Oakwood Branch, on 31st April 1961. One of the smaller '16XX' Class pannier tanks, No. 1642, of Gloucester Horton Road shed but sub-shedded at Lydney at this time, is engaged in shunting duties at the colliery. No. 1642 was withdrawn from Gloucester in early 1962. The colliery spoil tip, which still remains today, dominates the horizon on the left. DEREK CHAPLIN

Back at Tufts Junction with No. 1664 and the Severn Boar II railtour. From left to right, the three lines are the former Down Main, latterly used as a siding, the Up Main, which had become the single running line, and the Up Loop, which effectively formed the end of the Mineral Loop. As the state of the rails indicates, it was only the Up Main which saw any regular use by this date. NPC

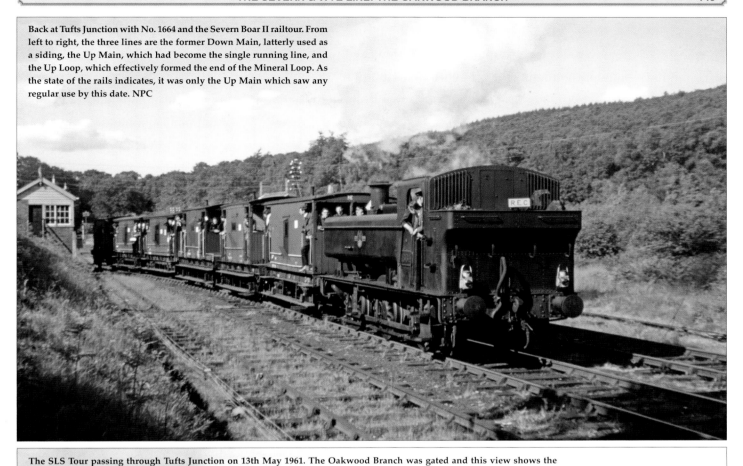

The SLS Tour passing through Tufts Junction on 13th May 1961. The Oakwood Branch was gated and this view shows the gates closed across the entrance to it. Also shown again are the wooden posted Tufts Down Starter signal of Midland Railway origin and the oil lamp and post just inside the boundary fence for the branch. ALAN JARVIS

LEFT: A view of the approach to Tufts Junction from the north, as seen from the brake van of an Up train circa 1967. The train is being hauled by an unidentified Series '63XX' diesel hydraulic. Although not of the highest quality, the view is useful because it also provides a glimpse of the plate girder bridge carrying the line over the Cannop Brook. The Oakwood Branch has been lifted – it was closed on 17th May 1965, the connection having been taken out the day before, and lifted the following year – but the signal box still operated as a block post. IAN POPE COLLECTION

BELOW: Passing the same spot on 29th October 1970 is blue liveried North British Type 2 No. 6338, hauling an Up train of hopper wagons with ballast from Whitecliff Quarry which, after closure of the Coleford Branch in 1967, was brought down by lorry and loaded at Parkend Marsh Sidings. The locomotive is passing the fixed Up Distant signal for Whitecroft. BILL POTTER/KRM

BELOW: The approach to Whitecroft from the south, as seen from the Lydney to Parkend road, looking across the valley to the Princess Royal Colliery spoil tip. On 30th March 1965, No. 3643 heads north with the 8.45am working from Lydney to Whitecliff Quarry. The fence curving round in the centre foreground to run just this side of the trees on the right marks the route of the Mineral Loop. The last vestiges of this, the short section serving Pillowell Drift, had been closed at the end of November 1957 and removed in 1959. JOHN DAGLEY-MORRIS

A second '57XX' Class 0-6-0PT was at work on the S&W line on 30th March 1965, No. 9616, here seen heading south through Whitecroft station and passing the pin factory with a short freight, possibly of free-mined coal loaded at Marsh Sidings, Parkend. JOHN DAGLEY-MORRIS

On 31st April 1961, No. 1642, which we saw a little earlier on the Oakwood Branch, trundles through Whitecroft station with just a brake van. It is possible that the locomotive has just deposited the coal wagons in the siding on the left, the yard being used for local coal merchants' traffic up until the autumn of 1967. The railwayman in the background, who was presumably in charge of the level crossing gates, seems to be inspecting the 'toe' of the point. DEREK CHAPLIN

RIGHT: A view north through the station circa 1961, showing it still in reasonably complete condition, with the S&W creosoted timber goods shed on the left. This was a smaller version of the shed which still survives at Parkend today and was a standard Gloucester Wagon Company product provided in 1890. The Down platform dated from 1897, when the line was doubled between Lydney and Parkend and was equipped with a small wooden shelter, although this was only added after criticism from the Board of Trade Inspector. The red brick building on the Up platform is the Gents urinal, which dated from 1899, being a replacement for the original facility in the main building, which again came in for severe criticism from the BoT. IAN POPE COLLECTION

BELOW: The Severn Venturer railtour calls at Whitecroft on 15th April 1956, in the charge of Class '16XX' 0-6-0PT No. 1625. Sadly, little of the station itself can be seen but some wagons can just be made out standing on the long Up siding in the right distance. T.B. OWEN

BELOW: Class '64XX' 0-6-0PT No. 6424 stands alongside the Up platform whilst heading the GRS railtour into the Forest of Dean on 23rd June 1962. The view provides good detail of the rear of the Down Starter signal and again a rake of wagons can be seen in the siding on the Up side in the distance. There is further interest in this picture, however, which provides proof that you can never start 'em too young. The clearly impressionable little five year old about to march over the boarded crossing is none other than Forest railway and industrial historian Ian Pope, in the capable charge of his mother Helen following on behind. We shall encounter Ian's father, Alec, a little further on in these pages. BILL POTTER/KRM

Such scenes of well managed landscape and permanent way are rare on our railway system today, as surrounding trees and hedges are allowed to grow unchecked for much of the time, often to the detriment of performance when the now infamous cry goes up of "leaves on the line". Special railhead treatment trains are sent out nationwide to help alleviate the problem but, in days gone by, it was the job of the local permanent way men to keep the undergrowth cut back from the lineside. Here, in a wonderfully picturesque vista taken on 6th August 1965, ex-GWR '57XX' class 0-6-0PT No. 4698 heads a ballast train from Whitecliffe Quarry between Parkend and Whitecroft. Note the permanent way (pw) hut hiding in the bracken on the left. This remains a most beautiful stretch of railway line to travel along today, courtesy of the DFR. BILL POTTER/KRM

LEFT AND BELOW LEFT: The same stretch of line as in the previous view but showing signs of the lack of maintenance that characterised the railways from the late 1960s on. In September 1970, North British Series '63XX' Type 2 No. D6331, in rail blue livery, heads south with a train of ballast hoppers that will have been loaded at Marsh Sidings, Parkend. In the lower view, it can be seen that the train is just approaching the Whitecroft Up Distant signal, which was permanently fixed at caution. No. D6331 was new from North British Loco in July 1960 and was working from Gloucester at the date of this picture, although was officially based at 82A Bristol Bath Road shed. Withdrawn from there in March 1971, after languishing for a few weeks, the locomotive was transferred to Plymouth Laira, setting out on 2nd May 1971 with classmates No's D6336 and D6356 in tow. However, whilst *en route*, No. D6331 caught fire at Sampford Peverell and was subsequently dumped in Exeter Yard. Towed back to Bristol St. Phillip's Marsh, it was still out of use there in late Octover 1971 but had been taken to Swindon for scrapping by the end of the year. It is recorded as being cut up in March 1972. R.H. MARROWS

ABOVE: A similar view to that on the left but with slightly less vegetation and without a train. Taken on 3rd March 1966, the pw hut features again. ROBIN BARNES

RIGHT: Also on 3rd March 1966 but looking north, No. D9503 heads away from Parkend with a rake of hoppers loaded with ballast from Whitecliff Quarry. ROBIN BARNES

This is one of those 'skew-whiff' pictures that, whilst I have straightened it up on the computer using picture editing software, to then square it up as well would have involved such severe cropping that it was decided to simply place it on the page as it was. We shall meet the train again on page 174, which will be seen in its entirity as it makes its way through Parkend station but here it heads slowly away towards Whitecroft, where we saw it a couple of pages ago making its way over the level crossing. The entrance to the short Parkend Goods Branch leading to Marsh Sidings was gated, a precaution in the Forest that was as much to do about roaming sheep as anything else. Note, too, the concrete sleepered track in the foreground and also the remains of the Down line (a remnant of the period when the railway here was double track) terminating at the buffer stop just beyond the single slip point. DAVID BICK/NPC

On 30th March 1965, ex-GWR 0-6-0PT No. 9616 departs Parkend with a short train of just two mineral wagons and a brake van, forming the 12.55pm return goods to Severn Tunnel Junction. The signal in the foreground is a tubular post LM&SR upper quadrant (the arms of upper quadrant signals moved upwards for 'off'), which dated from the singling of the line in 1930. The post carried the Down Main to Siding signal – the small arm on the bracket – with the Advanced Up Starter facing in the opposite direction above it. At the very top of the post, and just visible in the top picture, is the Down Home signal, which again faced south. This very tall signal was fitted with four bracing wires, one leading to the wooden post on the left, two down to the ground in front of and behind it, and one over the line to the bank on the right. Note also the wooden posted ex-MR Up Starting signal, on the correct side of the line, just beyond the locomotive. JOHN DAGLEY-MORRIS

RIGHT: Parkend station from the south in May 1963, showing the junction for the Parkend Goods Branch. The picture was taken on the occasion of a group visit, possibly the Gloucestershire Industrial Archaeology Society. DAVID BICK

BELOW: No. 3775 ambles slowly southwards through the station in 1965. Progress was leisurely enough for photographer Bob Marrows to photograph it twice at Parkend and twice more passing through Whitecroft. Note the pw hut on the right, which also features in the top view. R.H. MARROWS

BELOW RIGHT: A close up of the shunt signal for the Parkend Goods Branch, seen just inside the gate in the picture below. IAN POPE COLLECTION

BOTTOM: The lower quadrant ex-Midland Railway Up Starter signal is 'off' for Class '57XX' No. 3643 on 30th March 1965, as it makes its way through the platforms with a train of ballast hoppers which have been loaded at Whitecliff Quarry. JOHN DAGLEY-MORRIS

A lengthy freight of loaded ballast hoppers and mineral opens for Class '57XX' No. 4698 at Parkend on 3rd August 1965. The train will pause here in order that No. 4698 can shunt the two loaded coal wagons at the front into the siding behind the Down platform. BILL POTTER/KRM

No. D9555 has stopped at Parkend whilst working a Coleford to Lydney Junction goods on 31st March 1967. The locomotive is about to perform the same manoeuvre as the pannier tank in the picture above. It would appear that the two or three loaded wagons that it will place into the siding are being uncoupled from the engine as well as from the rest of the train. This is presumably so they can be gravity worked behind No. D9555 past the point, then propelled back into the siding and simply deposited there. JOHN TOLSON/TREVOR DAVIS COLLECTION

Viewed from partway down the footbridge steps, No. 4698 shunts a wagon load of coal up the Parkend Goods Branch on 6th August 1965. As we shall see, the arrangement of level crossings here was one of the most complicated and intensive anywhere in the country, with two gated crossings within fifty yards of each other on the branch, plus another on the main line at the far end of the station. Whilst something unique and quite special has been lost with the closure and final removal of the Parkend Goods Branch, it is probably also fair to say that many local residents did not mourn its passing. Bill Potter/KRM

The fact that, to this author's knowledge, no one has yet recreated the Marsh Wharf at Parkend in model form is rather surprising when one sees scenes such as this. Moments after the previous view, No. 4698 shunts the two mineral wagons, which appear to be loaded with pit props for use in one of the local free mines, along the centre road of the Marsh Sidings. Note the timber blocks in use across the tracks, to prevent wagons running away down the branch; these were provided in 1922 following a runaway of six loaded wagons in 1921, which damaged the crossing gates on Fountain Way. Parkend was a centre for industry in the Forest and the Marsh was an historic location, the wharf having been built in 1869 as a transshipment point between the Milkwall Branch tramroad and the broad gauge line of the Severn & Wye. The tramroad to Milkwall was abandoned in 1876 but the lower portion of it remained in use connecting the Oakwood Tramroad to the wharf, the tramroad rails running onto the top of it. A wooden Eassie design goods shed had also been provided here in 1871 but was later moved to the station goods yard. The siding on the right served a stone sawmills and was thus always known as 'Sawmills Siding'. A wooden derrick for lifting the stone was in use on the wharf until at least the late 1940s and was still here in 1966; it can be seen in the picture on page 168. BILL POTTER/KRM

ABOVE: Shunter Ferdie Wilkins pinning down the brakes on one of the last wagons to be loaded here, with what the wagon label referred to as 'FOD Small Mines Coal', bound for Uskmouth 'A' Power Station at Newport in 1976. It was unusual to see a van here by this date, so the vehicle on the right may have belonged to the pw department. COLEFORD GWR MUSEUM (MIKE REES)

LEFT: Looking from the coal loading dock in June 1968, with a Class '63XX' diesel shunting a rake of empty ballast hoppers onto the middle road and a batch of loadeds waiting to be collected alongside. The hut, presumably built in connection with the transfer of the ballast traffic down from Whitecliff, does not feature in any other picture taken here and may not have been in use for long. ARTHUR DAY, COURTESY MONMOUTH MUSEUM

Whilst the nostalgic pull of the steam locomotive remains as strong as ever, there is now a growing body of interest in the green diesel era on British Railways and in the early classes of diesels, many of which failed to survive beyond the early to mid 1970s. There are numerous evocative views of various types of green liveried diesels at work in the Forest within these pages but this lovely shot of NBL-built Type 2 diesel hydraulic No. D6319 shunting Marsh Wharf sidings in glorious summer sunshine on 10th June 1968, is undoubtedly one of the best and can only further fuel this interest. No. D6319 was delivered new to Plymouth Laira (83D) on 11th April 1960 and was withdrawn on 22nd May 1971. It was cut up at Swindon Works. Having shunted the empty ballast hoppers into position on the centre road, the locomotive will then collect the rake of steel mineral wagons on the left, which are loaded with free mined coal. The man on the left is operating the point levers. Bill Potter/KRM

Tatty looking North British Type 2 No. D6354 shunts a train of hopper wagons along the Goods Branch on 26th November 1970. One of the train crew holds the level crossing gate closed to traffic. However, the other gate appears to have been removed and can be seen leaning against the fence on the right. It is thought that the damage to the locomotive's paintwork may have been caused by a fire. New into service in August 1962 and first allocated to Bristol Bath Road shed (82A), No. D6354 was withdrawn in May 1971 and cut up at Swindon Works during February 1972. BILL POTTER/KRM

On 6th July 1971, Type 2 No. 7625 is seen in a similar position with another lengthy train of ballast hoppers. Despite the later date, the locomotive is still sporting BR two tone green livery, albeit in an extremely careworn condition; a BR lion emblem can also just be discerned on the bodyside. Clearly, a repaint into blue livery was imminent. This BR/Sulzer Type 2 was one of the first two of the class to be built by Beyer, Peacock in Manchester, being delivered new to Tinsley depot (41A) on 30th July 1965. It was working from Newport Ebbw Junction shed at the time of this view and later spent time at Bristol, Cardiff and Laira. Becoming part of Class '25' (later Class '25/1') under TOPS, the locomotive was renumbered No. 25275 in April 1974. It was withdrawn on 18th April 1982 and eventually broken up at Swindon in July 1985. BILL POTTER/KRM

At Marsh Sidings a short while later, where No. D7625 has just completed shunting the empties along the centre road. The engine will shortly uncouple and then run forward clear of the points, which will be switched over to the siding on the right. It will then reverse back to collect the train of loaded hoppers from this siding and draw forward once more. Next, the point will be switched again and the loaded train will reverse back to attach the empties (minus the brake van) on the end. The engine will haul both sets of wagons clear of the points, which will be switched back again, so that the train can reverse and deposit the empty wagons alongside the wharf. Having then drawn forward once more, the final manoeuvre will be another reversal to attach the brake van to the rear, before proceeding back down the branch. On the right, stored at the far end of the Sawmills Siding, is a Fowler 0-4-0 diesel shunter that was an early acquisition by the Dean Forest Railway but which is no longer a part of their stock list. BILL POTTER/KRM

LEFT: A view along the branch from Fountain Way level crossing in the autumn of 1966. JOHN STRANGE/NPC

ABOVE: The then heavily grass-grown sidings at Parkend Marsh in the early 1960s, with just a few wagons in attendance. DEREK CHAPLIN

BELOW: A view off the end of the wharf towards the Fountain Inn on 21st July 1974. Crown Lane runs along on the left. Loading of Whitecliff ballast from here began in August 1967 and led to the state of the track being improved. BILL POTTER/KRM

RIGHT: Another view of the sidings but from a little further along the wharf, with the vegetation threatening to take over again in August 1974. R.H. MARROWS

BELOW: In its pre-TOPS guise, BR Sulzer Type 2 No. 7520 shunts four steel mineral wagons that will most likley be loaded with free mined coal at the Marsh Sidings on a bright sunny day circa 1973. As No. D7520, the locomotive was new to Nottingham shed on 22nd December 1964 and was a well travelled machine, finding its way to Cardiff shed by July 1972. Under TOPS, it was redesignated as Class '25' (later Class '25/2') and as such was renumbered to No. 25170 on 4th July 1974. It left Cardiff for Laira depot, Plymouth, in October 1975. The engine was withdrawn from Crewe depot on 2nd August 1982 and had been broken up at Derby Works by early April 1983. NPC

The history and rights surrounding the free mining of coal in the Forest of Dean are briefly touched upon in the Introduction, on page 12. They are one of the traditions within the Forest that proclaim its uniqueness and the rights are both jealously guarded and also protected for the future by those few hardy individuals who still crawl underground to mine coal. Here, on 5th November 1968, a green liveried tipper lorry from Farmers Folly Colliery at English Bicknor, near Coleford, has just emptied its load into the mineral wagon below. The coal, of poor quality from a domestic point of view, was destined for the furnaces of either Uskmouth A or Uskmouth B Power Station at East Usk, near Newport. Farmers Folly Colliery had been quite a productive little mine, first established in 1841. Worked intermittently throughout the 19th century and changing hands several times, as was usual for these small Forest mines, by 1900 it had come into the ownership of the Gwilliam family, with an output for the previous year of some 5,750 tons. The colliery was still owned by the Gwilliams at the date of this photograph but was listed as being deregistered from the List of Companies in 1979, coal production probably having ceased a few years earlier. BILL POTTER/KRM

Having expressed surprise that no one has yet made a model of the Marsh Sidings, this wonderful shot begs the question as to just how you would replicate in miniature form the motive power on show here. In spring 1976, three men attempt to push this empty steel mineral wagon, weighing around seven tons, on a slight rising gradient towards the buffer stops at the end of the Parkend Goods Branch. Taken on Friday 25th March 1976, the day of the last ballast train from here which Ian and Alec Pope had come along to record, this wagon was waiting to be loaded with free-mined coal but the train was late arriving. Consequently, the three men decided to manhandle it into position for loading. Note the shack alongside the coal loading wharf. IAN POPE

Later on that day, Class '25' No. 25155 had finally arrived and stands at the very end of the branch, straddling the three-way point, at the head of a brake van and half a dozen steel mineral wagons, which will be left here for loading with coal. Delivered new to Toton shed from BR's Derby Works on 22nd October 1964 as No. D7505, the locomotive was based at Cardiff at the time of this view. The windscreen configuration marks this out as one of the engines that were later designated as Class '25/2'. It will be noted that the Class '25/1' seen on page 157 has the smaller centre windscreen, fitted above the nose end doors. It was realised that these doors were no longer required after the original members of the class had been in use for a while, so later examples were fitted instead with a flush front end and a larger centre windscreen, as exhibited here and also by No. 7520 on page 165. Parkend Sawmills is visible through the trees in the background. Having been established on here since just after the First World War, a timber company still uses the site today. The branch to Coleford ran just behind it as it climbed the hill up to Milkwall. IAN POPE

ABOVE: No. D9555 shunts the Sawmills Siding on 21st July 1966. Note the wooden derrick used for unloading stone blocks still in existence. Also shown are the stone steps at the apex of the wharf. R.H. MARROWS

LEFT: A view of the three way point at the end of the branch from just above the buffer stop in August 1976, with mineral wagons still in evidence awaiting loading with free mined coal. DENNIS PARKHOUSE

BELOW: One of the lorry loads forming the last load of ballast to be shipped from Marsh Sidings being tipped into a hopper wagon on 25th March 1976. The lorry belongs to local hauliers N. & G. Bradley. Note the nearer 'Dogfish' wagon is still lettered 'RETURN TO COLEFORD', some nine years after the line to Coleford had closed. IAN POPE

LEFT: This noticeboard lettered for the LMS & GW RLY Cos SEVERN & WYE JT RLY was a remarkable survivor alongside the signal box at Parkend in 1958. T.B. OWEN

BELOW: A general view of the station looking north from the footbridge circa 1962. The goods shed was – and still is – another remarkable survivor, being the original Eassie building erected at Marsh Wharf in 1871 and then moved to this new site behind the station in 1897. The signal box had been repainted around 1960, from the brown and cream livery glimpsed in the picture left (and also shown on page 179), to the all over cream style seen here. DEREK CHAPLIN

The track recovery train seen previously at the south end of the station and on the crossing at Whitecroft, eases through the platforms in summer 1964. The slightly foreshortened aspect emphasises the curve in the line, past the site of Parkend Ironworks, over the crossing and through the station. DAVID BICK/NPC

LEFT: A view of the back loop siding looking north towards the level crossing, showing the separate gate that was provided to protect it. Also shown is the ground level shunt signal just in front, which was operated by lever No. 11 in Parkend Signal Box. The wooden posted Down Starter positioned on the end of the platform was again of Midland origin and worked by lever No. 21. In the left background, there is a glimpse of the staff instrument through the open window of the signal box. NPC

BELOW LEFT: A close up of the 'S' pattern Miniature Electric Train Staff (METS) instrument glimpsed in the picture left, which was provided when the section of line from Parkend to Tufts Junction was singled as an economy measure with effect from 30th November 1930. It was a product of the Railway Signal Co. Ltd of Fazakerley, Liverpool. This instrument was provided (on the right hand side) with a tapper key for sending bell signals but no bell (the bell was on the block instrument shelf). The driver in charge of each train entering on to the single line had to be in possession of one of the staffs. The instruments were so arranged that although there were a number of staffs, only one could be released at any time – a staff could be obtained at either end of the section, so long as no staff was already out. To obtain a staff, the signalman raised one of them to the top of the column and waited a few moments for his counterpart in the next box along to react. On receiving an electric release from the signalman at the other end of the section, he then moved the staff round the quarter circle slot until it could be withdrawn through the opening at the 'nine o'clock' position. If the system was operated correctly and the rules obeyed, no two trains could be in the same section at the same time. DEREK CHAPLIN

BELOW RIGHT: Part of the instrument shelf above the lever frame, with the Midland Railway pattern block instrument for accepting Up direction trains from Travellers Rest Crossing Signal Box in the centre. The bell, with tapper key, for working to Travellers Rest Crossing is on the left. On the right is a bell without tapper key, working to Tufts Junction Signal Box in connection with the METS staff instrument. DEREK CHAPLIN

LEFT: As the Dean Forest Railway occupied the station yard from 1971, whilst the branch was still in operation, it would be wrong not to feature some of their early operations, which served in any case to generate a certain amount of traffic on the line. Here, in 1972, the Peckett 0-4-0ST *Uskmouth 1* gives brake van rides along the short length of the back siding. Built in 1952, to Peckett Works No. 2147, *Uskmouth 1* went new to Uskmouth Power Station at Newport. In 1971, it was bought by Mike Rees, who is seen on the footplate, arriving here at Parkend on 10th May. The engine was subsequently purchased from Mike by the DFRPS. DEREK KNIGHT

RIGHT: Ex-GWR 'Manor' Class 4-6-0 No. 7812 *Erlestoke Manor* at Parkend during an open day on 19th May 1974. Purchased by the Erlestoke Manor Fund, a group including DFRPS members, it was brought here especially for this open day, after which it was removed to the Dowty RPS site at Ashchurch for restoration work to begin. It had relocated again to the Severn Valley Railway by April 1976, where it was brought back into service in 1979. It remains there today and is currently again in use following an overhaul in 2008. Coupled behind it is 'Large Prairie' No. 4150. BILL POTTER/KRM

OPPOSITE PAGE TOP: No. 3775 heads a train of ballast hoppers from Whitecliff through the station in 1965. This is another train we have seen already as it made its way southwards from here and, indeed, will come across again. R.H. MARROWS

OPPOSITE PAGE BOTTOM: As a contrast and from a similar viewpoint, Type 1 diesel hydraulic No. D9555 rumbles through with loaded ballast hoppers from Whitecliff on 21st July 1966. Apart from the motive power, little if anything had changed here in a year and the yard was still busy with local coal traffic. Indeed, the two mineral wagons laden with coal behind No. D9555 will shortly be dropped here, having been worked north to Coleford Junction on a Down train. It was preferred practice to shunt them in to the siding from the Up working, as the locomotive simply had to detach from the train with the two wagons and reverse them into the siding. The north end of the looped back siding had been removed by this date. R.H. MARROWS

RIGHT: Looking over the level crossing to the DFRPS site, on the same occasion as the top picture, showing the terminus of the branch in the station on the left. DEREK KNIGHT

ABOVE: A final view of DFR operations in Parkend goods yard in 1972, looking from part way along the Goods Branch, between the two level crossings. The length of track that *Uskmouth 1* had to run over was little more than fifty yards. DEREK KNIGHT

RIGHT: In the 19th century, the centre of Parkend village was dominated by the ironworks. Iron making had begun on the site by 1799 and had expanded from the original single furnace to two in 1827 and three in 1870. The furnaces were charged from above with a 'covered way' or bridge extending over the railway to the hillside behind. The ironworks closed in 1877 and was subsequently demolished, the tall chimney that stood next to the engine house eventually being felled in 1908. The engine house was left standing, however, and was later converted for use as a Forestry School and is now the Dean Field Studies Centre. This view of it is looking north east across the Goods Branch in February 1970. DAVID BICK

BELOW: A rare but poor quality colour view along New Road, looking south towards the old engine house and railway station, circa 1960. Nearer to the camera, with the awning shielding the main window from the sun, is Parkend stores and post office, which is still open today. New Road, running between Mierystock and Lydney, was built by the Crown in 1902-04. NPC

Another of Bill Potter's early colour pictures, with one of the '16XX' Class of small pannier tanks, No. 1632, on a short freight from Coleford, halted alongside Parkend Signal Box so fireman and signalman can exchange tokens on 7th August 1957. The box, here seen in its 1950s chocolate and cream livery, was provided in 1897 and was to a standard GWR design, in a similar style to the brick boxes seen elsewhere along the route but constructed instead of timber. Situated adjacent to the gates to the north of the crossing (the new DFR box here at Parkend is immediately to the south), it originally housed a wheel for operating the gates but when the double gates were replaced in the last few years by wide span single ones, hand operation took over instead. The north end of the loop siding and the Down to Up line crossover by the locomotive were all removed in December 1963, after which wagons had to be shunted into the goods yard from the south. Note, too, the Down Advanced Starter and Travellers Rest Distant signals positioned on the same post and 'wrong side' for sighting purposes, due to the curvature of the line at this point. A BR build, in January 1951, No. 1632 spent much of its career allocated to Gloucester but sub-shedded at Lydney, the '16XX' Class being seen as ideal replacements for the '2021' Class 0-6-0 tanks which had previously worked in the Forest for many years. The engine had migrated to Croes Newydd shed, Wrexham, by the time of its withdrawal in 1965, however. The retaining wall seen just beyond the train is the last remains of the 'covered way' bridge over which the ironworks furnaces were charged. BILL POTTER/KRM

Parkend Signal Box from the north, with No. D9555 heading past on 21st July 1966 with another short freight. The signalman, with hand aloft as he waits to collect the token, is probably Fred Wilkins, whose brother Ferd was signalman at Travellers Rest Crossing. Both men were later taken on as shunters at Parkend, working at the Marsh Sidings, after closure of their respective signal boxes. R.H. MARROWS

There was clearly a sharp frost on the morning of 30th March 1965 as No. 3643 storms north through Parkend with a train bound for Coleford Junction. The two loaded coal wagons will be left there whilst the rest of the train, empties for Whitecliff Quarry, will be taken up to Coleford. They will later be collected by the return working, which will pause here at Parkend to shunt them into the siding behind the platform. JOHN DAGLEY-MORRIS

The Severn Boar II railtour heads along the causeway between Parkend station and Travellers Rest Crossing. This was a most attractive stretch of double track railway, which this author fervently hopes will be brought back into operation by the DFR before too long. The line currently terminates just on the other side of the buildings in the right background. The patch of ground on the right edge of the picture marked by the stone retaining wall is the site of 'The Square', two terraces of three storey houses built in 1851 to house workers at Parkend tinplate works and demolished in the 1950s. T.B. OWEN

Photographer Bob Marrows worked mainly in black & white in the 1960s, so his colour output of the Forest amounts to little more than a couple of handfuls of slides. It can only be regretted that he was not more prolific when presented with pictures such as this, showing No. D9501 approaching Travellers Rest Crossing with a single brake van in tow on 27th May 1966. Just behind where he was standing is the route of the Parkend Royal Branch, the remaining stub of which can be seen with wagons parked in it beyond the signal box; running behind the box it then curved to the right, on the other side of the fence. The building beyond the locomotive is the old Railway Inn, originally named The Travellers Rest and from which the adjacent railway crossing took its name. Its name had changed by 1884, when it was put up for auction, and it continued to trade as a public house until 1959. Up on the hillside top left is York Lodge, one of the six lodges (of which the Speech House is the most well known) built between 1670 and 1680, when the Forest of Dean was divided into six 'Walks', the Crown's intention being to provide better management of the woodlands. The fencing running along the bottom of the field below York Lodge marks the route of the Coleford Branch. R.H. MARROWS

RIGHT: The GRS's Severn Venturer railtour on the causeway on the approach to Travellers Rest in 1962. JOHN STRANGE/NPC

BELOW: On 13th May 1961, pannier tank No. 8701 is seen travelling 'light engine' up from Lydney shed and about to be signalled over the crossing by an ex-LM&SR upper quadrant tubular post signal. Below the Home arm is the Distant arm for Coleford Junction, which was fixed at 'caution'. The closed Parkend Royal Branch ran on the low embankment seen behind the locomotive, on the other side of the fence, and then climbed through the shallow cutting beyond, just above the line of gorse bushes. ALAN JARVIS

No apologies are made for this run of full page views taken around Travellers Rest Crossing; it was a highly picturesque location and they are all superb studies. Here, a few moments after the previous picture, No. 8701 trundles over the crossing on its way to Coleford Junction to wait for the arrival of the SLS Special, which it would then be attached to in order to assist on the steep climb up to Fetterhill and Milkwall on the Coleford Branch. Travellers Rest Crossing Signal Box matched those provided in 1897 at Lydney Town, Tufts Junction and Whitecroft in design and construction, and would have been a delightful location for a signalman to go about his duties – but then you could say that about almost all of the Forest signal boxes! DEREK CHAPLIN

The SLS Special makes its way over the crossing as it heads for Coleford Junction. The Parkend Royal Branch ran behind the box at the approximate height of the top of the steps. The trip was blessed with very favourable weather, perfect for colour photography at this time. ALAN JARVIS

Travellers Rest Crossing looking up the Parkend to Blakeney road, with a Class '57XX' pannier tank heading across some time in 1965. The Railway Inn on the left had been closed for some years by this date, having served its last pints in 1959. It has since been converted into a private residence. COLEFORD GWR MUSEUM (MIKE REES)

RIGHT: Travellers Rest Crossing and signal box on 2nd August 1967, two days before the last train passed through. Oddly, whilst the line wass officially closed on 14th August, official closure of the box did not take place until 2nd October. This was another of the crossings where double gates had been replaced by a single large gate hung from a substantial post, which required some considerable bracing. Hand operation then came into use as well. This view is useful because it also shows the remains of the gate for the Parkend Royal Branch, behind the box. IAN POPE COLLECTION

LEFT: This ground signal was operated from the box and was positioned about 100 yards along the line towards Coleford Junction. It can be seen by the rear of the train in the pictures which follow overleaf. Operated by lever No. 9 in the box, it controlled access over the crossover from the Up line to the Down line and was matched by a similar signal, facing north and operated by lever No. 11, which controlled movments in the opposite direction. There were two further adjacent northward facing ground signals at the end of the Down loop sidings, controlled by levers No's 13 and 15.

BELOW LEFT: A rear view of the same signal. These pictures were again taken on 2nd August 1967.

BELOW: Looking the other way on the same day. It will be noted that the box retained chocolate & cream livery on its wooden upper storey to the end, albeit somewhat faded by this time. The GWR-built boxes at the southern end of the line, between Lydney Town and Travellers Rest, were unusual in controlling Midland Railway signals, a result of the line's post-1894 Joint status. Whilst on a short cycling tour round the Forest of Dean in 1967, your author passed over this crossing. He has vague memories of the signals and the line on the causeway between here and Parkend but, sadly, no recollection of the box whatsover. The small shack behind the steps housed the signalmen's privy. ALL IAN POPE COLLECTION

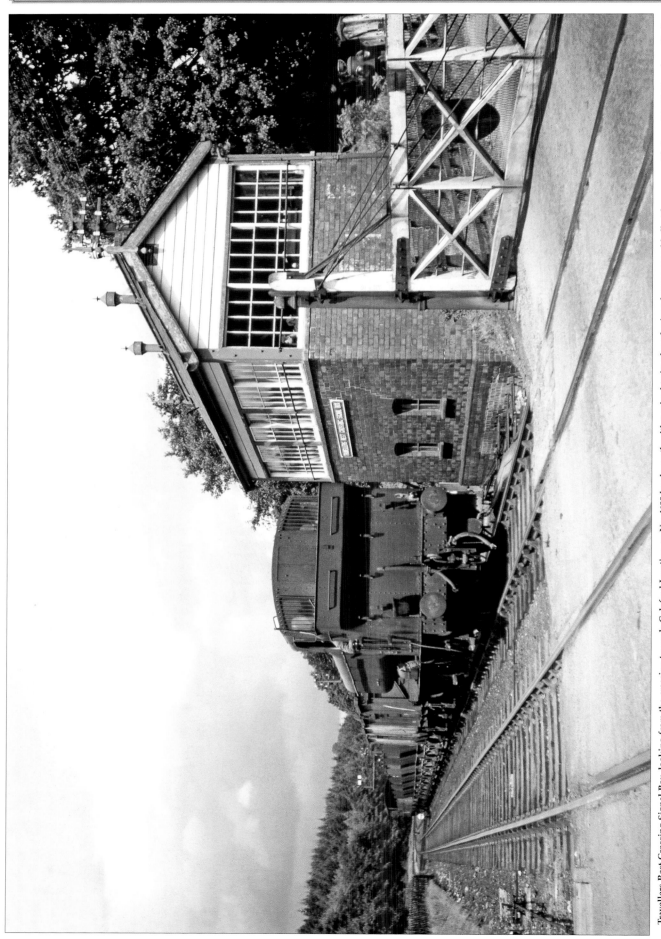

Travellers Rest Crossing Signal Box, looking from the crossing towards Coleford Junction, as No. 4698 heads south with a mixed train of steel mineral wagons and ballast hoppers on 6th August 1965. Signalman Ferd Wilkins, the last man to work the box, can just be glimpsed through the windows but, in this pre-Health & Safety conscious age, no one seems bothered that the photographer is standing inside the crossing gates. Just by the end of the train is the crossover and single slip connecting the Up Main, Down Main and Down Loop lines, with the attendant ground signal. Also by this date, the southern end of the Up Loop had been taken out; removed on 7th July 1974, the point can be seen beneath the wheels of the locomotive in the top picture opposite. The ground signal by the end of the train is that shown in close-up on the previous page. BILL POTTER/KRM

Later on 3rd August, having come down the branch from Coleford with eight loaded ballast hoppers and under the watchful eye of the Coleford Junction signalman, No. 4698 begins the process of arranging its train for the journey down to Lydney. Having first dropped the brake van and now running forward, the engine will shortly shunt the wagons onto the loop siding to the right of the signal. It will then come back for the brake van and add it on the end of the rake of hoppers, before running round the whole ensemble to attach itself at the far end. Note that No. 4698 is facing 'downhill' from Coleford. Traditionally, the locomotives working to Coleford faced 'uphill', so that water in the boiler was always maintained over the firebox. As a consequence, the Coleford Branch engine could always be distinguished at Lydney shed because it faced the opposite way to the rest of the stud. However, after the closure of the shed in March 1962, locomotives worked out and back daily from Gloucester and this general rule was subsequently not rigorously followed. Bill Potter/KRM

No. 4698 again but a couple of weeks later, on 18th August, with a train from Lydney Yard consisting of some open wagons bound for Coleford S&W and behind a rake of empty hoppers for Whitecliff Quarry. The locomotive is shunting the train onto the Down Main line and is part way through the sequence that all trains had to go through at Coleford Junction. Essentially, with a complete change in direction being required here, on arrival from Lydney both the engine and brake van were at the wrong ends of the train for the journey up to Coleford, so shunting was required to correct this and place both in the right position. These manoeuvres were reversed for trains heading back down to Lydney. In earlier, busier times, when the main line was still in operation north from here to Lydbrook (and pre-1951 to Cinderford), traffic from Coleford would often be deposited in the yard for southbound trains to collect. Earlier still, when the regular passenger service was still in operation, although there was never a public platform here, passenger trains would drop off Coleford bound carriages for the Coleford Branch engine to collect; this operation not taking place at a public station was quite a rare working practice on a British railway. With the yard by this date only being used by Coleford Branch traffic, there were no issues with blocking one of the main running lines. Note the two wagons in the Up Loop siding on the left; they appear to be carrying boilers and will have been loaded at Fred Watkins boiler works on the Sling Branch at Milkwall, which we shall visit later on in these pages. Bill Potter/KRM

Later the same day, having returned from Coleford, No. 4698 is seen part way through the reverse process of arranging its train for the journey back down to Lydney, watched by the guard waiting patiently in his van. BILL POTTER/KRM

Finally, all shunting manoeuvres now completed and with the brake van reattached at the far end of the train, driver and guard have a chat prior to departure for Lydney yard. It would appear that a crew of four was required to work these trains, with a driver and fireman on the footplate, and a guard and shunter travelling in the brake van. BILL POTTER/KRM

ABOVE: No. D9555 at Coleford Junction with the 09.00am freight from Lydney Junction on 31st March 1967. The empty mineral wagons are being deposited here for collection later, as they are destined for Marsh Sidings. The brake van will then be reattached to the empty hoppers which are bound for Whitecliff Quarry, so the engine will need to run round the train first. JOHN TOLSON/TREVOR DAVIS COLLECTION

BELOW: No. D9555 now shunts the hoppers and brake van back through the yard towards Coleford Junction Signal Box, in order that the train can gain the Coleford Branch and then proceed locomotive leading up the steep climb. JOHN TOLSON/TREVOR DAVIS COLLECTION

ABOVE: This rather incongruous looking BR (WR) design bracket signal, on a very short post to allow sighting through the road bridge just to the north of it, was a late 1950s replacement for an earlier wooden posted GWR bracket of rather more elegant appearance. The ringed arm on the left controlled entry to the Up Loop siding, the Home and Distant arms in the centre referred to the Up Main line and the arm on the right to the Coleford Branch. The picture was taken in July 1967. IAN POPE COLLECTION

ABOVE: Another view of the signal, taken on 1st February 1961, when the line north of here was still in use. Also shown is the permanent way hut and maintenance trolley, along with the boarded area which aided mounting of the trolley on the rails. Note the 'ENGINES MUST NOT PASS THIS BOARD' sign propped upside down against the end wall of the hut. B.J. ASHWORTH

ABOVE: This view of the north end of Coleford Junction yard was taken in July 1967 from the old lamppost next to the water column. The signal post in the foreground holds the Down Starter, whilst the two ground signals control access to the Down Loop siding, left, and exit from the Up Loop siding, right; note the catch point next to the signal. In Joint line days, the boundary between Midland Railway and GWR maintenance responsibilities bisected the yard just behind the photographer's position. IAN POPE COLLECTION

ABOVE: North British Type 2 No. D6329 shunts wagons on the Down Main on 24th July 1967, under the control of the Down Starter signal. The signal in the foreground is the Up Inner Home and Distant for Travellers Rest Crossing, which again was a late 1950s replacement for an earlier wooden posted signal; it applied to the Up Main, the line between the diesel and the wagons on the right. R.H. MARROWS

OPPOSITE PAGE BOTTOM LEFT: The interior of Coleford Junction signal box in the mid 1960s, with relief signalman 'Bruce' on duty. IAN POPE COLLECTION

OPPOSITE PAGE BOTTOM RIGHT: 'Bruce' with his master, signalman George Cooke, outside the box in June 1967. ARTHUR DAY, COURTESY MONMOUTH MUSEUM

This delightful view of the old Severn & Wye main line heading north into the Forest was taken from the New Road bridge on 26th April 1961 and shows No. 1631, ambling south past the Coleford Junction Advanced Starting signal (the arm of which which later received a fresh coat of paint as the picture on the previous page shows), with the short train seen previously at Travellers Rest Crossing. Note the also the milepost in the right foreground. To lessen the angle at which the bridge passed over the railway, the road executed a sharp S bend as it crossed, as indicated by the 'elbow' jutting into the picture on the left. Sadly, as road traffic into the Forest increased it was deemed dangerous for road users, as a consequence of which, in the early 1990s, the bridge was demolished and the road here realigned. A new bridge will therefore be required when the DFR extends the line back up to Speech House Road. As an aside, the ashes of the author's late father, some of whose pictures grace these pages, were scattered in amongst the trees up on the right as he requested. DEREK CHAPLIN

The Severn Boar II tour departing from Bicslade Wharf, midway along the line between Coleford Junction and Speech House Road, in June 1964. This view is useful because it shows the connection between the siding serving the wharf and the main line, and the short headshunt. These arrangements dated from December 1952, when the loop siding running south from the end of the headshunt was taken out, along with the connection to the main line at the end of it and the South Ground Frame that controlled it. The point lever on the far side of the line just ahead of the engine, originally the Middle Ground Frame, was then renamed as the South Ground Frame. NPC

Taken on the same occasion, this view shows that the tour stopped here in order that the participants could explore the remains of the wharf, which was provided circa 1875 as a transshipment point between the railway and the Bicslade Tramroad. Bicslade Stoneworks, which was established in 1901, shipped out dressed stone from here that had been cut from Bixhead Quarry, further up the valley. Coal was also delivered here for use in the Stoneworks boiler house. The horse-drawn tramroad which delivered the stone blocks to the Stoneworks and then brought the dressed stone to the wharf, onto which it ran, continued in use from the quarry until 1944 and between the works and the wharf into the 1950s, although tractors had taken over from horses by then. On the left is the remains of one of the two wooden derricks that were erected for loading stone into railway wagons. They were provided around 1900, the one as a replacement for an earlier crane which had become defective. The course of the tramroad up the valley is still easily followed today, with many of the distinctive stone sleeper blocks still remaining in position. JOHN RYAN

Bicslade Wharf on 26th April 1961, with No. 1631 pausing as it heads south with a short freight from Speech House Road. As we shall see overleaf, photographer Derek Chaplin had already taken one view of the train here from further along the wharf, with the shots then to follow at Coleford Junction and Travellers Rest which we have already seen. Clearly, all of these pictures could only have been taken with the collusion of the footplate crew, taking their time or even pausing along the way to allow the photographer time to get into position. However, with Speech House Road being serviced by just one train a week by this date, such a leisurely schedule was not a problem. Of interest here are the new girders just in view on the left. Delivered presumably for the Stoneworks, it is entirely likely that they could have been the last consignment to use the wharf. The siding had originally continued on beyond the buffer stop to join the main line again past the end of the wharf but this section was removed in July 1959. DEREK CHAPLIN

ABOVE: A view through the main gate of Bicslade Stoneworks in July 1976. Apart from the mobile crane in the yard, little had changed here for decades and the works looks pretty much as it would have done when still sending out stone by rail. The Stoneworks was established in 1901 by E. Turner & Sons, quarry owners from Cardiff, who had taken out a lease on Bixhead Quarry at the top of the Bicslade Valley, in order that they could process the rough hewn stone blocks prior to sending them out by rail. The works was taken over by United Stone Firms Ltd in 1910, as part of a general takeover of the stone industry in the Forest of Dean. United Stone Firms (1926) Ltd took over in that year and then, in 1939, Bicslade was acquired by Forest of Dean Stone Firms Ltd, the name under which it still operates today. Sadly for industrial historians who used to enjoy the sight of the old works and its machinery, Bicslade Stoneworks was extensively modernised in the 2000s. Its high quality Pennant sandstone products are today much in demand, however, for prestige building projects, whilst the company has, since 2010, installed a micro hydro turbine generator on the nearby Cannop Brook to generate its own power. DAVID BICK

RIGHT: A view of one of the two massive stone cranes then in use at Bixhead Quarry, in July 1976. There are three quarries at the head of the valley but this one, also known as Barnhill Quarry, is the only one in operation today. DAVID BICK

OPPOSITE PAGE TOP: Another view of the REC tour whilst at Bicslade. A waymarked path crossed the line just beneath the locomotive, the gate for which can be seen just behind it, along with a cast iron notice no doubt exhorting users to close the gate. There were steps in the face of the wharf in order for the footpath to carry on across it. NPC

OPPOSITE PAGE BOTTOM: As referred to on the previous page, this is the first shot of No. 1642 passing the wharf. The northern end of the loop siding, removed in 1959, had connected with the main line a short distance beyond the end of the train; it was controlled by the North Ground Frame. The distance between the main running line and the siding were a result of the former being slewed over in 1906, to guard against an accident in the event of a stone block falling from the wharf. Like many old railway locations within the Forest, the site of the wharf is heavily overgrown today but the remains of it can still be found and much of the stone facing wall still survives. DEREK CHAPLIN

LEFT: No. 8701 potters light engine past Cannop Ponds on 13th May 1961. It would appear from this shot that No. 6437 was left to manage the southwards journey of the SLS Special from Speech House Road on its own. The trackbed north of Coleford Junction is today a footpath and cycletrack, so has been put to good use but unchecked tree growth alongside it over the decades since closure means that much of it is hidden from general view. B.J. ASHWORTH

BELOW: The SLS tour negotiates its way through typical Forest of Dean scenery near Cannop Ponds as it heads south on the same day. B.J. ASHWORTH

BELOW: The REC Severn Boar II tour heads north along a distinctive section of the S&W main line between Bicslade and Speech House Road in June 1964. The elevated viewpoint was courtesy of the Speech House Road Down Distant signal, another which was permanently fixed at 'caution'. Note that the width of the formation was sufficient for a second track but the line north of Coleford Junction was always single. T.B. OWEN

The photographer remained at the top of the signal post but turned round to capture this second view of the tour heading towards Speech House Road station. T.B. Owen

The SLS tour arriving at Speech House Road station in May 1961, in another view which shows much else of interest. In the right foreground is the overgrown Howlerslade or Cannop Siding, which branched off the Up Loop line near the far end of the train and terminated where the photographer was standing. The loading wharf which it ran alongside was a transshipment point with the Howlerslade Tramroad, which was in existence by 1877 and served Cannop Chemical Works, as well as a colliery and a quarry further up the Howlerslade Valley. Around the same time, Messrs Trotter, Thomas & Co. also established a Stoneworks adjacent to the wharf. The company were bankrupt by 1891 but became part of David & Sant Ltd in 1892, this concern in turn being acquired by Forest of Dean Stone Firms Ltd in 1900. By 1910, the wharf had been extended and now included a steam powered gantry crane straddling the siding, as well as a wooden derrick crane on the wharf itself. The Stoneworks is believed to have closed around 1925, not becoming a part of the reconstituted United Stone Firms (1926) Ltd concern. The tramroad, which ran in just on the right by the fence, was out of use by circa 1920 but the tramplates were not actually taken up until January 1941; the lower section of it serving the wharf may have lasted a little longer. The last use of the wharf may have been for shipping sawn timber from a saw mills established during the Second World War near the site of the chemical works, which could have used the lower section of the tramroad. There was also a permanent way hut at the far end of the wharf, which can just be glimpsed here. In the centre foreground is Speech House Road Siding Ground Frame, which controlled access to the wood distillation works sidings, installed circa 1917. The train is approaching the Up Advanced Starting signal, which was controlled from Speech House Road Signal Box. Alan Jarvis

Speech House Road station was situated right in the heart of the Forest and had a character all its own. This view is looking north towards Serridge Junction and Lydbrook in 1961. The Down Loop on the left continued on beyond the level crossing gates to serve Cannop Colliery but this had closed in 1960, traffic ceasing in the September, with the last train running on 21st November. The tubular post, ringed bracket signal on the left and the signal on the right both dated from circa 1959, and were replacements for wooden posted signals, the rings denoting that the arms referred to goods lines. Quite why BR decided to spend money renewing the signals here at this late date is not known. Official records note the level crossing gates as being operated from the box but, as far as is known, the gates were in fact always hand operated. Note that the gates and station building had recently been repainted too. IAN POPE COLLECTION

No. 1631 makes its way back down the short branch to the wood distillation works on 26th April 1961, having probably dropped a few wagons loaded with coal in the siding. In the left background is the small wooden goods shed, just 20 feet in length, another Eassie design supplied by the Gloucester RC&W Co. in late 1889. Note the pronounced drop down from the main running lines for both the goods yard siding and the wood distillation branch; the latter then climbed again just out of picture on the left, on a short embankment to reach the works. The photographer was standing on the course of the Howlerslade Tramroad, which crossed over the line beneath the wheels of the locomotive. The signal on the right, the Up Starter, had not been replaced by a more modern example. DEREK CHAPLIN

RIGHT: This wooden, gilt lettered nameboard is a remarkable survivor from the short lived period between 1923, when the London, Midland & Scottish Railway superceded the Midland on the Joint Committee, and 1929, when the S&W passenger service ended (the Midland became a part of the LM&SR at the 1923 Grouping of railway companies). It is not known from which station this board came but it is believed to have formed the header to a noticeboard. NPC

Having assembled its short train, No. 1631 makes ready to leave. Note the siding and the wood distillation branch were gated, although the numerous gates and fences could not prevent roaming Forest sheep from wandering on to railway property. The middle gate had been provided for the tramroad, the route of which had then been through the goods yard and across the Speech House Road, before curving left to head up the Howlerslade Valley. The station had originally opened as a temporary platform in 1875, a new permanent station being provided from August 1878. Note the standard S&W wooden station building still extant on the platform. Just visible beyond the signal box is the stationmaster's house, which was provided in 1888 and was the only dwelling in the vicinity of the station. It was an attractively designed property but did not survive the closure of the railway. The Speech House, the grand Forest lodge after which the station took its name, is situated nearly a mile away at the top of a steep hill off to the right. DEREK CHAPLIN

ABOVE: This view of the SLS Special arriving at the station was taken from the bracket signal just in front of the signal box, on which lofty perch Bill Potter and Derek were stood side by side. The yard was full with loaded coal wagons delivered here for local merchants, whilst a van stands by the gated entrance to the wood distillation branch. The bracket signal beside the far engine was the Down Home, with the arm 'off' for the main line. DEREK CHAPLIN

RIGHT AND BELOW: Two views of the wood distillation works in 1970. Again the author cycled past it in 1967 but has little recollection of it. The works was built between 1911 and 1913 by the Office of Woods, with the aim of using the large quantities of waste wood generated during felling operations for the production of charcoal, acetate of lime, wood spirit and wood tar. From 1915, acetone was also produced, used in the production of cordite for use in shells during the First World War, which was somewhat ironic considering that the internal machinery had been supplied and fitted by a German company. The works closed down in 1927 when the then owners went bankrupt but were subsequently bought by Shirley Aldred & Co. Ltd, who modernised the plant before reopening it. A further reconditioning was carried out in 1950 but in 1960 the plant was reduced to the production of charcoal only, until final closure in June 1972. Nothing remains at the site today. DEREK KNIGHT

LEFT: The Severn Venturer tour at Speech House Road station on 15th April 1956. Note that a short length of the Down Loop line in the foreground was laid on concrete sleeper pots, with the gauge being held by metal tie bars. Lengths of track at various locations in the Forest were relaid in this manner during the Second World War. T.B. OWEN

BELOW: The GRS tour at the station on 23rd June 1962. The gentleman chatting to a lady whilst leaning against the fence with his hand on his neck – a distinctive pose – is Alec Pope, Ian's father, who maintained a lifelong interest in the railways of the Forest and who saved many interesting items of local railwayana and industrial history interest from being lost forever. BILL POTTER/KRM

BELOW: The closure in November 1960 and subsequent lifting of the line north of Speech House Road a year later did little for the aesthetics of the station, with the loss of the level crossing as the road was relaid. The signal box was another standard GWR design (and perhaps the most handsome on the entire Forest system), opened on 11th August 1908 as a replacement for an earlier, smaller wooden box situated on the platform. Its career came to an end on 12th August 1963, when the line north of Coleford Junction was closed, although it was unlocked for the benefit of the enthusiasts on the brake van tour in June 1964. Note that the station building had also been removed by this date. In the right background, the wood distillation branch can be seen curving away from the goods yard on a low embankment. T.B. OWEN

LEFT: By the time of the REC's Severn Boar tours in June 1964, the line up to Speech House Road had been closed for ten months as the rust covered rails and grass grown tracks indicate. Here, as the tour prepares for departure, one intrepid photographer climbs the ladder of the Up Starting signal for a better viewpoint. Note the signal has lost its finial since the earlier pictures; does it still survive in a collection or as an ornament somewhere? T.B. OWEN

ABOVE: The departure of the last train to call at Speech House Road, on 20th June. The piles of coal in the goods yard would indicate that deliveries were still being made here but now by road. In the distance beyond the signal box there is another glimpse of the stationmaster's house. Although the box was opened up for tour participants to have a look round, it was not in use so the train was not signalled away. T.B. OWEN

RIGHT: The demolition contractors were to move in almost immediately, track removals commencing in the following month. The buffer stop in the centre foreground is that at the end of Cannop or Howlerslade Siding, serving the old transshipment wharf. T.B. OWEN

Moving back in time to 1957, these two rare colour views show No. 1642 shunting wagons over the level crossing and on to the Wimberry Branch, bound for Cannop Colliery. In the top picture, the fireman is about to exchange tokens with the signalman, whilst the train heads over the scissors crossing that formed Wimberry Branch Junction. On the right is the wooden posted bracket signal which was replaced circa 1959 by the signal seen in the later pictures. The photographer was positioned on the bracket signal next to the box, which was also renewed at the same time. COLEFORD GWR MUSEUM (MIKE REES)

RIGHT: A full frontal study of Speech House Road Signal Box circa 1960, with the 'S' and 'T' plates in position. These were used by the GWR and other railways from the later 19th century to give a visual indication as to the state of the equipment to linemen or an Inspector in a passing train, as to whether a visit was required from the Signal & Telegraph Department. The Signal plate was round and the Telegraph plate diamond shaped, and they were reversible; the white letter on a black background on the one side (as the 'S' plate here) meant that everything was in order but the red letter on a white background on the flip side (as displayed by the 'T' plate) meant there was a fault. However, their use seems to have been discontinued around the time of the First World War, when more reliable methods of communication became commonplace. After this, their continued display at boxes which still had them is likely to have been purely decorative, on the whim of the signalmen inside. The isolated location belied the fact that this was the largest signal box in the Forest. COLEFORD GWR MUSEUM (MIKE REES)

LEFT: On the occasion of the Severn Boar II tour, Gloucester Traffic Inspector Allan poses in the upper right window of the box, whilst down below are three Lydney-based men, Inspector Tony Crabbe, shunter Bill Tyrell and guard Bill Gregory. The box nameplate survived – just. When Alec Pope arrived to collect it, he discovered that the demolition gang had broken it into pieces with a sledge hammer but it has recently been repaired and is now on display in the DFR Museum at Norchard. COLEFORD GWR MUSEUM (MIKE REES)

BELOW: A rare view just to the north of Wimberry Branch Junction, with the SLS tour arriving back from Serridge in May 1961. The centre line heads to Cannop Colliery whilst that on the left was a refuge siding, which the colliery company had ceased using circa 1940. In the right background, just above the level of the tops of the locomotive's tanks, was Speech House Hill Colliery, closed in 1910 and the site of which is now a Forestry Commission visitor site, Beechenhurst Lodge. The colliery was served by a branch running uphill from a junction with the main line beyond where it curves out of sight in the distance. COLEFORD GWR MUSEUM (MIKE REES)

ABOVE: Next to the Howlerslade Valley was the Wimberry Slade Valley, which was penetrated by the Wimberry Branch tramroad and later by a railway branch (originally broad gauge), running to Wimberry Colliery. This pit ceased operations in the early years of the 20th century but around the same time a new deep mine was sunk at the head of the valley, Cannop Colliery, where construction began in 1906. Sinking of the pit was bedevilled by water incursion problems, something that was to effect the mine throughout its life but coal raising eventually began in 1912. New sidings for the colliery were laid in along the Wimberry Branch. The colliery was one of the most productive in the Dean Coalfield but closed in September 1960, the cost of the pumping operations to keep it dry eventually proving too much; the last train of coal departed from the colliery on 21st November. This 1962 view looking down the Wimberry Slade Valley shows the headgear in the centre distance, which had yet to be removed. The site is today mainly in use as a council depot but a cycle hire centre has also been established here, for those wishing to cycle along the route established on the old S&W railway line. In the right foreground is the spoil tip for Wimberry Drift Mine. ANNE BEAUFOY

LEFT: The entrance to the drift mine, showing that it was disused at this time. The construction is typical of a Forest free mine. ANNE BEAUFOY

BELOW: Burrowing even deeper into the Forest, half a mile further on from Speech House Road, the SLS tour climbs the long straight 1 in 40 gradient, mostly on embankment, up to Serridge Junction in May 1961. BILL POTTER/KRM

ABOVE: The Severn Venturer tour made for a splendid sight with its red and cream coaches as it stood near the summit of the line at Serridge Junction in April 1956. The line actually continues climbing towards Cinderford, curving round to the right just behind the photographers on the far left, but that section had been out of use since 1949. The train is here paused just above the junction, alongside the site of Serridge Platform, which stood on this side of the line and was provided for the benefit of the keeper at Serridge Lodge but which was only open from September 1878 to November 1879. T.B. OWEN

BELOW: The special then reversed back through the junction to stand on the line to Lydbrook. This was in order that the locomotive could run round the carriages and then propel them back up the bank towards Cinderford, after which it would be at the correct end of the train for the trip back down to Lydney but, in so doing, it also became the last passenger train to venture onto the Lydbrook extension. The initial plan for a triangular junction here did not come to fruition and the difference in height between the two lines indicates why the junction faced the way it did, so it was always something of an operational headache. The Mineral Loop was never signalled for use by regular through trains, so traffic could not be routed along the S&W main line to Drybrook Road. Plans made prior to the First World War to improve the siding accommodation here, to aid in the reversal of heavy coal trains coming off the Lydbrook Branch bound for Lydney, were also in the event not proceeded with and the junction remained a difficult piece of railway to work, which brought out the best (and occasionally the worst) of train crews and signalmen. The water tank dated from the later 1890s, replacing an earlier structure. The siding on the left of the picture belonged to the Crown and ran through a gate to a short loading bank used to load timber and pit props. Added in 1903, it had fallen out of use circa 1952 but was left *in situ* until closure of the line. It was controlled from a separate ground frame. Note the fresh ballast on the main line beyond the point for the siding. T.B. OWEN

RIGHT: No. 6437 takes a breather having brought the SLS tour up to Serridge Junction with the assistance of No. 8701 in May 1961. The S&W line up to Drybrook Road had opened in June 1872 but Serridge Junction did not come in to operation until 1874, when the branch to Lydbrook opened in August of that year. NPC

ABOVE: Enthusiasts from the SLS tour inspect the sidings at Serridge Junction which were used to sort trains. The method of operation for a loaded Up coal train from Waterloo Colliery at Lydbrook was for it to come to a halt first on the running line, the leftmost of the three lines. The locomotive would then uncouple from this end of the train and run round to the rear to collect the brake van. After depositing this in one of the two loop sidings on the right, it would then run round the brake van in order to be on the right side of it to haul it to this end of the train. The locomotive would then run round again and couple up to the far end of the train, ready for the tricky bit. The 1 in 40 gradient of the main line meant that the loaded wagons had to be propelled up the bank towards Cinderford, clear of the junction points, before they could be changed and the train could proceed southwards. This required a run up so the train would set back round the curve towards Lydbrook first, before charging the bank. Often, particularly in bad weather, the train would slip to a halt, meaning that more than one go would be required. Once clear of the junction, the two guards carried would jump down and quickly start pinning down wagon brakes, in order to hold the heavy train on the gradient. Meanwhile the signalman would smartly change the points, so that if the locomotive was forced back down the bank it would be heading towards Lydney. The guards would quickly climb back into their van and this potentially dangerous operation would have been safely completed once again. JOHN RYAN

LEFT: The SLS tour parked just above the junction. Unlike the Severn Venturer trip, it did not need to run up onto the Lydbrook line. JOHN STRANGE/NPC

A last look at the junction from the start of the Lydbrook Branch, with the SLS tour easing its way downhill towards Lydney, leaving the railway here to the sheep and its ultimate fate. It is presumed that a signal box was provided to control the junction from when the branch opened in 1874 but nothing is known of it. The box which existed here in later years comprised a brick built ground floor topped by a wooden superstructure that is believed to have come from Lydney Town, when the new box was built there in 1897. Serridge Junction Signal Box was closed on 12th December 1951, following the official closure of the line to Drybrook Road and Cinderford three days earlier, and replaced by a new ground frame. The box stood on the far (Up) side of the S&W main line, behind the first coach but had clearly been demolished by the date of these pictures; exactly when it was removed is not known. Passenger trains were never reversed at Serridge, instead being run another 1³/₄ miles further on to Drybrook Road, which had a loop for running round. The runaway siding on the left beyond the permanent way hut was added in 1880. These pictures show the area around here as quite open but today it is all heavily wooded and the site of the junction is well hidden. BILL POTTER/KRM

A rare colour view of the remains of Drybrook Road station circa 1961, after removal of all the track and buildings but with the platform still in situ. Another Eassie wooden station building had been provided here; it was removed to a builder's yard after closure and can be found today at the DFR's Norchard site. A signal box of similar design to that at Speech House Road but constructed of timber stood at this end of the platform, overlooking the junction with the Mineral Loop, which can be seen heading off to the right on its way to Tufts Junction. Still standing at this time in the left distance is the stationmaster's house but this too has since gone. Drybrook Road was at the very summit of the S&W main line. Behind the photographer to the left, the short branch from Trafalgar Colliery joined with the main line; the pit had closed in 1925 but a short stub of the branch survived until closure. The Mineral Loop had served Crump Meadow, Foxes Bridge, Lightmoor and New Fancy collieries but as they closed so use of it declined. A brief final flourish

took place when Acorn Patch munitions depot was established on the line in 1943. The last train from the depot ran in 1953, via Drybrook Road and Bilson, after which the Mineral Loop closed, apart from a short section at the southern end to Pillowell Drift mine. The line was not signalled for through running and tended to be worked in two halves, with traffic originating at the top end being worked out to the north and from the southern end to the south. IAN POPE COLLECTION

ABOVE: After leaving Serridge Junction in a south westerly direction, the Lydbrook Branch turned sharply through 180 degrees via Speculation Curve, to head almost due north to Mierystock. Hidden in woodland and away from the roads, a number of photographs were taken along this section of line but none in colour when it was in operation. The only architectural feature of note before Mierystock Tunnel was this fine stone bridge, carrying a Forest track over the line, just to the south of the tunnel. This view looking through the bridge dates from circa 1967; happily, it still stands today. Mierystock Sidings, serving Arthur & Edward or Waterloo Colliery, branched off on the Down side of the running line behind the photographer and crossed the Forest track on the level just to the left of the bridge. BILL POTTER/KRM

BELOW: The south portal of the 242 yards long Mierystock Tunnel, as viewed from the bridge probably in the early 1970s. The level indicated by the yellow gorse and fence just above the tunnel marks the route of the empties road curving round to the colliery screens, which were situated to the right. The colliery itself lay in the valley far down below to the left, at the far end of the tunnel, coal being hauled up to the screens in tubs on an endless ropeway known as 'The Creeper'. BILL POTTER/KRM

One of the most remarkable pictures in the book is this view of Upper Lydbrook station, dating from circa summer 1959, with the track still *in situ*, nearly all the buildings still extant and the level crossing gates closed across the line. Track lifting along here commenced in October 1959. The signal box, with its unusual narrow lower storey – dictated by the need to still allow access to the Down platform – was provided in 1912, as a replacement for an earlier box of 1892 sited on the Up platform, which in turn had replaced North and South signal boxes at either end of the station. The box seen here was reduced to ground frame status with the ending of the passenger service in 1929. On the right are the two sidings running in to the goods yard, with the roof of the goods shed just visible above the Down platform. A small wooden shelter provided on this platform was removed shortly after the passenger service ceased. The section of railway down through the Lydbrook Valley was the most spectacular in the Forest and equalled some of the most picturesque lines to be found anywhere in the UK. Carried on a ledge which was carved out of the northern side of the valley, in places supported by stone buttresses and tunnelling through a rocky outcrop just to the south of the station, trains running along here must have made a fine sight. Much of the route is still clearly visible today. In the background here is Lydbook's Holy Jesus church, which pre-dated the railway, being built in 1850-1, and in which the author and his wife were married in 1994. MICHAEL HALE

After closure of the passenger service, the station building, another standard William Eassie design as supplied at all the other S&W stations, was fenced off along the platform edge and rented out as a private dwelling. However, it was clearly unoccupied by the date of this October 1966 view, looking north towards Lower Lydbrook through the abandoned platforms. Today, the station site is occupied by three new houses. JOHN STRANGE/NPC

A first view of Lydbrook Viaduct, a beautifully proportioned girder bridge of three spans supported on two lofty stone-built central piers, with stone buttresses and arches at either end. The viaduct spanned the northern end of the valley as it carried the S&W line from the west side to the east on its way to Lydbrook Junction. IAN POPE COLLECTION

7

Lydbrook Viaduct from the south in 1965. The viaduct was designed by George W. Keeling, the Severn & Wye Railway's Engineer. The foundation stone was laid on 9th November 1872, the masonry work contract being awarded to J.E. Billups, who was contractor for the Lydbrook Extension, whilst the ironwork contract was awarded to the Crumlin Viaduct Works Company, who at £7,396 had submitted the lowest tender. The two outer spans were 120ft wide whilst the central span was 150ft and at its highest point the viaduct was 90ft above the valley floor. It opened on 26th August 1874 but it was not until 23rd September 1875 that the first passenger train crossed it. The line across the viaduct closed officially on 30th January 1956. The flat ground in the foreground is part of the old Lydbrook Tinplate Works site. The works closed in 1925 but the derelict buildings remained for many years afterwards. A short branch from the S&W line ran down a steep incline to serve the works. R.H. MARROWS

A closer circa 1964 view from the B4234 road, which runs right down the centre of the Lydbrook Valley from Mierystock crossroads. There was a 5mph speed restriction for trains running across the viaduct. Flood water regularly causes the River Wye to burst its banks and inundate this end of the village. NPC

SECTION 3

The SEVERN & WYE LINE
The COLEFORD BRANCH

The Coleford Branch, as it existed for the last fifty years of its life, was actually a combination of the remainder of two lines that reached this market town situated in the heart of the Forest of Dean, which arrived from opposing directions. Both were authorised by Act of Parliament on the same day – 18th July 1872. The Severn & Wye proposed a line from a new junction just north of Parkend, to a station on the south east side of Coleford's town centre. The GWR line was part of a proposed railway from Coleford to Pontypool via Monmouth and Usk but also included the possibility of an extension to Milkwall, part way down the S&W's intended route.

Progress with the Severn & Wye line was relatively straightforward. Commencing at Coleford Junction, from just north of Parkend, it largely paralleled the course of the Milkwall Tramroad as far as Darkhill but from there it took a more direct route to Coleford. It was steeply graded for much of its route, the line only reaching its summit a short distance before reaching Coleford, and there were a number of severe curves along the way. Unlike the competing GWR sponsored route, the S&WR had the twin benefits of serving local interests and building over Crown land. Construction was completed in the summer of 1875, with the line opening to goods traffic on 19th July but not until 9th December for passengers.

The story of the GWR branch to Coleford is rather more complicated. As recounted in Volume 1 of this series, the Monmouth Railway, a 3ft 6ins gauge horse-drawn plateway, authorised in 1810 and opened in 1812, had been the first line to serve Monmouth. However, preceded just by the Severn & Wye and Forest of Dean tramroads, it could not claim to be the first line to serve the Forest. Running from pits to the south east of Coleford, it was built to transport coal down to Monmouth. The Coleford,

Monmouth, Usk & Pontypool Railway was authorised on 20th August 1853, being promoted to transport Forest of Dean iron ore and timber to the hungry furnaces and mines of South Wales. It had grown out of an earlier scheme, the Dean Forest, Monmouth, Usk & Pontypool Railway, which was intended to link up with the South Wales main line near Blakeney but which had been modified in the face of opposition from the Severn & Wye Railway. Truncated back to Coleford, the name was changed to the CMU&PR and the Monmouth Railway's tramroad was purchased in order that its route could be used for the section into the Forest of Dean. The CMU&PR line was completed as far as Wyesham, having managed to bridge the River Wye, by early 1861 but then money ran out. An interchange wharf with the tramroad was opened but there was no money left to rebuild the tramroad and make it suitable for locomotive operation.

As noted above, the Coleford Railway Company was formed by Act of Parliament granted on 18th July 1872, with powers to rebuild the tramroad, thus completing the line to Coleford but also to extend beyond, as far as Milkwall. There was strong GWR interest in this little railway, however, with the chairman being Sir Daniel Gooch, who was also chairman of the GWR, whilst another of the directors, C.A. Wood, was also a GWR director. The Parliamentary Select Committee considered both the CR and S&WR Bills together and effectively left the duplicated section between Milkwall and Coleford for the two companies to sort out. They made the stipulation that, if the S&WR had managed to get their line open to Coleford before 1st August 1874, the CR would not be empowered to construct their extension to Milkwall. If the CR reached Milkwall first, however, the S&WR would be permitted running powers over the line as far as Coleford.

The Severn & Wye had, as previously noted, opened their extension to Lydbrook Junction in August 1874. This, coupled with a general economic depression at the time,

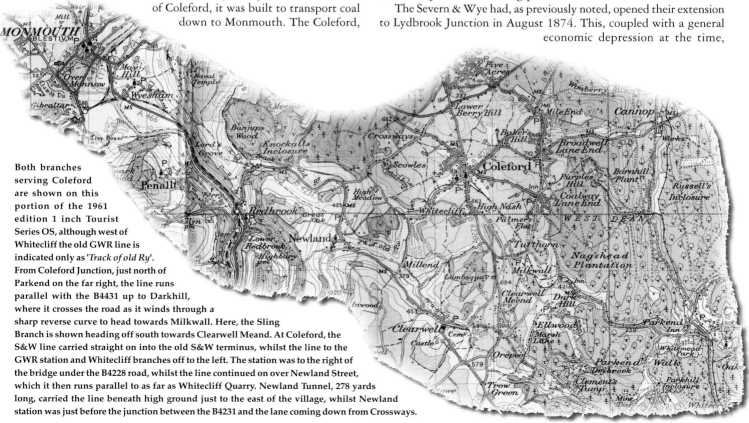

Both branches serving Coleford are shown on this portion of the 1961 edition 1 inch Tourist Series OS, although west of Whitecliff the old GWR line is indicated only as 'Track of old Ry'. From Coleford Junction, just north of Parkend on the far right, the line runs parallel with the B4431 up to Darkhill, where it crosses the road as it winds through a sharp reverse curve to head towards Milkwall. Here, the Sling Branch is shown heading off south towards Clearwell Meand. At Coleford, the S&W line carried straight on into the old S&W terminus, whilst the line to the GWR station and Whitecliff branches off to the left. The station was to the right of the bridge under the B4228 road, whilst the line continued on over Newland Street, which it then runs parallel to as far as Whitecliff Quarry. Newland Tunnel, 278 yards long, carried the line beneath high ground just to the east of the village, whilst Newland station was just before the junction between the B4231 and the lane coming down from Crossways.

ensured that little progress was made with the Coleford Railway scheme, whilst the opening of the S&WR's Coleford line in 1875 further slowed matters. The GWR applied for a three year time extension for building the line on 28th June 1877 but it was not until January 1880 that they moved onto the land adjacent to the S&WR station to begin construction. Progress, on what was a short but difficult line to construct, continued to drag, however, with the result that the GWR had to apply for yet another extension, of two years, this further Act being granted on 10th August 1882. The line was finally opened for goods and passenger traffic on 1st September 1883, whilst on 7th August 1884, the Coleford Railway Company was formally absorbed by the GWR.

The new station was situated about 100 yards to the west of the S&WR's facility but, despite their proximity, initially no connection was made between the two stations, the GWR not wishing to encourage traffic onto the S&WR line. Common sense finally prevailed just over two years later, with a connecting line being laid in that was brought in to use on 7th December 1885. However, this was by no means a direct connection, transfer traffic having to be reverse shunted through both company's yards. Despite the GWR becoming a joint owner of the S&WR in 1894, more than sixty-five years were to pass before BR finally brought this unsatisfactory arrangement to a close, with the opening in 1951 of a direct connection from the ex-S&WR line to that through the old GWR station, by which time passenger services had long since disappeared from both stations. Proposals for a single joint station serving the town were never proceeded with.

Coleford's era as a town with two passenger terminii was to be relatively short lived. The population was not huge in any case but, apart from market days and for some school children, Monmouth was not a direction in which many Coleford folk needed or wanted to travel. This is borne out by the passenger service provided, which comprised two morning and two afternoon trains, each way, on weekdays only. After 1894, the GWR's interest in the S&WR line left the company with little appetite for the branch up the valley from Redbrook. There was only one intermediate station, at Newland, and little opportunity for developing new traffic. Freight traffic came mainly from the sidings at Whitecliff, which were taken over by the Whitecliff Lime & Stone Co. in 1912, a new Private Siding Agreement being signed on 13th June 1914. The quarry was well established, having been supplying lime to local kilns when the railway was built. There is a relatively well known photograph of a GWR train in the station at Coleford circa 1915, preparing to carry away local menfolk who had volunteered to join up for the war. This was to be a last hurrah, however, the First World War ironically proving the death knell for much of the branch. As an economy measure, the line between Whitecliff and Wyesham Junction was closed on 31st December 1916, the track being removed for use in France soon after. In his book *The Great Western Railway in Dean*, Harry Paar notes the rumour, still unconfirmed, that the ship carrying the rails was sunk *en route*. Thus, for the remaining fifty-odd years of its life, traffic over the remaining section of the GWR line between Whitecliff and Coleford was worked out of the Forest via the S&WR line, to Coleford Junction and Lydney. It was a small and much belated victory for the Severn & Wye Railway.

A second equally small victory was obtained by the S&WR's passenger service, which outlasted that of the GWR by twelve and a half years, passenger trains over the line to Coleford Junction and on the Severn & Wye main line being withdrawn on 8th July 1929. It is difficult to think of another town with two stations which lost all of their passenger trains quite so early.

COLEFORD JUNCTION AND COLEFORD

Coleford Junction Milkwall	...	...	...	...	13	Whitecliff Sidings...	...	...	...	...
Sling...	...	...	...	...		Coleford Stop Board	...	...	...	5
Stop Board Coleford	...	...	...	...	2 4	Sling...	...	...	...	...
Whitecliff Sidings...	...	...	...	...		Milkwall Stop Board Coleford Junction	... ...	... ...	... ...	2 8 9

ABOVE: No. 3775 arrives at Coleford Junction with a train of empty coal wagons from Coleford on 9th April 1965. Some maintenance work is underway on the track alongside – grease by the look of it, in the process of being applied to joints and the moving parts of the points. HOWARD BURCHELL

INSET ABOVE: Time allowances for trains on the Coleford Branch, from the *Working Time Table,* September 1958. NPC

LEFT: With No. 1664 leading No. 1639, the Severn Boar tour of 6th June 1964 poses at Coleford Junction. This slide is the one mentioned on page 14, which first put me on the track of No. 1639 being the second engine used on that day and the one that failed at Coleford Junction, leading to No. 1664 working the rest of the trip, including up to Coleford, on its own. The weather was much poorer on the day of the first run than on the occasion of the second trip two weeks later, as this view indicates. However, what is happening here? No. 1639 is still in steam and the train is posed as if it has just come back down from Coleford. According to the report in the REC's Newsletter, on arrival back at the junction No. 1639 was found to be still not fit for travel, so presumably was left there. So on the face of it, this picture does not appear to make sense, just another indication of the difficulties which can be experienced when trying to unravel what happened on a particular day over fifty years later. JOHN STRANGE/NPC

ABOVE: The unidentified NBL 'D63XX' Series diesel, that we previously saw running round at Coleford Junction on page 199, now waits to leave with empty hopper wagons for Whitecliff Quarry. It is possible that this was the first visit of one of this class of locomotive to the branch. There is quite a group around the signal but it is not clear whether they are enthusiasts or railwaymen. The 'D95XX' 'Teddy Bears' held sway almost until the end of workings on the Coleford Branch in 1967 but were falling out of favour with BR generally due to their unreliability, so in the last few weeks, members of the 'D63XX' Series appeared on the S&W and Coleford Branch services in their stead. NPC

LEFT: No. D9555 pictured at the limit of working on the S&W main line on 26th April 1967, having journeyed back down the branch from Coleford with just the brake vans full of photographers in tow. NPC

Coal and general goods to Coleford, coupled with the traffic from the boiler works served by the short Sling Branch, would undoubtedly have kept the Parkend to Coleford line in operation up until the late 1950s. However, it was Whitecliff Quarry, which produced stone for railway ballast, as well as for road making and blast furnace flux, that was responsible for the continued use of the section west of Coleford and probably for the last few years of operation of the whole of the branch. The steep gradients, severe curves and shunting required at Coleford Junction meant the branch was costly to operate though and consequently, in 1967, BR transferred ballast loading at the quarry from rail to road, with the loaded lorries then tipping in to wagons

at Marsh Sidings, and so were able to close the line north of Parkend. The last ballast train ran on 11th August and the final few empty mineral wagons were collected from Coleford four days later, the line then being officially closed. The rails were lifted in 1969. The trackbed today is used as a foot and cyclepath but the bridges have gone and there is little sign of Milkwall station. However, the large skew arch which carried the line to Whitecliff over Newland Street in Coleford still stands, whilst ex-local railwayman Mike Rees mounted a successful eleventh hour campaign to save the GWR goods shed in the town from demolition in the late 1980s, opening it up as a museum to the railways of the Forest of Dean in 1988.

ABOVE: An unusual aspect of the junction, from the top of the ladder of the Up Branch Home signal on 13th May 1961. In the foreground is the point leading to the sand drag, provided in January 1923, to halt any prospective runaway vehicles coming down the Coleford Branch; note the points were always set into the drag, except to allow trains to pass over. In the background, enthusiasts mill around No. 8701, which will shortly be coupled to the nearer end of the auto trailers forming the SLS Severn & Wye tour, prior to leading it up the branch. Beyond the railway is the Remploy factory, part of a nationwide network of factories that were established after WW2 to employ disabled workers. At one time there were eighty-three factories spread across the country but, following reviews into the business and how people with disabilities should be employed and treated by main stream society, most have since closed, the Parkend factory in 2008. DAVID BICK

RIGHT: No. 3643 at the bottom of the Coleford Branch on 30th March 1965, with a short train of three loaded ballast hoppers from Whitecliff Quarry, the second trip back down the branch that day. Behind the train is the Up Branch Home signal, from which the previous picture was taken. Unusually, it had a concrete post. All Up trains had to stop on arrival here and give two loud whistles to let the Coleford Junction signalman know that they had come to a halt before the points. These would then be switched and the signal pulled off, allowing the train to proceed. In the background are some of the cottages of Stampers Row, Parkend. JOHN DAGLEY-MORRIS

Amidst a kaleidoscope of late autumn colours on 1st November 1961, No. 8701 rounds the curve past the disused Point Quarry with a very varied train comprising two container wagons, three empty steel-bodied opens, five assorted vans, four loaded ballast hoppers and a 'Toad' brake van. Although the gradient was on a climb from near Parkend to Fetterhill at 1 in 30 and 1 in 31, locomotives still had to work quite hard when going down hill, as the wagon brakes would be pinned down to prevent the train from running away and the drag caused by the check rails on the sharp curves were capable of bringing a train drifting down the gradient to a halt. B.J. ASHWORTH

LEFT: Inside Point Quarry circa 1964, which was gradually being reclaimed by nature. The remains of the stone loading bank feature in the left foreground; stone was loaded onto railway wagons here from Point and other quarries up until the 1930s. ANNE BEAUFOY

BELOW: From a slightly different viewpoint to the picture on the previous page and just over a year earlier, No. 1623 eases past Point Quarry on its way back down from Coleford and Whitecliff, on 12th October 1960. The gate on the right just in front of the train marked the rail entrance to the quarry; the connection was taken out in 1953 but had been out of use for many years prior to that. Photographer Ben Ashworth had mounted his camera on a tripod and set the timer to capture himself taking a black & white view of the same scene. B.J. ASHWORTH

RIGHT: A second view inside the old Point Quarry, with the indentations of railway sleepers still evident in the foreground. In the late 19th century, the quarry was owned by the Payne family but was bought at auction by Forest of Dean Stone Firms in 1909. Later that year, this became part of United Stone Firms Ltd but that company went into liquidation in 1913. The quarries were worked under the receiver until 1926, when United Stone Firms (1926) Ltd was formed but that too failed in 1931. Point Quarry continued to operate under the receiver's control until 1939, after which all working ceased. ANNE BEAUFOY

ABOVE: The SLS Severn & Wye tour climbs up past Point Quarry in May 1961. Of additional interest here is the stonework just visible on the far right, part of the portal of the tramroad tunnel. The tramroad remained open whilst the branch was constructed, the tunnel being built at this time as the railway was carried over it. After the tramroad closed it was used for road access to the quarry and this portal survives in good condition, albeit well hidden, today. BILL POTTER/KRM

TOP LEFT: Point Quarry curve from the same train, providing a closer view of the top of the tramroad tunnel portal. JOHN RYAN

ABOVE: The SLS tour makes its way up through the valley at Fetterhill. Whilst Point Quarry had been abandoned over twenty years earlier, the hillside further up was still being worked for stone as can be seen. This area, which appears on older maps as Futterill, the name by which it was also known by older Forest folk, was once a hive of industrial activity, the site of two small collieries, a brickworks and a stoneworks, as well as the quarries. Photographer Derek Chaplin was standing on the site of Wanklyn & Grindle's Brickworks, established in the mid 1850s but which had closed around 1900. The embankment running down from right to left between the railway and the road carried the siding originally serving the brickworks and later the stoneworks. Today, this view would be impossible to capture, as both sides of the valley are now heavily wooded but some of the scars left by the quarrying are still just visible. DEREK CHAPLIN

ABOVE: The Severn Boar II tour makes its way up to Fetterhill just over three years later. Note how the quarry workings had extended even further along the side of the valley. T.B. OWEN

OPPOSITE PAGE TOP: Another view of the SLS trip at Fetterhill but a little further up, with the stoneworks in the foreground. Pullen's Stoneworks was in operation by 1909, having been started by Samuel Clothier from Somerset but he assigned it to Thomas Pullen in 1920. Access to the sidings serving the stoneworks was controlled by Darkhill Siding Middle and West ground frames but traffic dwindled to only a couple of wagons a month in the late 1940s and then one wagon a year by 1956. With the ground frames imminently in need of renewal, it was decided to remove the sidings instead and they were taken out in April 1957. The stoneworks were taken over by a Mr B. Simpson circa the late 1960s but he went bankrupt in 1971 and the works, along with six quarry leases, were offered for sale by auction in 1972. The works did not reopen and nothing now remains of them. ALAN JARVIS

OPPOSITE PAGE BOTTOM: More detail of the stoneworks, as the 20th June 1964 Severn Boar II trip makes its way up the steep climb behind. T.B. Owen

RIGHT & BELOW: Although of poorer quality, these two shots of the Gloucestershire Railway Society's Forest of Dean railtour of 23rd June 1962 heading back down the branch past Fetterhill were considered worthy of inclusion as few views of this trip were taken along the Coleford Branch. BOTH JOHN STRANGE/NPC

BOTTOM: Back on the SLS train, this view is looking across towards Ellwood and the abandoned Darkhill Quarries on the hillside. In the right middle distance can be seen black spoil from Darkhill Level Colliery, which was worked sporadically from the 1840s up until the early 1950s. This pit, which was operated for a time by the Darkhill & Ellwood Colliery Company who owned their own wagons, shared use of Fetterhill Sidings with the brickworks and later the stoneworks. JOHN RYAN

OPPOSITE PAGE TOP: Viewed from the top of Darkhill, an unidentified '57XX' Class pannier tank climbs past the George Inn in August 1965 with a short freight bound for Coleford. The George had opened by 1876 but closed circa 1970. It was converted to a private house in 1973 and has since been substantially rebuilt, with new windows and losing the distinctive twin gabled roof. The site of Wanklyn & Grindle's Brickworks lay beneath the trees on the right. BILL POTTER/KRM

Another lovely panoramic view, looking down the Fetterhill Valley on 3rd August 1965, with Class '57XX' No. 4698 at the head of a train of empty mineral wagons bound for Lydney yard. The bungalow in the foreground remains, although has been much expanded from the property seen here. The railway curved round right behind the photographer, who was standing just above track level near where the branch crossed over the road up to Coleford. BILL POTTER/KRM

Taken a few moments before the previous picture, No. 4698 and its train clatter across the bridge carrying the line over the B4431 road to Coleford. BILL POTTER/KRM

Looking over the timber deck of the bridge towards Coleford Junction circa 1964. The lower slopes of Birch Hill (which gave its name to the bridge) in the background again show signs of having been worked for stone in years past. The bridge rails are a later replacement; the form they originally took is not known. ANNE BEAUFOY

ABOVE: Birch Hill Bridge is another of the Forest railway bridges which has been demolished since the closure of most of the lines in the 1960s. With a relatively low headroom, its going was probably inevitable but with its handsome Forest stone abutments, it is another sad loss nevertheless. The abutments have of course been completely removed as well, so cyclists on the foot and cycle path along the trackbed now have to brave crossing the steeply climbing road a little further up. Perhaps the funds will be found one day to put some sort of bridge back but it won't look anything like this. No. 3643 makes its way over on 30th March 1965 with its first Up (downwards) train of the day from Whitecliff Quarry. The junction with the road coming down from Sling and Ellwood is just behind the photographer. JOHN DAGLEY-MORRIS

RIGHT: North British Loco Type 2 No. D6329 crosses the bridge with empty hoppers for Whitecliff Quarry. This was one of the last trains up the branch in early August 1967. COLEFORD GWR MUSEUM (MIKE REES)

The SLS tour on the reverse curve at Darkhill, showing the check rail on the inside, another curve so severe that it was capable of bringing to a halt a goods train travelling down hill with its brakes pinned down to prevent it running away. Note the difference in vegetation and undergrowth compared to the lush scene in the picture below, just three years later. It is little surprise that this section is so heavily wooded today. COLEFORD GWR MUSEUM (MIKE REES)

A rare colour view of the first run of the Severn Boar, on 6th June 1964. The weather was much poorer on this day than was experienced on the second trip two weeks later. As detailed in the REC's post-run write up of the tour reproduced in the 'History of Rail Tours in the Forest of Dean' section at the beginning of this book, No. 1639 had failed with a hot box at Coleford Junction, so No. 1664 worked the train up the Coleford Branch on its own. One of the brake vans was first dropped off the train, however, with the participants crowding into the other five, the decision being taken to allow for the steep climb, sharp curves and the wet greasy rails. NPC

Two weeks later, on 20th June, the Severn Boar II tour winds its way round the Darkhill curves, as a couple of lads with bicycles watch its stately progress from the lane below. With double the motive power this time and on a fine dry day, the two pannier tanks had little trouble making the climb up to Milkwall. T.B. OWEN

No. 3643 negotiates the reverse curve at Darkhill on its first trip up the branch on 30th March 1965. In the left background can be seen the ruins of Darkhill Ironworks, an industrial site of international importance and now a scheduled monument. It was built as an experimental coke fired furnace by Scottish metallurgist David Mushet in 1818-19, who had moved to the Forest of Dean in 1810 to become manager of Whitecliff Ironworks. Whilst some iron was produced here for sale, Mushet also used much of the works for experimental research. After he retired, his youngest son Robert carried on experimenting on part of the site in the production of steel alloys and the development of steel, for which he is now internationally acclaimed. In 1857, he sent ingots to Ebbw Vale for rolling, producing the first durable steel rails, which the Midland Railway laid at Derby station. He also made crucial improvements to the Bessemer process, which dramatically improved the quality of malleable steel produced and made it commercially viable. Mushet opened a new works, the Titanic Steel Works, at Milkwall in 1862 and sold the Darkhill site in 1864. It was out of use by 1874, when it was sold to the Severn & Wye Railway, who built the Coleford Branch through part of the site. In 1871, Mushet joined Samuel Osborn & Co. at their Clyde Works in Sheffield and the two men collaborated on the development and production of Osborn-Mushet high speed tool steel. Both men died in 1891 but the Osborn Company continued in operation until the mid 1960s, when it merged with Hadfields Ltd but this concern has since closed. JOHN DAGLEY-MORRIS

This scenic vista was captured by Bill looking north west from the top of Darkhill on 6th August 1965 and shows No. 4698 climbing bunker first towards Milkwall with a freight for Coleford. On a wet day, the climb through these curves could cause train crews severe problems. A section of steel rail from a point has been mounted on a plinth on the old trackbed just by the road here, as a monument to Robert Mushet and the pioneering work he carried out at Darkhill. Bill Potter/KRM

A few of the local inhabitants show little interest in No. 3643's progress up the branch with its second trip of the day. The engine is about to pass over an occupation crossing for a pathway between Ellwood and Milkwall. Beyond is the site of Robert Mushet's Titanic Steel Works of 1862, so named because the alloy he had most success with was made using titanium. The new works was built with rounded corrugated iron roofs, state of the art at the time but a factor in their deterioration after they had been abandoned. Some 300 men were employed here, so it was a sizeable operation but sadly it was not profitable and the company was wound up in 1874. Mushet, meanwhile was poverty stricken and in poor health but his daughter Mary managed to persuade Henry Bessemer, whose steel making process Robert had been instrumental in making commercially viable, to pay him a royalty of £300 a year, a handsome sum for the time. Mushet died in 1891 and is buried in Cheltenham, along with his wife and daughter. Much of the remains of the works had been demolished shortly before this photograph was taken, having been deemed unsafe, the stone being used as hardcore in the construction of the approach to the Severn road bridge. What remains today is now a scheduled monument. John Dagley-Morris

ABOVE: A view over the occupation crossing to the Titanic Steel Works circa 1964, with the ground just beyond the gates showing evidence of having recently been cleared. ANNE BEAUFOY

LEFT: A closer view of the remains of the works on 6th January 1977. The white painted cottage is the old works office. It is now a private house. To date, no survey of the uses to which other buildings on the site were put has been carried out. NPC

Leaking steam, No. 4698 heads bunker first up to Coleford propelling a brake van before it; clearly there were no wagons to be delivered on this occasion, so the trip will be to collect any downwards traffic from Coleford and Whitecliff. The photograph was taken on 3rd August 1965 from the occupation crossing seen above. Milkwall lies at the top of the rise, just beyond the tree on the far right. BILL POTTER/KRM

The Severn Boar II tour arrives at the long closed Milkwall station on 20th June 1964. The line continued to rise on a 1 in 31 gradient right through the platform. The Sling Branch heads off sharply to the right, whilst immediately to the right of the train is the loop which was provided to give access to the branch in the days of passenger services. As can be seen from the rust covered rails, it had not been used for a while, although there is photographic evidence of wagons in the loop in March 1962. Section 37 of Tony Cooke's *Track Layout Diagrams*, covering the Forest of Dean, states that the loop was removed ten days after this tour, on 30th June. However, as we shall shortly see, it was still *in situ* in March 1965. Also noted as being taken out at the same time was the connection seen heading off to the left, behind the train. This had been a short siding serving an interchange wharf between the S&W and a tramway from Gorsty Knoll Quarries but the tramway had gone by 1898. The siding remained for many years afterwards and may still have been there as late as 1950. T.B. OWEN

LEFT: The train paused at Milkwall for those on board to explore the station and this view looks in the opposite direction, towards the road bridge from which the previous picture was taken. This carried Station Road, which runs between Milkwall and Broadwell. It was demolished some years after the line was closed and the road lowered. Early plans indicate that a level crossing may have been provided here when the line first opened, the bridge being built a few years later. The loop extended up the slope beyond the bridge for another 100 yards. JOHN RYAN

No. 3643 coasts gently downhill through Milkwall on 30th March 1965, on its second return trip of the day. This view proves the loop had not been removed in late June 1964, although it had clearly not been used in the interim. Milkwall station opened to passengers on 10th December 1875 and was provided with a standard 20ft wooden Eassie building in the same style as those found elsewhere on the Severn & Wye. A slightly larger wooden structure alongside, believed to have been provided as a goods shed, survived until the 1950s but had gone by 1962. For many years, entreaties by local folk and Coleford Urban District Council for improved station accommodation had gone unheeded by the Joint Committee, so it was indeed fortuitous that the wooden building was destroyed by a fire in late June 1923, which was just five years after the similarly complained about Coleford station building had also gone up in flames! However, as these views show, the brick-built replacement did little to improve the station's overall appearance or importance but perhaps that was just as well given its closure to passengers just six years after the fire, although it remained in use as a goods office. Note the photographer's green MGB sports car hiding in the forecourt. JOHN DAGLEY-MORRIS

No. 4698 steams in to Milkwall with a freight for the Sling Branch on 18th August 1965; the branch was trip served from Coleford Junction. The wagons contain boilers for repair at Fred Watkins engineering works at the terminus of the branch. Note that the loop had now been removed. BILL POTTER/KRM

The start of the Sling Branch, as seen from the approach road for Milkwall station, a view again taken on 18th August 1965 which also provides some detail of the rear of the replacement brick building. The lane is now covered with a layer of tarmac and leads to a mobile home park. BILL POTTER/KRM

SECTION 3A
The SLING BRANCH

The gate across the entrance to the branch had not been used for some years by this date. The three open wagons stand on the Milkwall Colour Works siding and we shall see them being collected by No. 4698 on its way back down the branch shortly. Most of the colour works buildings still survive today, albeit somewhat modernised from how they appear here but the derelict cottage on the left unsurprisingly no longer exists. BILL POTTER/KRM

Whilst the Coleford Branch had closely followed the route of the Milkwall Tramroad up the Fetterhill Valley from Parkend when it was built, once it reached Milkwall the Severn & Wye's main aim was to head directly to Coleford. This left the last part of the tramroad serving various industries around Milkwall isolated, although the S&W did provide an interchange wharf and loading chute to assist in the transshipment of iron ore. Even before the branch had opened, however, there were complaints that these facilities were not sufficient. With the S&W pleading that funds were not available to permit the conversion of the rest of the tramroad to a railway, W.H. Fryer, who owned several iron mines in the locality, offered to loan the company £1,000 to pay for the work to be done. In return, the S&W would carry his traffic for free or at reduced rates until the loan was repaid. The conversion of the tramroad at Sling to a railway would save Fryer a great deal of money, as he otherwise faced the costs of horse haulage

from his mines as well as the transshipment costs at the exchange wharf. The S&W were happy to take up his offer and the work of converting the tramroad commenced in October 1875, being completed in the summer of 1876. At its terminus, Sling Sidings served the adjacent Dun Pit Iron Mine, whilst tramways brought ore from other local mines. The Crawshay family acquired Dun Pit circa 1875 and leased it to Richard Watkins; they subsequently assigned their interests in the mine to Messrs Watkins & Sons in 1902. When the market for local iron ore collapsed in the late 1920s, Watkins diversified into second hand machinery, so beginning the engineeering industry with which the Sling Branch was latterly connected and which continues to this day.

The Sling Branch was 1,150 yards long and unfenced for its entire length, although was gated at its junction with the line to Coleford. It climbed away from the Coleford line on a 1 in 40 gradient, which itself was dropping away towards Darkhill at 1 in 31, so the difference in levels between the two lines was marked. The steep nature of the branch meant that all traffic had to be propelled up it, with the engine at the lower end as it were for safety purposes. However, as we shall see, certain liberties had to be taken with these instructions on occasion, in order to be able to work the branch successfully.

MILKWALL

The points connecting the Loop Siding with the Main Line are worked from the East and West Ground Frames which are locked by a key on the Staff.

Before any shunting is done by trains travelling in either direction, the train including the Guard's van must be first placed in the Loop Siding or on the Sling Branch and the wagons put off where required. No vehicle must, under any circumstances, be left on the Main Line uncoupled from the engine.

Sling Branch

The gradient is 1 in 40 falling to Milkwall, and great care must be exercised by all concerned.

Wagons for Sling Sidings and Sand Sidings must always be coupled to, and propelled by, the engine. During the propelling movement the Guard must walk in front of the leading wagon.

Colour Works Siding

The connection to this Siding is from the Sling Branch. Wagons must remain coupled to the engine until they are brought to a stand in the Siding.

The Guard of the train is responsible for seeing that there is no obstruction in the Siding before any shunting operation is made.

The instructions for working the loop at Milkwall station and the various sidings on the Sling Branch, from the *Appendix to the Working Time Table*, October 1960. NPC

A few minutes after the top picture on page 250 was taken, No. 4698 propels its train of open wagons loaded with boilers up the branch to Fred Watkins engineering works. The point lever for the nearer end of the loop siding serving the colour works was just inside the gate on the left; it can be seen on the left of the picture on page 249, albeit apparently disconnected. It had originally enjoyed the luxury of being housed inside a small shed but this was dismantled some time after 1962. On the skyline on the right of the picture is the engine house for Easter Iron Mine, first galed in 1846. Nicholls's *Forest of Dean* (1866) gives output figures for Easter Mine for 1864 and notes that *'a light steam-engine of 14 horse power is used'*. A report of 1880 mentions an Inverted Cornish Beam Engine with 42ins cylinders, which is believed to have been installed circa 1873 and the engine house may well date from then. The mine was subject to the vicissitudes of the iron industry but it finally ceased production circa 1923. The engine house still stands, now protected by listed building status. BILL POTTER/KRM

To make best sense of this sequence of photographs, we now move to the end of the branch and follow No. 4698's progress back down it on this day. The branch terminated in the yard of Fred Watkins (Engineering) Ltd, where No. 4698 is seen having deposited its train load of boilers, on the right, and is now in the process of collecting some wagons full of scrap metal. As well as boilers and tanks, the company repaired, hired and dealt in steam and diesel cranes and railway locomotives, as well as being steel stockholders, fabricators and erectors. We shall encounter one of their 'stored' steam locomotives at Whitecliff a little later on. The siding on the right ran alongside the wharf provided by the S&W for public use, at the far end of which can be seen one of the company's steam cranes, used around the site for general lifting and shunting wagons. BILL POTTER/KRM

INSET TOP RIGHT: An example of a Fred Watkins worksplate. NPC

No. 4698 rattles back down the Sling Branch with two wagons collected from Fred Watkins engineering works. The locomotive is about to pass over the ungated level crossing which carried Ellwood Road across the railway and is passing the Sand Siding, which clearly had not been used for a while. This siding had been laid in by 1898 and may have been put in as early as 1878, which date was to be found cast into the point lever that allowed access to it. Little is known of its early history but it seems likely that it was provided to serve a nearby sand quarry. Foundry sand and stone may also have been loaded here from Lambsquay and Clearwell Meend quarries but this all seems to have ceased around 1923. The siding was left *in situ*, however, and found work again in the early 1960s when it was used for loading scrap metal for a short period, although it could only hold a maximum of three wagons. Contrary to normal operating practice on the branch, certainly in later days, trains serving this siding had to work up locomotive first, in order to shunt wagons back in to it. In a further example of unusual operating methods, No. 4698 will shortly detach from its train to collect the three wagons from the colour works siding. The stone face of the wharf is still partly visible today, whilst there is a 30 yard length of concrete 'pot' wartime sleepers clearly to be seen on the old trackbed just behind where Bill was standing. BILL POTTER/KRM

BRITISH
COLOUR & MINING
LTD.

Having originally stopped short of the siding, No. 4698 had uncoupled from the brake van and two wagons brought down from Watkins Works. Once the engine was safely ensconced in the siding, the guard unscrewed the brake enough to allow the brake van and two wagons to run gently down the gradient past the point, before screwing the brake back on again and bringing them to a halt. No. 4698 was then able to draw forward with the three wagons from the colour works siding, before gently reversing back to attach them to the rest of the train. The Easter Iron Mine engine house features again on the left. BILL POTTER/KRM

OPPOSITE PAGE TOP: Milkwall Colour Works was established in 1927 by the British Colour & Mining Co. Ltd, to make red oxide and to mix ochre produced from Old Ham Iron Mine, with an ochrous clay that was surface mined in the Oakwood Valley. Some ochre was also produced from Lambsquay Mine, whilst the Easter Iron Mine tips were worked as well. The new works was built on the Easter Mine wharf, which had been served by the siding since the railway opened in 1875 and from which No. 4698 is seen collecting three wagons to add to its train. The colour works was still in operation at the date of this picture and is believed to have continued until circa 1970, latterly using ore brought in from elsewhere. Amazingly, looking at how dilapidated these buildings are here, they still survive in slightly modified but recognisable form, in industrial use today. BILL POTTER/KRM

INSET OPPOSITE PAGE TOP: This painted sign for British Colour & Mining Ltd, still to be found on the gable of one of the old sheds, is another remarkable relic of the company's existence. NPC

ABOVE: To complete this sequence, No. 4698 is seen reversing its train off the branch back at Milkwall, with the locomotive facing downhill for the journey back to Coleford Junction. The Sling Branch was never to see diesel working, the last train up the branch being worked by Class '57XX' No. 3675 on 31st December 1965, the final day of steam on British Railways Western Region. However, it was only officially closed with the rest of the Coleford Branch in August 1967. BILL POTTER/KRM

At the summit of the line, between Milkwall and Coleford and 650ft above sea level, both Up and Down goods trains had to stop to pin down brakes before descending. On 16th August 1965, No. 4698 is again providing the motive power but has stopped with its train of loaded hoppers from Whitecliff whilst one of the crew pins down the wagons' brakes to assist in controlling the 1 in 31 descent down through Milkwall and on down the Fetterhill Valley. Behind the brake van can be seen the stop board advising Up goods trains to stop dead, in order to carry out the same procedure before heading down the 1 in 47 slope to Coleford. BILL POTTER/KRM

RIGHT: In the early 1960s, opencast coal mining was carried out in fields to the east of the railway, close to the S&W station at Coleford. The land was part of Edenwall Farm which was owned by the Ludlam family. After the opencast mining finished, Henry Ludlam landscaped the site to become part of Bell's golf course. This circa 1964 view shows these workings, with a Ruston-Bucyrus model 54-RB dragline crane in operation in the foreground and a Class '57XX' pannier tank leaving Coleford with a goods train behind. One of these model 54-RB cranes was on display until recently at Snibston Discovery Museum but this was closed by Leicestershire County Council in summer 2015, with the site earmarked for redevelopment. The houses on the skyline run along High Nash road. ANNE BEAUFOY

LEFT: A rare early colour view of Coleford S&W station in 1950. It is a still taken from a 16mm colour ciné film made of the Wye Valley railtour, which was organised by the Gloucestershire Railway Society. As detailed in the section on railtours in the Forest at the beginning of this book, in fact two tours were run, on 22nd July and 23rd September and this picture is believed to show the second of those trips. The railcar is No. W7W, which was still in GWR chocolate and cream livery, although that company had ceased to exist from 1st January 1948, upon Nationalisation of the railways. Note the goods shed in the far left background is also painted chocolate and cream. COLOUR-RAIL

RIGHT: No. 6417 with the Severn Rambler railtour at Coleford S&W station on 20th April 1958. Were enthusiasts more orderly in these earlier railtour days? A few years later they would swarm all over any site visited as some of the following pictures show but, apart from the headboard, you would not know this was a special. This is another photograph giving a flavour of how things would have appeared if a regular passenger service on the S&W lines had lasted into BR days. T.B. OWEN

A general view of the station and goods yard circa the summer of 1959. At some point in the later 1950s, repairs to the rotting planking of the Eassie-built wooden goods shed provided by the S&W had been effected by the simple expedient of nailing sheets of plywood or hardboard over the affected areas. The goods shed siding ran in front of it. MICHAEL HALE

A general view of the S&W passenger station prior to the arrival of the SLS tour on 13th May 1961. The goods yard is here behind the photographer and, as the top picture shows, had four sidings but the one holding the further line of box vans in that view, had been lifted by the date of this picture, as the empty chairs in the left foreground indicates. However, this was only to be a temporary measure and why is not known. DEREK CHAPLIN

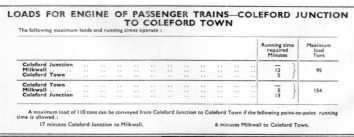

LOADS FOR ENGINE OF PASSENGER TRAINS—COLEFORD JUNCTION TO COLEFORD TOWN

The following maximum loads and running times operate :

											Running time required Minutes	Maximum load Tons
Coleford Junction Milkwall Coleford Town	..	..	..	..	..	..	..	..	..	..	13 } 5	95
Coleford Town Milkwall Coleford Junction	..	..	..	..	..	..	..	..	..	..	5 } 13	154

A maximum load of 110 tons can be conveyed from Coleford Junction to Coleford Town if the following point-to-point running time is allowed :

17 minutes Coleford Junction to Milkwall.   6 minutes Milkwall to Coleford Town.

TOP: The SLS tour departing from Coleford S&W in May 1961. The train is passing the goods and livestock loading dock, on the right; the crane on the goods dock was of 1½ tons capacity. ALAN JARVIS

INSET ABOVE RIGHT: This gradient sign, indicating where the 1 in 47 gradient changed to a gentle 1 in 200 through to the end of the platform, can also be seen almost hidden in the grass on the far left of the picture above. T.B. OWEN

INSET ABOVE: Maximum permitted loads and running times for passenger trains on the Coleford Branch, from the *Working Time Table*, September 1955. NPC

RIGHT: The SLS special alongside the old S&W platform. The change in gradient is evident just beneath the second coach. DEREK CHAPLIN

LEFT: The GRS tour at the station on 23rd June 1962. The lengthy climb away from the platform is evident in the picture, left, and the 1951 connection to the GWR station can just be made out above the heads of the group on the tracks in the right middle distance. Of particular interest here is that the lifted siding had been laid back in by this date and not that recently by the look of it, so it can only have been out of use for a short time. NPC

BELOW LEFT: As the tour departs, it is about to pass the pw trolley hut, off picture to the right; the boards were to assist in getting the trolley on and off the rails. NPC

BELOW: The typewritten itinerary sheet for the tour. IAN POPE COLLECTION

GLOUCESTERSHIRE RAILWAY SOCIETY

FOREST-OF-DEAN RAILTOUR
SATURDAY JUNE 23rd 1962

The Society have organised a special steam train covering the following branch lines which are now closed to passenger traffic:-

Gloucester Central - Dymock, now terminus of the Ledbury line, Newnham,- Bullo Pill,- Cinderford, Lydney Junction, Lydney Town, Coleford Junction - Coleford, and Speech House Road Lines.

The train will call at intermediate stations for photographic purposes.
A G.W.R. 64XX class 0-6-0 PT will be used for motive power, and the train will be made up of two auto-car coaches. Should bookings warrant it an additional coach will be provided and the train will be assisted from Coleford Junction.
A detailed Itinerary will be distributed on the train.
The fare is £1-5s, children under fourteen half fare. The timings are as follows:-

Gloucester Central	dep 1/30 p.m.			
Over Junction Pass	1/34			
Barbers Bridge	arr 1/43		dep.	1/50
Newent	arr 2/01		dep	2/10
Dymock	arr 2/20	N	dep	2/30
Over Junction	arr 2/59	N	dep	3/03
Bullo Pill East	arr 3/21	N	dep	3/30
Cinderford S & W	arr 3/50	N	dep	4/00
Bullo Pill East	arr 4/20	N	dep	4/25
Lydney Junction	arr 4/40	N	dep	4/45
Whitecroft	arr 5/02		dep	5/10
Parkend	arr 5/15		dep	5/25
Coleford Junction	arr 5/27	N	dep	5/35
Coleford	arr 5/35	N	dep	6/10
Coleford Junction pass	6/35			
Speech House Road	arr 6/45	N	dep	6/55
Coleford Junction pass	7/08			
Lydney S & W	arr 7/20	*		
Lydney Junction G.W.R.	dep 7/35		N ...Reverse	
Gloucester Central	arr 8/05			

* Passengers alight at Lydney S & W and entrain at G.W.R. station
----
Application to Mr.D.B.Lyall,   Tickets will not be sent out
              Highercombe,   until approx. one week
              52, Hall Road,   before tour.
              Leckhampton,
              Cheltenham, Gloucestershire.
                              With S.A.E. please
NOTE: The MID-WALES RAILTOUR has been postponed until Saturday
      8th September 1962.

LEFT: The Severn Boar II tour at the station in June 1964. The platform line seems to have been out of use by this date, so the train stopped adjacent to the loading dock. As indicated earlier, the original Eassie wooden building, which was even less popular that that at Milkwall, burnt down on 20th July 1918. The Joint Committee made no rush to replace it, however, first providing a temporary wooden building six months later, although a brick built ladies waiting room and WC was constructed at the same time. It was not until late 1924 that a new brick station building was provided (the nearer building here), at the same time as the similar new station at Milkwall was built. Surprisingly, the S&W Joint Committee, of which the GWR was a part, seems to have given no thought to approaching that company to use the far better passenger facilities at their station instead, which had been out of use since 1917. T.B. OWEN

No. 3643 shunts the S&W goods yard at Coleford on 30th March 1965. A further mystery surrounds the siding behind the goods shed, the one which had been partially removed for a time around 1961. G.W. Keeling's 1877 survey of the S&W shows it extending a short way beyond the station's boundary, into an adjacent yard. It is believed that it may have been extended into a local coal merchant's yard but the siding extension is not shown on the 1881 25ins OS. The goods yard was mainly used by coal traffic by the date of this picture, for deliveries of house coal. The sidings were well spaced out, so wagons could be accessed for unloading from either side. However, the nearer siding, which No. 3643 is shunting, had a ramp installed alongside it in later years, it is believed for loading free mined coal. The goods shed was leased to a local builders' merchants, so the van alongside was presumably delivering building materials of some description. JOHN DAGLEY-MORRIS

Another view of No. 3643 shunting the S&W yard; the locomotive has just placed the box van by the goods shed. John Dagley-Morris

A general view of the station and goods yard in 1965, with the rails in front of the platform starting to become overgrown. The photographer sent this picture to the author as a Christmas card in the early 1980s, fortuitous as the whereabouts of the original slide is currently not known. Bill Potter/NPC

A rare view of one of the North British Type 2 '63XX' Series diesels, No. D6329, at Coleford S&W on Monday 24th July 1967. Members of this class first appeared on the S&W line in early July 1967, apparently taking over completely from the '95XX' 0-6-0s for the last few weeks of operations on the Coleford Branch. No. D6329 was new into service in June 1960 and its short career came to an end just over a year after this picture was taken, in November 1968. It was cut up by Cashmore's of Newport six months later. The overgrown state of the track indicates that, with closure on the cards, BR had applied no weedkiller in this year. R.H. MARROWS

OPPOSITE PAGE TOP: No. D9500 shunts loaded coal wagons into the S&W sidings on 28th March 1966. The road on the left led from the station entrance onto the loading platform, whilst in the foreground are the dismantled remains of the livestock pens. The ramp for loading coal is just out of sight round the bend in the road. As its number indicates, D9500 was the first of the '95XX' Series of Type 1s, completed at Swindon in July 1964 and sent to Cardiff where it spent much of its early career and where it was possibly still based at the date of this view. It was put into store at Worcester about three months later but was then returned to traffic early in 1967 and spent time at Bristol and Cardiff. Back in store again by December 1967, it returned to traffic one last time ten months later in October 1968, again at Cardiff, but was stored in February 1969 and finally withdrawn two months later. Sold to the NCB, it was allocated to their North East Area and became Ashington Colliery No. 1, in which guise it was painted NCB blue. After closure of that system, the engine was bought for preservation in 1987 and is currently under long term restoration at Peak Rail in Derbyshire. R.H. MARROWS

ABOVE: Discussions are in progress as No. D9555 shunts the yard on 26th April 1967, the first day of the photographers' charter utilising three additional brake vans. The generally good condition of the structures attests to the fact that the railway had rented out the station building and ladies waiting room for much of the time since the cessation of the passenger service. The nearer block, the gents urinals, was provided in 1897 and was not affected by the 1918 fire. BILL POTTER/KRM

A second view, looking towards the buffer stops. The building just glimpsed beyond the goods shed and which looks to be connected with it was not actually on railway property. Note the local coal merchant's delivery lorry behind the goods shed. Behind that, the church tower visible is situated in Market Square, right in the centre of the town, giving an indication of how well situated both stations were, little good that it did either. The tower is all that remains of a church knocked down in 1882, because it was too small to accommodate the growing local congregation. BILL POTTER/KRM

A close up of the water crane and fire devil – provided for when the temperature dropped below freezing – in summer 1965. The stone base for the water tank on the right dated from the opening of the station in July 1875, although the tank was originally made of wood. This was replaced with the iron tank seen here in 1895, with those at Lydbrook Junction and Serridge Junction being similarly upgraded at the same time. As the later views show, these facilities remained until final closure, although steam finished at the end of 1965. In 1929, at the time the passenger service was withdrawn, the staff here at the S&W station totalled six, including the stationmaster and two porter/signalmen. By the end no one was positioned here, all necessary procedures being carried out by the train crew and a shunter. The station was always rather inconveniently situated, on the farthest side of the line from the town, access to the goods yard being deemed more important. BILL POTTER/KRM

Coleford S&W station awaits its fate in March 1968. Apparent in this view is the decorative pattern in the blue engineering brick bases to the newer buildings. Passenger access was a little hidden away, being via a narrow fenced footpath from the buffer stops end of the station, which opened out on to the end of the platform. The track was lifted soon after this picture was taken and the buildings demolished it is believed in the early 1970s. The site of the platform now lies under the south western side of the Pyart Court development, a small parade of shops, whilst the goods yards and the GWR station site were levelled and are now a car park. Old Station Way, a new road by-passing the town centre, bisects the trackbed about where the pine trees are in the right distance; beyond this point, the route of the railway up to Milkwall, on to Darkhill and Fetterhill, and down to Parkend is a foot and cycle path. IAN POPE COLLECTION

ABOVE: Bell's Grammar School from Cinder Hill circa 1962, with the railway in the bottom of the valley and the GWR goods shed on the left. The school was founded in the village of Newland in the 15th century and the completion of a new building for it was funded by the will of Edward Bell in 1576; it became a charitable trust in 1627. In 1876, the school moved to a new building on Lord's Hill, in Coleford, the site seen here. Enlarged in the 1920s, it became a grammar school in 1944, with 300 pupils attending in 1959. However, it was closed in 1968 upon opening of the Royal Forest of Dean Grammar School at Five Acres. Henry Ludlam subsequently purchased the school buildings and playing fields to create Bell's Golf Club, which is today known as the Forest of Dean Golf & Bowls Club. The large stone building is now Bell's Hotel. The opencast mining seen earlier was carried out in the fields to the right, where the cows are grazing. ANNE BEAUFOY

BELOW: The view from the school, with a rainbow in the sky after a recent shower and the school tennis courts and outdoor swimming pool in the foreground. In the centre distance is the rear of the S&W station, with the GWR station visible just above it and the rail side of the goods shed to the left of the trees. ANNE BEAUFOY

As mentioned at the beginning of this chapter, it was not until 1951 that British Railways finally did what neither the GWR or the Severn & Wye Joint Committee had ever managed, which was to lay in a direct connection between the two stations at Coleford. However, the fact that it took so long and happened so late probably made little difference to the history of the railway at Coleford or the eventual demise of both stations. The connection was made by extending the headshunt for the GWR goods yard to the S&W line. A new connection was also made with the siding running in front of the S&W loading dock, so both sets of sidings – there were only two on the GWR side – could now be directly accessed by trains approaching Coleford. Previously, even the line serving the loading dock had only been accessible by shunting back from the S&W goods loop. The Severn Boar II tour is here seen negotiating the connecting line and is about to pass the 1883-built GWR goods shed. Although in a parlous state, it was saved from imminent demolition in 1986 by local businessman and ex-Forest of Dean railway lineman Mike Rees, who has subsequently established a superb little museum here. Now bordered by a car park and a new by-pass road, and hemmed in by architecturally inappropriate modern buildings, it has lost much of its context but none of its relevance; it is by far the most important railway building surviving in the Forest today. T.B. OWEN

A leisurely break at Coleford GWR station for the crew of '57XX' Class 0-6-0PT No. 7750, as they head for Whitecliff Quarry with empty ballast hoppers in 1961. The line from Coleford to Whitecliff was worked as a separate section, so whilst paused here the locomotive crew will also collect the single line staff permitting them to proceed. The staff was held in the stationmaster's office here and its handover to and from the footplate crew was conducted by a Coleford-based railwayman. The Coleford Junction to Coleford staff was supposed to be left at the station whilst the train went down to Whitecliff but, in later days, it was often left in the ground frame where the 1951-built link to the GW diverged from the S&W. The moped on the platform most likely belongs to the man based here. The use of the staff allowed a second engine – trains up the branch from Coleford Junction were often double-headed – to shunt the goods yard whilst the line down to Whitecliff was occupied by the first engine. DEREK CHAPLIN

The station building, to a GWR design brought in during the 1880s, was of a much higher standard than its S&W counterpart, which makes the decision not to combine the two stations when the line to Monmouth closed at the end of 1916 seem all the more obtuse. Two lorries were also based here for local road deliveries, a service maintained until January 1966; one of these can be seen behind the station building, with the trailer for the other at the far end. DEREK CHAPLIN

The station from the opposite direction, looking along the line towards Whitecliff in August 1965. There had originally been a loop line on the left, although the station had only ever had one platform; the loop was removed in 1951, at the same time as the new connection to the S&W line was laid in. BILL POTTER/KRM

Although a typical railtour shot with enthusiasts everywhere, this was worth including for the glimpse it provides of the otherwise little photographed GWR sidings, complete with box van, on the left. The section of the loading dock on the extreme left was part of a siding extension added in 1913. JOHN RYAN

Having breasted the climb up from Whitecliff with the eight loaded hopper wagons which constituted its first trip of the day to Coleford Junction, No. 3643 makes its way along the level run through the station on 30th March 1965. After passing the goods yard and weaving its way across to the S&W line, the crew will then be faced with the short but stiff climb up to Milkwall, where they will have to stop and pin down the wagon brakes before the descent. The ballast hopper wagons seen in most of the steam era views are 'Herrings', probably BR-built but to a GWR design. JOHN DAGLEY-MORRIS

This panoramic view of both stations was taken about half an hour before the previous view, showing No. 3643 heading through on its way down to Whitecliff with empty hoppers. The loading ramp mentioned earlier, for loading free mined coal, can be seen with a wagon alongside on the far left. The goods yard was still busy at this date, with coal stockpiled on the various loading docks, a yellow liveried parcels lorry backed up to the road entrance to the goods shed and another trailer parked near the feed store. These distinctive concrete buildings, made of pre-fabricated sections to a standard design, could be found all over the railway system by the late 1950s as BR installed them at hundreds of rural stations. As they were made of pre-cast sections, their size could vary as necessary and they were produced at three locations: Exmouth Junction, Lowestoft and Newton Heath, Manchester. This particular shed was a very late addition, provided by BR in 1959, so had a very short life indeed. Many have survived across the country, having found other uses since closure of the stations they once served but this example, along with everything else seen in the picture – apart from the GWR goods shed in the right background – has long gone, the station site having been landscaped out of existence. JOHN DAGLEY-MORRIS

ABOVE: No. 4698 works through the station on 16th August 1965 with a single empty hopper wagon for Whitecliff Quarry. BILL POTTER/KRM

BELOW: Two days later, the same engine is framed by Cinder Hill Bridge as it tops the climb up from the quarry with a train load of ballast. BILL POTTER/KRM

Having dropped off the loaded coal wagons in the S&W sidings, the photographers' charter of 26th April 1967 waits to head down to Whitecliff behind No. D9555. Attentive readers will have realised that these two trips, out and back from Gloucester on consecutive days, used different locomotives, No. D9502 handling the journey up to Cinderford on the following day. The GWR signal box had stood on the platform between the nearer telegraph pole, erected after its removal, and the white Hillman Imp. Having been reduced to ground frame status after the station had closed to passengers, it remained in use controlling the points and signals on the GWR side until the track alterations carried out in 1951; it survived for a while longer but had been removed by 1960. Note the mobile crane in the background, beside the feed store. BILL POTTER/KRM

Despite the imminent closure of the railway north of Parkend, the goods yard was still well used by local coal merchants, with piles of coal visible on the loading dock. In point of fact, the Coleford coal merchants were stocking up with vast quantities of house coal before the cessation of rail deliveries just three weeks later; the nearest rail-served coal depots thereafter would be at Abergavenny or Stonehouse. No. D6329 has arrived with nine more wagons loaded with various grades of coal on 24th July 1967. The photographer recalls: 'The arrival of a loaded coal train at the GW station was indeed unusual, though forty-eight years on I cannot recall the reason. The train must have been sitting there for at least 10-15 minutes, for I had photographed its departure from Coleford Junction and then cycled up to Coleford. It is possible that the run round loop at the S&W station was blocked up with coal wagons, so the train crew may have intended to run through to Whitecliff to run round their train. However, the train then reversed back towards the junction with the S&W.' Members of the '63XX' Series Type 2s first appeared on the S&W line in early July 1967, seemingly taking over completely from the '95XX' 0-6-0s for the last few weeks of operations on the Coleford Branch. The final load of BR ballast to leave Whitecliff Quarry by rail ran on Friday 11th August 1967, whilst the very last train on the branch ran engine and brake van to Coleford S&W only on Tuesday 15th August, to collect the remaining empty mineral wagons. R.H. MARROWS

Coleford GWR station in March 1968, some seven months after closure. In 1933, the GWR station building was adapted for use by the S&W Joint Committee staff at the station. Parcels traffic was also concentrated on this side of the station, with the S&W buildings being rented out, as mentioned earlier. For the last eighteen months or so of its existence, traffic on the Coleford Branch had comprised ballast from Whitecliff Quarry and coal to Coleford, with a small amount of free mined coal heading out, British Railways having terminated the general goods and parcels traffic to and from here on 3rd January 1966. IAN POPE COLLECTION

ABOVE: The other side of Cinder Hill Bridge, with No. D9555 about to head beneath on its way down to Whitecliff of 26th August 1967. The abutments were constructed of local sandstone, whilst as can be seen, the wrought iron girder span was on quite a pronounced slant as it carried the road down Cinder Hill. With the redevelopment of the sites of both stations for retail use and car parking, the bridge was demolished and a roundabout built in its place. This provides access to the car park from its eastern arm. BILL POTTER/KRM

COLEFORD

The Line from Coleford Station to Whitecliff Quarries is connected to the Main Line at Coleford by points worked from a Ground Frame locked by a key on the Wooden Train Staff for the Coleford Junction—Coleford Station Section.

INSET RIGHT: The instructions for working the line from Coleford to Whitecliff, from the *Appendix to the Working Time Table*, October 1960. NPC

This view of the Severn Boar II tour was taken from Cinder Hill Bridge and is looking towards Whitecliff, showing the cutting through which the railway climbed to reach the town. In 1990, new offices for the Forest of Dean District Council were completed, on land at the top of the cutting on the right. These offices are accessed from a fourth road leading off to the west from the roundabout, whilst the car park serving them has been built in this cutting. NPC

Traversing another highly picturesque piece of line, the Severn Boar II tour crosses the skew arch over Newland Street as it heads down to Whitecliff. It is about to run on to the section of railway that was built on the Monmouth Tramroad, the route of which comes in from the right behind the locomotives. T.B. OWEN

Still leaking steam badly (see page 247), No. 4698 struggles up the grade across the skew arch with eight loaded hoppers on 16th August 1965. BILL POTTER/KRM

LEFT: Having crossed over Newland Street, the line was perched on a ledge on the north east side of the valley as it followed the route of the Monmouth Tramroad for most of the way down to Whitecliff, as this view looking up to see No. 3643 heading towards Coleford shows. This was the engine's second Up trip of the day, with an additional three loaded hoppers from the quarry. JOHN DAGLEY-MORRIS

BELOW: The Severn Boar II trip paused at a similar point on the line, with Newland Street on the right. The houses still remain, whilst the building with the corrugated iron roof is now also converted as a private residence. The cutting leading to Coleford GWR station can be seen in the centre right distance, directly above the cab of the leading engine. T.B. OWEN

RIGHT: The historic Whitecliff Ironworks site in May 1976, prior to any remedial work being carried out on the furnace to stabilise and preserve it. Built between 1798 and 1802, the ironworks was rebuilt under the advice of David Mushet in 1808-10, who became a partner in the concern and moved to Coleford in 1811 to manage it. However, despite numerous attempts, he was unable to make the works profitable and soon parted company with his new partners, although seemingly on good terms. The problems are believed to have been a combination of the local coal being of poor coking quality and the alkaline nature of the iron ore. The period of iron making here was thus extremely short; it may have finished by 1812 but certainly by 1816. Much of the blast equipment was transferred to Cinderford Ironworks in 1827 and the site here was then abandoned, although was periodically robbed for building stone. Emergency repairs to the remains were carried out in the early 1980s but it was not until the Wye Valley AONB provided funding in 2010-11 that a full programme of conservation work was carried out to the furnace. It is now owned by the Forest of Dean Buildings Preservation Trust. The Monmouth Tramroad ran on the ledge behind the ironworks, although this did not open until 1812. DAVID BICK

LEFT: No. 3643 leaves Whitecliff Tunnel with its first Up working to Coleford Junction on 30th March 1965. The tunnel was very short, just 55 yards, but on a sharp curve hence the lack of light coming through from the other end. There was a catch point at this end of the tunnel, installed in 1938 to protect against any runaway wagons coming down the gradient from Coleford and smashing into the quarry sidings. The single lever frame for this, named Quarry Sidings Ground Frame, can be seen beside the locomotive. All Down workings had to stop for the point to be set and it was then reset immediately the train had passed over it. However, the point blades were sprung so that Up trains could just run through without having to stop. JOHN DAGLEY-MORRIS

WHITECLIFF QUARRIES

A spring catch point is provided at the entrance to the Quarry Siding, and is worked from Whitecliff Quarry Ground Frame which is locked by a key on the Wooden Train Staff for the Coleford Station—Whitecliff Section.

All trains must stop at the Stop Board on the Coleford side of the Catch Point.   The Guard in charge must walk through the tunnel and satisfy himself that all is clear, close the Catch Point, and signal the Driver to proceed.

Before an engine is allowed to pass under the screens at the Quarries the Guard must notify the Quarry staff in order that they may raise the chutes clear and secure then to the girder provided before the shunting movement proceeds.

After trains have been formed ready to leave Whitecliff, up to 12 empties may be attached behind the brake van, drawn into the tunnel, secured, and detached at the Coleford end.

ABOVE: The instructions for working the sidings at Whitecliff Quarry and the catch point on the approach, from the *Appendix to the Working Time Table*, October 1960.

RIGHT: A view of the heavily overgrown entrance to the sidings in June 1964, as the Severn Boar II tour exits the tunnel. Note that the rake of hopper wagons seen in the view below do not feature here, yet in that picture they clearly straddle the point partly seen on the left. The only explanation seems to be that the point was switched and the tour train was used to shunt the wagons clear, in order that it could then gain access to the quarry sidings. T.B. OWEN

LEFT: Another view of the tour in a similar position but seemingly perilously close to a rake of empty 'Herring' ballast hopper wagons that do not appear in the picture above. There was obviously no way past, so the wagons must have been moved. Both tunnel portals are still accessible, although this end is within the boundaries of the old quarry, now an industrial site, whilst the other end has been roughly blocked off with old bits of corrugated iron. JOHN RYAN

ABOVE: In early 1962, a rake of load hopper wagons ran away from Whitecliff Sidings, down the bank and into the Peckett, pushing it through the buffer stops, where it was photographed the following year. Built in 1941 (Works No. 2013) and used at the Royal Ordnance Factory at Llanishen, near Cardiff, the locomotive was cut up on site shortly after this picture was taken. NPC

ABOVE: Dog Kennel Bridge, in the background, takes this narrow lane linking Newland Street with Scowles Road through the railway embankment. The railway again took an easier curve here than the tramroad but this necessitated building the substantial embankment and bridge to carry it. The tramroad followed the contours of the hillside and crossed the line by means of a timber span bridge, the stone abutments for which can be seen in the foreground of this 1976 view. They still remain today. DENNIS PARKHOUSE

LEFT: Dog Kennel Bridge, seen here circa 1964, was one of three substantial stone bridges built for the Coleford Railway, the others being the skew arch crossing Newland Street and the lofty arch below Newland, which we shall see shortly. The origins of the bridge's name are lost in the mists of time. Note the height difference between the two arches due to the steeply climbing nature of the lane. This view is today almost completely obscured by trees. ANNE BEAUFOY

RIGHT: Another aspect of Dog Kennel Bridge, taken in 1976 and showing the massive retaining walls which were required to carry the weight of the embankment on the eastern side. Again built of local sandstone, the arch is lined with brick. DENNIS PARKHOUSE

BOTTOM: Knockalls Bridge, carrying the railway over a minor lane about a mile west of Newland station, was another considerable construction, out of all proportion in many ways to the inconsequential little branch line it carried. The arch is wider than that of Dog Kennel Bridge and slightly higher, rail height at the top of the embankment being around 40ft above the roadway. The lane, leading to Staunton from the Redbrook to Coleford road, is now a footpath having been closed some years ago amid concerns that the bridge might be unsafe but it still stands today. DENNIS PARKHOUSE

ABOVE: Newland station building disappearing into the undergrowth in 1960. Opened on 1st September 1883, it was the only intermediate station on the branch and closed with the line on 1st January 1917. It was of a similar design to the building at Coleford, although smaller and built of stone. The view is looking west towards Monmouth and to drive from Coleford down to the River Wye at Redbrook today, following the route of the railway for most of the way, is to wonder why it was ever built at all. It rises through challenging terrain, whilst Newland station was situated over half a mile from the village it was built to serve and generated little in the way of either goods or passenger traffic. In the 1970s, the station, along with the surviving stone shelter on the Up platform, were joined together by building across the space in between and made into a sizeable residence. The small stone built goods shed and the stationmaster's house, here hidden behind the main building, also still survive. MICHAEL HALE

SECTION 4

LINES AROUND BLAKENEY
The PURTON STEAM CARRIAGE ROAD and the
FOREST OF DEAN CENTRAL RAILWAY

The three-arch Purton Steam Carriage Road bridge or viaduct of 1832 spans a minor lane running from Etloe to Purton. It is seen here, looking towards Etloe, on 2nd October 1971, at which date it was quite heavily overgrown and at some risk. It was Grade II listed by English Heritage in 1979, the description for the listing reading: 'Red sandstone rubble with dressed voussoirs. 3 arches of diminishing heights, main pier wedge shaped, so that the viaduct is slightly angled: the tallest arch spans road; centre one damaged on NE side. South east wall continues as retaining wall for some distance, slightly curved return to NE. Part of the parapet survives at the north west end. This viaduct is of considerable historical and industrial archaeological interest.' BILL POTTER/KRM

The poor relation of the Forest's railways, as compared to the Severn & Wye Railway and the GWR's Forest of Dean Branch, was the Forest of Dean Central Railway, the route of which was first proposed in 1849, with the Act for its construction eventually being secured on 11th July 1856. It was to be a further twelve years before the line opened, however, on 25th May 1868, due to difficulties in both financing it and building it. The FoDCR ran from Awre Junction station, on the South Wales Railway main line between Lydney and Newnham, to New Fancy Colliery, on top of the ridge to the north east of Parkend. Although a station was built at Blakeney, the only village passed on its short 4¾ miles route, the line was only ever used for goods traffic.

The FoDCR was, however, preceded by an even earlier scheme, one which, if it had been completed, would have seen the first use of steam locomotives for haulage in the Forest of Dean. Whether it would have changed the course of later railway history in the area though is debatable. The S&W Tramroad served the western side of the Dean and the Forest of Dean Tramroad the eastern valley but there

was nothing that accessed the relatively undeveloped central section. The first proposal to rectify this was made in 1826 and this scheme was revived in 1830, when it was decided to put forward a plan for a steam railway between Foxes Bridge Colliery, which had then just opened, to a new basin on the River Severn at Purton Pill. Reflecting the confused terminology then still in use at this very early date in railway history, the line was called the Purton Steam Carriage Road. It was to be just over 8 miles in length, including a short branch to another colliery, whilst the new dock at Purton Pill would be reached via a rope worked incline.

There was much support for the scheme, such as from noted Forest industrialist Moses Teague and many of the free miners, who struggled to sell their coal against the monopoly of the bigger colliery owners, to the inhabitants of Berkeley, across the river, and the woollen manufacturers of the South Cotswolds. However, there was also stiff opposition mostly from the S&W. The Bill was presented in 1832, the main promoter behind it being Charles Mathias of Pembrokeshire. He was confident enough of the Bill's success to purchase the land required

ABOVE: In the mid 1970s, prior to the listing being carried out, a group of volunteers led by the noted industrial archeaologist David Bick cleared all the scrub from around the bridge and also removed the worst of the plant life growing out of and on it. Around this time, the author visited the bridge in the company of his father, who took these photographs, and his young nephew. The fine stonework was exposed for the first time in many years, whilst this view also shows how the bridge was on a gentle gradient from right to left (west to east) as the intended line headed towards the river. Sadly, in the intervening years since this picture was taken, the bridge has become almost completely overgrown once more.

LEFT: Looking east across the bridge towards the River Severn and Sharpness, in the right background. The line was intended to reach the dock by means of a rope worked incline, which would have run down the hillside to the right from the far corner of the field, parallel to the later railway.
BOTH DENNIS PARKHOUSE

at the Purton end of the line and even to begin major construction works. However, further opposition appears to have come from the Commissioners of Woods, who at this period were opposed to further development of the Forest's mineral deposits. At a time when the King's Navy still comprised wooden-hulled ships, the conservation of the timber was deemed of far more importance. Consequently, the Bill failed to make its second reading, being withdrawn after this was deferred for six months.

Construction completed prior to the scheme collapsing included part or all of Nibley Hill Tunnel, south of Blakeney, and a shallow cutting or ledge cut into the hillside, to the west of the A48. The most visible reminder, however, is a graceful three-arch stone bridge over a minor lane near Purton, whilst the South Wales Railway's plans of 1844 show a dock at Purton, although how complete this was is unclear and any evidence of it was destroyed when the SWR was built.

The Forest of Dean Central Railway's fate was sealed just four years after it opened, when, in April 1872, the S&W completed their Mineral Loop line, which extracted all the coal traffic from the collieries that the FoDCR had been built to serve. After 1877, there was no traffic north of Howbeach Sidings and by 1911, and probably well before, the traffic level had dwindled to three trains a week. Howbeach Colliery did not reopen after the 1921 coal strike, after which working beyond Blakeney ceased, the track being lifted in 1942. Blakeney goods station enjoyed a brief 'Indian Summer' during the Second World War as a depot for charcoal, an important war material, but there was little traffic left when this finished and the last train ran on 29th July 1949. The stone station building has recently been dismantled for re-erection on the Dean Forest Railway, with a new housing estate being built on the station site. Much of the route can still be walked and several stone bridges also still survive along it.

The view from Viney Hill at 5.15pm on 17th May 1961, with the village of Blakeney on the left and Nibley Hill on the right. The northern end of Nibley Hill Tunnel, built to take the Purton Steam Carriage Road through the ridge on which the photographer was standing, was just off picture on the right (the two tunnel entrances, on opposite sides of the A48 road but around half a mile apart, can be found on 19th century 25ins OS maps marked as old quarries). The line would have run across the hillside from right to left about where the cows can just be made out in the centre of the picture. Further to the left, its route, if any of it was actually built, was taken by the Forest of Dean Central Railway, which arrived from Awre Junction in 1868. The hamlet of Awre can be made out on this side of the River Severn in the centre left distance. The site of Blakeney goods station is hidden in the trees to the right of the main part of Blakeney village, on the lower slopes of Nibley Hill. The line crossed the A48 by means of a three-arch bridge (two stone arches and a wrought iron span over the road), which was demolished in April 1959, and then followed an S shape as it made its way across the valley on the left. The railway was then carried over New Road and the Blackpool Brook on a viaduct which consisted of two stone arches, two metal spans and a further six stone arches. The two metal spans were dismantled in May 1959, leaving the abutments, prominent here on the left, and the stone arches which all still survive today. The Cock Inn, still open today, is the white painted building nearest the trees centre right, whilst the Severn Railway Bridge, still standing although damaged by this date, lay about half a mile downstream to the right. ANNE BEAUFOY INSET ABOVE: A detail from an 1892 painting of Blakeney from Viney Hill, which shows a coal train crossing the viaduct. No photograph of a train on the line north of Blakeney has ever been seen.

Looking north at Otterspool Junction, Lydney in the summer of 1964, with the Otterspool Junction Home signal prominent to the fore. The overgrown line in the right foreground, running past the 25mph speed restriction sign and directly in front of Otterspool Junction signal box, was that to the Severn Bridge, out of use since the accident which damaged the bridge in October 1960. The forge castings factory in the left background has been through various ownerships over the years but is still in operation by J.D. Norman Industries in 2015, although it is now separated from the railway by the Lydney by-pass. ALAN JARVIS

SECTION 5

The SEVERN BRIDGE RAILWAY
LYDNEY to SHARPNESS

The River Severn below Gloucester as far as the start of the Severn Estuary, which the Admiralty defines as commencing at Aust/Beachley, has long provided a barrier to transport. It is believed that the Romans may have been able to cross the river near Lydney with relative ease, as it was much narrower then but soon after wetland areas in the vicinity flooded and the Severn became much wider. Water levels may have risen at this time, whilst the twice daily 'bores' – when a wave of tidal water sweeps upstream – have always made the building of bridges and the operation of ferries difficult.

Thomas Telford's bridge over the Severn at Over, near Gloucester, became the lowest downstream crossing of the river when it opened in 1830. Prior to that, the proprietors of the Bullo Pill Tramroad had begun construction of a tunnel beneath the river, which would have run between Newnham and Bullo on the west bank, to Arlingham on the other side. Buoyed by the success of building their mile long tunnel beneath Haie Hill, construction began in 1810 but was brought to a halt part way under the river when water broke in and the workings flooded. Unable to pump the water out, the project was abandoned but some of the associated earthworks can still be seen today. Various railway schemes during the first half of the 19th century proposed crossings of the river but encountered opposition from the Severn Commissioners and the Admiralty, despite the opening of the Gloucester & Berkeley Canal in 1827, which effectively by-passed the Lower Severn and allowed ships to reach Gloucester by a safer and less tortuous route.

Brunel's South Wales Railway plans of 1844 originally envisaged a line from near Stroud crossing the Severn between Fretherne and Awre, nine miles south of Gloucester. He bought off the Commissioners with a proposal for a new cut straight across the meander at Arlingham but the Admiralty refused to accept this. Coupled with vehement opposition from the city of Gloucester, which the proposed route missed out, Parliament was persuaded to sanction the new railway's route from Fishguard only as far as Chepstow. Meanwhile, a railway crossing of the Severn was proposed by another new company, the Gloucester & Dean Forest Railway of 1846, which intended linking with the proposed Monmouth & Hereford Railway of 1844 at Grange Court. In the event, the latter was not proceeded with, whilst the former company's finances ran out once the line had reached Grange Court. A proposed six mile extension to meet with the SWR at Awre ened up being built by the SWR themselves. The railway crossed the Severn alongside Telford's bridge, the line opening in 1851.

Thus, as the 19th century moved into its second half, there was still no way of getting across the River Severn below Gloucester apart from a handful of small ferries. However, in 1857 came the first serious proposal for crossing the wider river, over the Severn Estuary between New Passage and Portskewett, south of Chepstow, by the Bristol & South Wales Union Railway. After gaining Parliamentary sanction, this line opened in September 1863 and ran from Bristol to a wooden pier at New Passage, with passengers then being carried

No. 1424 at Lydney Junction (S&W) in 1959, whilst working trailer first back to Sharpness and Berkeley Road with what was the last remaining passenger service on the old S&W Joint line. Trains shuttled between Berkeley Road and Lydney Town stations, calling at Berkeley, Sharpness and Severn Bridge on the way. The footbridge just glimpsed in the right background spanned the extensive yards here to link the S&W and GWR Junction stations. DAVID BICK

by steam ferry across to another lofty wooden pier at Portskewett; a short branch serving this had been built from the SWR main line. The need for a proper fixed crossing, however, was becoming more acute. The canal to Gloucester could not accommodate the larger ships that were being built and Sharpness Docks lacked a railway connection. Accordingly, six competing schemes were produced in 1871 but only two won Parliamentary sanction, the Severn Bridge Railway and the Severn Tunnel Railway, both securing their Acts in 1872.

The GWR were the promoters of the tunnel scheme and had already absorbed the B&SWUR, in 1868, intending to close the ferry once the tunnel was open. However, although work commenced promptly in 1873, problems encountered during the construction, including the complete flooding of the workings in 1879, when water from a spring on the Welsh side burst in, meant that the whole project took nearly fourteen years, the tunnel finally opening to traffic on 1st December 1886. Nevertheless, its construction was a major engineering achievement of the 19th century and it continues to carry trains between England and South Wales today.

In comparison, the Severn Bridge had a much less fraught birth, although nothing that involves building within the tidal reaches of the River Severn is ever easy. In 1865, G.W. Keeling, who had been Engineer of the Severn & Wye Railway since 1860, was asked by W.B. Clegram, Engineer of the G&B Canal, to survey the river near Sharpness as to its suitability for the site for a new bridge. Finding that it was indeed a good location and that the river bed was suitable for driving the piers, plans for a scheme were deposited with Parliament in 1870 but sufficient financial support could not be raised at this time. However, a year later, backing for the scheme, from the canal company, the Severn & Wye and the Midland Railway, ensured its success. The Severn Bridge Railway Act was granted on 18th July 1872, to build four miles of railway between Lydney and Sharpness, with a bridge over the River Severn, designed by G.W. Keeling, which included a foot/road toll bridge alongside, although in the event this latter was never built. A week later, the Midland received their Act to build a branch railway from Berkeley Road to Sharpness, which was opened for goods traffic to and from the docks in 1875 and for passengers to a temporary terminal station on 1st August 1876.

Contracts for the construction of the bridge were let in 1875. The river piers and girders were to be built by the Windsor Iron Company of Garston, near Liverpool, whilst the railway approaches either side, along with the stonework, were to be be built by Vickers & Cooke of London; the value of the two contracts were £190,000 and £90,000 respectively. The preferred method of construction would have been to have built the spans on the shore and floated them into position but the tides and currents mitigated against this, so huge timber stagings had first to be erected and then the spans built over them. In 1876, the two main piers were washed down and had to be dismantled by divers before they could be re-erected. Meanwhile, Vickers & Cooke failed to meet their obligations, having secretly sub-let the contract to someone else. Griffith Griffiths of Yorkley took over building the Sharpness side approach in 1876 and was then given the contract for the Lydney side as well in 1878. Construction of the bridge had now fallen well behind but, by means of electric lighting, then very much a novelty, a night shift was able to work on the staging in conjunction with favourable tides, thereby saving around eight months from the schedule.

The bridge was completed in 1879, being inspected by Colonel Rich of the Board of Trade on 3rd-4th October and then formally opened for traffic on 17th. A special train ran from the Midland Railway's terminus station at Gloucester, via Berkeley Road to Sharpness and over to Lydney, exploding a fog signal at each of the twenty-one spans on its way. On the return journey, the train stopped on the bridge and everyone got off to watch W.C. Lucy, Chairman of the Severn Bridge Railway Co. and also of the G&B Canal Co., drive in the last rivet. This was followed by lunch at Sharpness.

The final piece in the jigsaw concerned the two railway companies who had collaborated under Keeling to build the bridge. By an Act of 21st July 1879, the SBR and S&WR were amalgamated to form the Severn & Wye & Severn Bridge Railway. In point of fact, this move had been forced on them by the Midland Railway refusing to take up its preference share options on the bridge in 1878, unless they were granted running powers over the S&W system. The latter were granted running powers on the Midland branches in the Stroud valleys in return but these were clearly not as advantageous as gaining access to the Forest of Dean coalfield. Prior to this, the Midland had rebuilt Sharpness station on a new site, in readiness for the start of the through service between Berkeley Road and Lydney and the Sharpness Branch was combined with the S&W&SBR's passenger services in *Bradshaw's* time tables. The S&W&SBR company was now hemmed in on all sides by the GWR and the Midland, both geographically and economically but they managed to remain independent until 1894.

The new bridge soon became an accepted part of the railway scene, useful for diversions as it proved in 1881 when fire wrecked Portskewett pier. The GWR were granted permission to run four trains a day each way over the bridge until the ferry service could be resumed three weeks later. Even after the opening of the Severn Tunnel in 1886, there were occasions when trains were diverted via the bridge but, more importantly, Forest coal now had a new outlet to a deep water port in comparison to Lydney and Bullo, the S&W building a coal tip alongside the old canal dock. Frequent diversions over the bridge, along with regular goods services from Lydney to Bristol and beyond followed from the opening of the Berkeley Loop in 1908, which allowed direct running from Sharpness towards Bristol. However, in relation to what it had cost the company to build, the bridge never lived up to the predicted traffic levels.

Costing around a third of what the Severn Tunnel was estimated at and with easier gradients either side, coupled with the advantage of being finished seven years earlier, the Severn Bridge promoters expected to take the lion's share of the cross river traffic. However, in their eagerness they ignored other crucial factors. The Severn Tunnel provided a more direct route, it was not hampered by having only a single line of rails and it was not affected by weight restrictions. A nationwide economic depression caused a slump in the Forest of Dean coal trade, which finally brought the S&W&SBR to its knees and saw it jointly taken over by the GW and Midland railways. The S&W had hoped that the bridge would lift their company out of the financial mire. Instead, the cost of building it and the lower than hoped for returns saw the S&W&SBR brought to its knees in 1894, to be somewhat reluctantly jointly taken over by the Midland and the GWR; although something of a liability,

An invitation ticket for the reporter from the *Dean Forest Guardian* newspaper at Coleford, to ride on the inaugural train over the Severn Bridge on 17th October 1879. The paper continues today as *The Forester*. NPC

The Severn & Wye & Severn Bridge Railway, from Lydney Junction to Berkeley Road, as shown on the 1961 edition 1 inch Tourist Series OS. Note the Berkeley Loop line of 1908, bottom right, which allowed trains to run direct from Lydney and Sharpness to Bristol and *vice versa*. The Ridge sandbank, on the eastern side of the river just above the bridge, is where the two tanker barges which collided with it ended up and their remains still lie today. Also shown is the remaining portion of the Forest of Dean Central Railway's line from the closed Awre Junction station to Blakeney; this had originally extended up to near Brandricks Green.

Just north of the bridge on the western bank is Purton, destination of the Purton Steam Carriage Road. The route of this had been west to Etloe and then a tunnel underneath Nibley before heading west again into the Forest. Finally, across the Arlingham peninsula at top right was where Brunel proposed driving his new cut to eliminate the river meander, in return for being allowed to build a bridge.

INSET ABOVE LEFT: S&W&SBR ticket issued on the first day. NPC

22698 Blakeney. The Severn Bridge

LEFT: Although the Severn Bridge could not claim the iconic status enjoyed by Brunel's Royal Albert Bridge, Stephenson's Menai Bridge or the Forth Bridge, it was certainly in the second string of important viaducts. As such, it could be measured alongside the Tay Bridge, Barmouth Bridge or Crumlin Viaduct and constitutes a major engineering achievement by such a small company. It certainly attracted the attention of picture postcard photographers and publishers, as this beautifully tinted circa 1905 view shows. It was published by the Photochrom Company of Tunbridge Wells, who also produced similar tinted views as carriage prints for the pre-Grouping railway companies. The station is seen in its original form, with the Eassie buildings, fencing and tall signal box all supplied by the Gloucester Railway Carriage & Wagon Company. The latter was replaced by the smaller standard Midland Railway box, opened on 12th November 1911, which is seen in the following photographs. NPC

BELOW: An Edwardian period china tea pot, with an applied transfer image of the Severn Bridge based on the picture left. NPC

neither were prepared to see the other take all of the potentially rich Forest of Dean coal traffic. The Sharpness Branch was transferred to the ownership of the Joint Committee at the same time

The takeover did not improve the fortunes of the bridge, however. Restrictions in regards to the locomotives that could work over the bridge came from the Midland Railway, Derby having imposed quite stringent maximum axle loads in 1894. 'Dean Goods' 0-6-0s and the '2021' Class 0-6-0PTs were the heaviest permitted GWR locomotives, at 37 and 38 tons respectively, whilst the Midland used nothing heavier than lightweight Johnson 0-6-0s. There was a 15mph speed restriction on the bridge but there was also an instruction that trains were to take no longer than 3 minutes when crossing it. Regular winter Sunday diversions to allow maintenance on the Severn Tunnel began after Grouping in January 1923, usually in the hands of 'Dean Goods' 0-6-0s. The LM&SR were to prove equally as 'windy' as regards what they believed the bridge was capable of, preventing the GWR from using heavy tank engines of the '42XX' and 72XX' classes during the early years of the war, in the light of the need for 'extensive alterations and heavy expenses'. Even the Collett 0-6-0s were barred and double heading of any sort was also not permitted.

It was not until the last decade of the bridge's working life that it started to come into its own and it must have finally been with some relief that the Western Region of British Railways got its hands on it following Nationalisation of the railways. With the prospect of any further objections from the Midlands now past, Class '43XX' 2-6-0s were used from October 1950 but the big news came in August 1956,

when tests were carried out with two 'Castle' Class 4-6-0s, No. 5018 *St. Mawes Castle* and No. 5042 *Winchester Castle*, both light engine and hauling a train of loaded ballast wagons. Despite the two locomotive weighing a combined near 250 tons including their tenders, the tests were deemed a success and the bridge acquitted itself well.

Amongst the interesting data which was gathered at this time was an estimate of the annual number of crossings by the various locomotives types using the bridge, which is shown in **Table 1**, below. This gives an estimated annual total of 5,250 crossings or 100 a week. Sixty of these were the Lydney Town to Berkeley Road auto trains, whilst the rest would break down as one a week being diverted passenger workings hauled by '63XX' 'Moguls', four a week were the 9.45pm Lydney to Stoke Gifford goods headed by Collett 0-6-0s and the rest local goods services worked by various types of pannier tanks. The estimates were based on a year from the early 1950s, so include '2021' Class panniers and their direct replacements the '16XX' Class. Within a couple of years, the '2021' Class engines had been withdrawn and '57XX' 0-6-0PTs would become commonplace. From early 1960 up until the time it closed, pairs of three car Class '119' 'Cross Country' DMUs on diverted workings were photographed crossing the bridge.

It was estimated that, allowing for the passage of up to four 'Castle' Class locomotives per week on top of the current usage, the bridge had up to fifteen years of life remaining without carrying out any additional work to it. However, if it was strengthened, a working life well beyond 1970 could be contemplated. The replacement of all the diagonal bracing struts on each span was therefore authorised, along with repairs to some of the expansion rollers and to some of the piers by fixing metal banding around them. The contract, worth £95,000, was won by the Fairfield Bridge & Shipbuilding Company of Chepstow and work started in early 1960. After over eighty years of life, it looked as though the bridge was at last going to be more fully utilised. Sadly, only three of the spans had been completed when disaster occurred. Having spent many years in Midland Railway brown and cream, it was a further irony that the bridge had been repainted in 1956, in the steel grey colour that it exhibits in the pictures that follow.

TABLE 1: ESTIMATED ANNUAL USEAGE OF THE SEVERN BRIDGE		
Class	Wheel Arrangement	Number of Crossings
'63XX'	2-6-0	50
'2251'	0-6-0	200
'16XX'	0-6-0PT	700
'2021'	0-6-0PT	1,300
'14XX'	0-4-2T	3,000

RIGHT: Few photographs were taken on the two mile section of line between Otterspool Junction and Severn Bridge Tunnel and none have so far been found in colour. Curving gently through an uninhabited landscape, the only other engineering feature apart from the tunnel was this bridge carrying Nass Lane over the railway, photographed here in 1996 shortly before the cutting was filled in and the bridge buried. The view is looking back towards Lydney.

BELOW: Looking east over the bridge towards Naas Lane level crossing, on the main line to Gloucester below and just past the house in the middle distance. There has long been argument locally about the spelling of Nass. On maps going back to the early 1800s at least, the spelling is Nass Lane and Nass House. However, locals prefer the quirkier Naas and, interestingly, so did the railway, referring to this as Naas Crossing. BOTH ALASTAIR WARRINGTON

BERKELEY ROAD JUNCTION TO MIERY STOCK SIDINGS
WORKING OF PASSENGER TRAINS WITHOUT GUARDS BETWEEN LYDNEY TOWN AND BERKELEY ROAD

Auto coaches, fitted for control from one end only, are used for the local passenger train service between Lydney Town and Berkeley Road. Not more than one coach may be propelled by the engine and all other vehicles must be attached to the rear of the train.

The trains are worked without guards provided the formation is restricted to three vehicles and all the vehicles are fitted with the continuous brake complete. In the event of any train exceeding three vehicles, a guard must be provided.

The following instructions will apply to trains worked without guards:—

In the event of an accident or failure, the train must be considered as coming within the category of a light engine.

Should a train be stopped by accident, failure, obstruction or other cause, the Driver and Fireman must carry out the provisions of Rules 178, 179, 180, 181.

At stations where the trains commence their journey, and at intermediate stations where staff are on duty, the responsibility usually attaching to the Guard must be carried out by the person starting the train.

Should a train arrive at a station, and there be no station staff on duty, the Fireman must attend to the opening and closing of the doors, and give the signal to the Driver to start.

The Station Master, or other authorised person must see that the tail lamp is in position (and burning properly when necessary) before the train leaves the starting point. Should a vehicle be attached or detached from the train at an intermediate station, the Station Master or person in charge at that station must see that the tail lamp is transferred to the last vehicle of the train before it leaves the station.

In order to ensure the safe custody of letter mails, etc., the brake compartments of each set of coaches in the working will be provided with special locks and keys. A supply of keys will be issued to each Station Master for the use of the staff at his station.

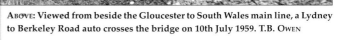

ABOVE: Viewed from beside the Gloucester to South Wales main line, a Lydney to Berkeley Road auto crosses the bridge on 10th July 1959. T.B. OWEN

INSET ABOVE: Photographed in January 1967, this original circa 1879 framed print of the bridge hung inside the swing section cabin. JOHN STRANGE/NPC

LEFT: Interestingly, the *Appendix to the Working Time Table for Passenger Trains*, October 1960, states that only one auto coach could be propelled over the bridge, other vehicles should be attached to the rear of the train but, as the picture overleaf shows, that was clearly not followed.

LEFT: List of signal boxes and their opening hours on the Berkeley Road to Lydney Town section from the September 1958 *Working Time Table*. NPC

BELOW: This lovely view of No. 1426 propelling the Lydney Town to Berkeley Road auto train into Severn Bridge on 10th July 1959 has been published several times before but it remains the best colour picture of the station seen to date. The bridge was 1,608 yards in length, with two larger spans of 327 feet over the main channel, plus nineteen smaller spans and the swing bridge over the canal. T.B. OWEN

K166

List of Signal Boxes—continued

Distance to Box			NAME OF BOX	TIMES DURING WHICH BOXES ARE OPEN					Whether provided with Switch
				Weekdays			Sundays		
				Opened at		Closed at	Opened at	Closed at	
M	C			Mondays	Other Days				
			BERKELEY ROAD AND LYDNEY TOWN						
—	—		Berkeley Road Junction	—	9.15 p.m.	Open continuously	9.30 a.m.A	4.25 p.m.A	No
—	—		Berkeley Road South Junction	—	—	4. 0 a.m. (Tues. to Sun.)	9.30 a.m.	4.25 p.m.	Yes
2	19¾		Berkeley Loop Junction	8.50 p.m.	—	10.45 p.m. or B	9.15 a.m.A	Until last train has cleared	No
2	24¾		Sharpness South	6.35 a.m.	—	8.50 p.m. Until last train has cleared	9.15 a.m.A	Until last train has cleared	No
1	8		Sharpness Swing Bridge	5.30 a.m.	4.40 a.m.	Until last train has cleared	8. 0 a.m.A	B	No
—	67⅜		Severn Bridge	6.30 a.m.	4.10 a.m.	B	9.15 a.m.A	B	No
2	30		Otter's Pool Junction	6. 0 a.m.	5.10 a.m.	B	9.15 a.m.A	B	No
—	41⅜		Lydney Engine Shed	6. 0 a.m.	5.10 a.m.	B	—	—	No
2	44		Lydney Town Station	6.45 a.m.	6.45 a.m.	B	—	—	No

A—During Engineers' occupation of Severn Tunnel only.

B—Until last train has cleared.

I.M.&S.&G.W
Severn&Wye Rly
MONTHLY RETURN
BERGN BRIDGE
Fare 11¼ P
OR CONDITIONS, SEE BACK

I.M.&S.&G.W
Severn&Wye Rly
MONTHLY
Severn Bridge to
LYDNEY TOWN
THIRD CLASS
Fare 11½d P
SEE BACK W.D

J166

J166

Gt. Western Ry. | Gt. Western Ry
Severn Bridge | Severn Bridge
TO
LYDNEY JN
THIRD CLASS
8d. Z Fare 8d. Z
Lydney Jn | Lydney Jn
FOR CONDITIONS SEE BACK C.L.

The view from the end of the Up platform in summer 1959. Note the check rails at the entrance to the stone viaduct to guide anything that derailed back onto the track and stop it from falling over the parapet. The siding which served the cattle dock on the left ran back from a second siding which was accessed from a point facing in the Sharpness direction; both were removed in 1956. MICHAEL HALE

21/2/60

SEVERN BRIDGE, Winter (Tunnel Maintenance) Season, 1960

All times herein are those (approximate or actual) at Lydney Jcn.

		5504 Fishguard Harbour - Paddington
	9.18	Cheltenham-Cardiff Diesel - (3) c 9.30
E	c10.8	Bristol-Cardiff Diesel (Chepstow) 8-car 8.10 2-way P
L	c10.18	Cardiff-Portsmouth (?) 626 (8) 625? 10.59 (Severn Bridge Tunnel) P
E	c10.58	Birmingham-Swansea Diesel 114 (9)
L	c11.5	Swansea-Birmingham Diesel - 1135 (C)
E	c11.8	Bristol-Cardiff Diesel 12.0 (C)
L	c11.30	Cardiff-Bristol Diesel 11.49 (Q) P
L	c11.55	Fishguard Harbour-Paddington 5077 029 (5) 12.23 P
E	c1.12	Paddington-Swansea (10) (1) 1.29 P
L	1.16	Swansea-Gloucester Diesel-(2) 1.46
L	c1.30	Cardiff-Bristol Diesel 5379 ? k.cσ (8) 1.57 P
E	1.48	Gloucester-Cardiff Diesel-(3+1) 2.51
E	c2.3	Bristol-Cardiff Diesel (Chepstow) (U-1) 2.13 P
L	c2.45	Carmarthen-Paddington × 7025 046 (6) 2.11 P
L	c2.48	Cardiff-Plymouth × 7322 (7) 2.4 1642 on Ballast P
L	c3.32	Cardiff-Bristol Diesel (2) 3.31 (Severn Bridge Tunnel) P
E	c4.6	Bristol-Cardiff Diesel→(6) 4.7 Mydney Jcn P
E	c4.15	Paddington-Carmarthen-(8) 4.31
	4.47	Cardiff-Cheltenham Diesel- (3) 4.47

Arrangements:-

Cheltenham (St. James)	Dep	8.30
Lydney Junction	Arr	9.18
Lydney Junction	Dep	4.47
Cheltenham (St. James)	Arr	6.5

SEVERN BRIDGE TUNNEL
506 YARDS

ABOVE: The typewritten schedule (with handwritten actual times and locomotive details added presumably by the Severn Bridge signalman) for winter diversions on 2nd February 1960, away from the Severn Tunnel and over the bridge, which shows how useful it could be. Note that no less than five 'Castle's appear to have crossed that day: No. 7025 *Sudeley Castle*, No. 5004 *Llanstephan Castle*, No. 5077 *Fairey Battle*, No. 7007 *Great Western* and No. 7009 *Athelney Castle*, and there were twelve DMU workings. IAN POPE COLLECTION

RIGHT: Looking east from the station again in 1959, showing the catch point on the Down line and its attendant sign. NPC

Disaster and Demolition

On the night of 25th October 1960, with a thick fog engulfing the river around Berkeley Power Station (then under construction), two tanker barges collided whilst attempting to enter Sharpness Docks. The two vessels were the *Arkendale H*, skippered by the experienced George Thompson, and the *Wastdale H*, whose captain, James Dew, had plenty of time in the job but who was only on his third day on the river. As with getting into the narrow harbour entrance at Lydney, the technique at Sharpness was to get upstream of the piers near the top of a rising tide and then to drive in against the flow, which gave steerage. Both barges were fully laden, the *Wastdale H* with 351 tons of petroleum and the *Arkendale H* with 296 tons of fuel oil. The Severn was still a busy waterway at this period and they were not the only craft on the river. Despite it being 10 o'clock at night, the tides of the Severn dictated when vessels sailed and there were fourteen other boats enveloped in this fog.

The collision itself was not a major one and did little damage to either vessel. However, the two craft seem to have become locked together, possibly as a result of a fierce current coming round the

RIGHT: Locomotives permitted to cross the bridge, as given in the *Working Time Table*, September 1955. The LMR list is detailed but it is doubtful if any of these types ever ventured over the bridge. NPC

BELOW RIGHT: In the September 1958 *Working Time Table*, the LMR list had been much simplified and BR Standard types were also now included. NPC

K128   ENGINE RESTRICTIONS—continued
THE SEVERN BRIDGE

The following engines only are permitted to pass over the Severn Bridge.

Western Region Engines.

Yellow and Uncoloured Groups.
Class 4300 (2-6-0) Tender (Blue Group). Subject to the strict observance of all Service Restrictions.

London, Midland Region Engines.

Class 1P (2-4-2) Tank (L.N.W. 5-ft. 6-in.).
Class 2P (2-4-2) Tank (Standard).
Class 2F (0-6-2) Tank (L.N.W., S.T.C.).
Class 2F (2-6-0) Tender (Standard).
Class 2F (0-6-0) Tender (L.N.W.).
Class 2F (0-6-0) Tender (L.N.W. 18-in.).
Class 2F (0-6-0) Tender (Midland) bearing numbers 58115 to 58228 and 22900.
Trains running over the Severn Bridge must not be worked by more than one engine in front. Two engines coupled together must not in any circumstances be run over the bridge.

The two 312ft spans viewed from below, as a goods train rumbles over towards Lydney on 10th July 1959. The two barges collided with the fourth pier along in this view; if they had collided with one of the double piers over the main channel, which were further protected by wooden pontoons, the likelihood is that the bridge would not have come down. T.B. OWEN

end of the old Sharpness dock entrance, which had the effect of slowly spinning the two barges across into the main tide. Dew, in particular, seems not to have known how to get out of this. A Marine Safety Division report after the event concluded that if the *Wastdale H* had gone full astern and the *Arkendale H* had gone full ahead on port helm, the two vessels could have disengaged and stood a chance of regaining control. Thompson did indeed

THE SEVERN BRIDGE

The following engines only are permitted to pass over the Severn Bridge:—

B.R. Standard Engines.
Class 4 (4-6-0) 75XXX } with light tender.
Class 4 (2-6-0) 76XXX }

Western Region Engines.
Yellow and uncoloured Groups.
Class 4300 (2-6-0) tender. (Blue Group.) Subject to the strict observance of all Service Restrictions.

London, Midland Region Engines.
Class 2. (2-6-2) tank (Standard).
Class 2. (2-6-0) tender (Standard).
Class 2F. (0-6-0) tender (Midland) bearing numbers 58115 to 58228.
Trains running over the Severn Bridge must not be worked by more than one engine in front. Two engines coupled together must not in any circumstances be run over the bridge.
In the event of the failure of an engine at either end of the bridge and it is necessary for such engine to be taken to the opposite end, or if an engine fails on the bridge, arrangements must be made for the engine to be worked specially, and 4 wagons must be placed between the assisting engine and the disabled engine. A competent man, must, in all cases, ride upon the disabled engine.

go full ahead port with his craft but Dew went full ahead starboard on *Wastdale H*, which was not sufficient for the forces holding the two vessels together to relent. Dew's inexperience on the Severn was to be costly. With the tide still flowing upstream at a fast rate, the two out of control vessels were now swept towards the bridge. The *Wastdale H* hit first, broadside on and turned over, to end up trapped beneath the *Arkendale H*. Almost immediately, the pier they had struck, No. 17, fell over, bringing two spans down on top of them. This was immediately followed by an explosion, probably caused by sparks generated by the falling ironwork, and with petrol and fuel oil spilling out of both barges, the river became a mass of flames.

A few minutes before the disaster occurred, the last train of the night, the 21.45pm Lydney to Stoke Gifford goods, had safely crossed over the bridge. Up at Severn Bridge station, Inspector T. Francis, having watched its passage, at 10.30pm collected the keys for the night occupation of the bridge by the workmen engaged in the strengthening work. As he walked along the Up platform, he saw the explosion as flames shot into the air, closely followed by its sound. He ran forward

to find that two of the spans were down and the barges burning fiercely in the river, so quickly made his way back to the signal box to phone the emergency services. There was little else he could do; the crews on the barges had to fend for themselves in the treacherous waters below.

Captain Thompson, despite being knocked out for a time, managed to get off his vessel. Having put on a lifejacket, he was swept three miles upstream before being deposited, alive, on the river bank. Captain Dew also survived, having first cajoled two of Thompson's crew into the water wearing life belts. Both were non swimmers and had ignored Thompson's instructions to get off the vessel, despite being told it was their only chance. One, engineer Jack Cooper, was immediately swept round the stern of the *Arkendale H* where he was caught by the still rotating propeller. Despite being severely injured by it, this probably saved his life, although he was to endure several more hours of terror before being rescued. The other, mate Percy Simmonds aged 34, was drowned. Also lost from the *Arkendale H* was second engineer Robert Niblett, aged 25. One act of bravery remembered from that night concerned two men who set out in a rowing boat from the Sharpness side

BRITISH TRANSPORT COMMISSION
British Railways (Western Region)

PASSENGER TRAIN ALTERATIONS
LYDNEY TOWN AND BERKELEY ROAD.

Consequent upon damage to the Severn Bridge, commencing forthwith and week-day until further notice, the following services will apply:-

SHARPNESS TO BERKELEY ROAD.

7.20am	7.55am	11.05am	1.20pm S.X.
1.25pm S.O.	4.15pm S.O.	4.40pm S.X.	5.59pm.

BERKELEY ROAD TO SHARPNESS.

8.22am	11.52am	1.40pm S.X.	2.10pm S.O.
4.50pm S.O.	5.10pm S.X.	6.28pm.	

S.X. Saturdays excepted.
S.O. Saturdays only.

The above trains will call at Berkeley. All other services between Berkeley Road and Lydney Town will be suspended.

An additional train will leave Lydney at 7.0am calling at Newnham, arrive Gloucester (Central) 7.30am for passengers to connect with the 7.42am train Gloucester (Eastgate) to Berkeley Road (Sharpness) etc.

Paddington Station.
October 1960.

J.R. HAMMOND,
General Manager.

BRITISH RAILWAYS

PASSENGER TRAIN ALTERATIONS

SUNDAYS

13th NOVEMBER until 5th MARCH, 1961
INCLUSIVE

(Except 18th & 25th December, 1960 & 1st January, 1961, when the advertised service via Severn Tunnel will apply)

Owing to

DAMAGE TO THE SEVERN BRIDGE

CERTAIN PASSENGER TRAINS

from

BRISTOL TO CARDIFF and

from

CARDIFF TO BRISTOL, PORTSMOUTH and SOUTHSEA and PLYMOUTH

shewn overleaf will run via an alternative route at amended times

NOVEMBER, 1960

AMENDED TIMES AND CONSEQUENT ALTERATIONS
BRISTOL, NEWPORT AND CARDIFF

9.0 am BRISTOL (Temple Meads) TO CARDIFF GENERAL
Runs as shewn in Time Table to Filton Jn., depart 9.20 am, Chepstow 10.49, Severn Tunnel Jn. arrive 11.0, depart 11.2, Newport arrive 11.14, depart 11.18A and arrives Cardiff General 11.34 am.
A—An additional train leaves Newport 10.49 am and arrives Cardiff General 11.5 am.

11.0 am BRISTOL (Temple Meads) TO CARDIFF GENERAL
Runs as shewn in Time Table to Filton Jn., depart 11.16 am, Severn Tunnel Jn. arrive 12.55, depart 12.57, Newport arrive 1.12, depart 1.16 and arrives Cardiff General 1.32 pm.

1.0 pm BRISTOL (Temple Meads) TO CARDIFF GENERAL
Runs as shewn in Time Table to Stapleton Road, depart 1.8 pm, Chepstow 2.45, Severn Tunnel Jn. arrive 2.57, depart 2.59, Newport arrive 3.12, depart 3.16 and arrives Cardiff 3.34 pm.

3.0 pm BRISTOL (Temple Meads) TO CARDIFF GENERAL
Runs as shewn in Time Table to Stapleton Road, depart 3.9 pm, Severn Tunnel Jn. arrive 4.50, depart 4.51, Newport arrive 5.7, depart 5.12 and arrives Cardiff General 5.35 pm.

CARDIFF TO BRISTOL, PORTSMOUTH & SOUTHSEA AND PLYMOUTH

8.10 am CARDIFF GENERAL TO BRISTOL (Temple Meads)
Runs as shewn in Time Table to Chepstow, depart 9.0 am, Filton Jn. 10.29, Stapleton Road 10.35, Lawrence Hill 10.38 and arrives Bristol (Temple Meads) 10.45 am.

9.10 am CARDIFF GENERAL TO PORTSMOUTH & SOUTHSEA
Runs as shewn in Time Table to Severn Tunnel Jn., depart 9.52 am, Stapleton Road 11.47, Bath Spa arrive 12.14 pm, depart 12.18, Trowbridge arrive 12.41, depart 12.44, Westbury arrive 12.52, depart 12.59, Warminster arrive 1.9, depart 1.12, Salisbury arrive 1.38, depart 1.48, Southampton Central arrive 2.29, depart 2.34, Fareham arrive 2.58, depart 3.0, Cosham arrive 3.9, depart 3.10, Fratton arrive 3.18, depart 3.19, and arrives Portsmouth & Southsea 3.22 pm.

12.50 pm WESTBURY TO WEYMOUTH
Leaves Westbury 1.0 pm and run 10 minutes later than shewn in Time Table to Yeovil (Pen Mill) arrive 1.58, depart 2.0, and runs 6 minutes later to Maiden Newton arrive 2.33, depart 2.34 pm, thence as advertised.

10.30 am CARDIFF GENERAL TO BRISTOL (Temple Meads)
Runs as shewn in Time Table to Severn Tunnel Jn., depart 11.6 am, Stapleton Road 12.54 pm, Lawrence Hill 12.58 and arrives Bristol (Temple Meads) 1.4 pm.

12.30 pm CARDIFF GENERAL TO BRISTOL (Temple Meads)
Runs as shewn in Time Table to Severn Tunnel Jn., depart 1.6 pm, Stapleton Road 2.46 and arrives Bristol (Temple Meads) 2.55 pm.

1.45 pm CARDIFF GENERAL TO PLYMOUTH
Runs as shewn in Time Table to Chepstow, depart 2.40 pm, Stapleton Road 4.21, Bristol (Temple Meads) arrive 4.29, depart 4.40, Bridgwater 5.27, Taunton arrive 5.49, depart 5.54, Exeter (St. David's) arrive 6.32, depart 6.38, Dawlish 6.54, Teignmouth 7.2, Newton Abbot arrive 7.12, depart 7.20, Totnes 7.39 and arrives Plymouth 8.24 pm.

2.30 pm CARDIFF GENERAL TO BRISTOL (Temple Meads)
Runs as shewn in Time Table to Severn Tunnel Jn., depart 3.6 pm, Stapleton Road 4.46 and arrives Bristol (Temple Meads) 4.54 pm.

NOTE
Except where otherwise shewn, passengers arriving too late for normal advertised connecting services will travel by the first available train shewn in the Time Tables dated "12th September, 1960, to 11th June, 1961 (or until further notice)" and Supplement thereto.

BERKELEY ROAD AND LYDNEY TOWN
The advertised weekday service is suspended. For details of the emergency service see local announcements.

---

to search for survivors – Charlie Henderson, on his first day at work at Berkeley Power Station, and Tommy Carter, skipper of one of the other tankers moored in the river. They had to row around burning debris and oil in the water but it was they who pulled Jack Cooper to safety.

The *Wastdale H* likewise had a crew of four, of whom only Captain Dew survived, found three hours later having also been carried upstream by the tide; engineer Alex Bullock aged 40, mate Bert Dudfield aged 46 and deckhand Malcolm Hart aged 17 all perished. The men who died were all from the Gloucester area and the bodies of all five were found over the next couple of days. The two barges came to rest on the Ridge sandbank, just above the bridge. They were fairly inaccessible there, so explosives were used to blast them open five days later, in order that they would settle in the sand and not float off and cause further damage elsewhere. Fused together in their final deadly embrace by the extreme heat, their remains can still be seen at low tide today. Ironically, when this occurs the *Wastdale H* looks over at the place of its birth, having been built at Sharpness Shipyard in 1951.

The disaster happened on a Tuesday night and numerous accounts state that the workmen on the bridge would have been out there sooner but for listening to a boxing match on the radio, between Henry Cooper and a Karl Muller, whilst ensconced in Severn Bridge signal box. In fact no such boxer exists, although Cooper did fight Karl Mildenberger in 1968. Cooper's boxing career is a matter of common public record and he did not fight on that date. The boxing match that took place on the night of 25th October 1960 was between Alphonse Halimi of France and Freddie Gilroy of Northern Ireland, fighting for the World Bantamweight title (Howard Winstone of Wales and Jean Renard of Belgium were on the undercard) and the *Radio Times* for that week lists the BBC broadcast as going out from 9.15 to 10.30, so it may well be that the men's lives were saved by listening to it.

Since 1954, the bridge had also carried the gas main over from Sharpness, so 6,000 households in the Forest of Dean awoke to cold

Typewritten passenger train alterations notice issued immediately after the bridge was damaged, TOP LEFT, and front and reverse of a printed notice of Sunday trains to and from Cardiff, diverted away from the Severn Tunnel and which would now have to travel via Gloucester. BOTH IAN POPE COLLECTION

breakfasts on the morning of 26th October. Bottled gas and appropriate appliances were delivered to schools and hospitals within two days, and to 3,000 other premises over the next nine days. A polyurethene pipe was strung across the gap in the bridge as a temporary repair and everyone had a gas supply by 12th November. Meanwhile, work was quickly put in hand laying in a new gas main from Gloucester. Further hardship was caused for Sharpness schoolchildren attending Lydney Grammar School, who now faced an hour-long train journey via Gloucester instead of the short hop across the river. After some deliberation, it was decided that students on their GCE courses would continue but those who had not yet started would transfer to schools on the Sharpness side. To accommodate this, the Sharpness to Lydney school trains continued to run via Gloucester until summer 1962, when all these students had completed their exams. A photograph of one of these trains at Gloucester can be found in Volume 1. The severing of the link proved quite an

TOP: Photographed from the top of the cutting leading to the tunnel, No. 1664 is seen arriving at Severn Bridge with the Severn Boar II trip. With all the points out of use, the tour was propelled up from Lydney so the engine could lead on the way back down. T.B. OWEN

ABOVE: A poor quality but extremely rare view taken from the SLS railtour as it passed by on 13th May 1961, which provides just a glimpse of the twin hulled floating crane *Tweedledum & Tweedledee*. It was only here for a month or so and this is the first known picture of it. DAVID BICK/NPC

RIGHT: The Severn Boar II at the Up platform. Only the signal box was left of the buildings and it remained for decades afterwards, only finally being removed a few years ago by a man who intended to restore it. T.B. OWEN

RIGHT: The last train to call at Severn Bridge prepares to leave on 20th June 1964. Special permission was granted for the Severn Boar tours to run up to here, with the decision having been taken that the bridge was going to be demolished and the line closed. NPC

BELOW RIGHT: From 2nd January 1961, BR ran a new Lydney Junction (GW) to Sharpness (via Gloucester Central, Eastgate and Berkeley Road) passenger service, to replace that which had run over the bridge, as shown on this notice. IAN POPE COLLECTION

BELOW: Another poor quality view, of the remains of the station in March 1964, included because it shows the cutting leading to Severn Bridge Tunnel in the left background. The site is now heavily overgrown but the platforms still remain. NPC

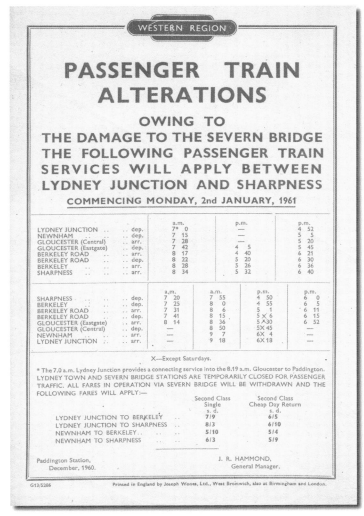

PASSENGER TRAIN ALTERATIONS

OWING TO THE DAMAGE TO THE SEVERN BRIDGE THE FOLLOWING PASSENGER TRAIN SERVICES WILL APPLY BETWEEN LYDNEY JUNCTION AND SHARPNESS

COMMENCING MONDAY, 2nd JANUARY, 1961

		a.m.	p.m.	p.m.
LYDNEY JUNCTION ..	.. dep.	7* 0	—	4 52
NEWNHAM ..	.. dep.	7 15	—	5 5
GLOUCESTER (Central)	.. arr.	7 28	—	5 20
GLOUCESTER (Eastgate)	.. dep.	7 42	4 5	5 45
BERKELEY ROAD ..	.. arr.	8 17	4 40	6 21
BERKELEY ROAD ..	.. dep.	8 22	5 20	6 30
BERKELEY ..	.. arr.	8 28	5 26	6 36
SHARPNESS ..	.. arr.	8 34	5 32	6 40

		a.m.	a.m.	p.m.	p.m.
SHARPNESS ..	.. dep.	7 20	7 55	4 50	6 0
BERKELEY ..	.. dep.	7 25	8 0	4 55	6 5
BERKELEY ROAD ..	.. arr.	7 31	8 6	5 1	6 11
BERKELEY ROAD ..	.. dep.	7 41	8 15	5 X 6	6 15
GLOUCESTER (Eastgate)	.. arr.	8 14	8 36	5 X 30	6 52
GLOUCESTER (Central)	.. dep.	—	8 50	5 X 45	—
NEWNHAM ..	.. arr.	—	9 7	6 X 4	—
LYDNEY JUNCTION ..	.. arr.	—	9 18	6 X 18	—

X—Except Saturdays.

* The 7.0 a.m. Lydney Junction provides a connecting service into the 8.19 a.m. Gloucester to Paddington. LYDNEY TOWN AND SEVERN BRIDGE STATIONS ARE TEMPORARILY CLOSED FOR PASSENGER TRAFFIC. ALL FARES IN OPERATION VIA SEVERN BRIDGE WILL BE WITHDRAWN AND THE FOLLOWING FARES WILL APPLY:—

	Second Class Single	Second Class Cheap Day Return
	s. d.	s. d.
LYDNEY JUNCTION TO BERKELEY ..	7/9	6/5
LYDNEY JUNCTION TO SHARPNESS ..	8/3	6/10
NEWNHAM TO BERKELEY.. ..	5/10	5/4
NEWNHAM TO SHARPNESS	6/3	5/9

Paddington Station, December, 1960.

J. R. HAMMOND, General Manager.

G13/5286 Printed in England by Joseph Wones, Ltd., West Bromwich, also at Birmingham and London.

emotional blow in other ways too, as many people from Sharpness came over to Lydney to shop or to work or to go out in the evening.

At first it was expected that the bridge would be repaired. A month after the disaster, BR published a sketch plan for a replacement span to fill the gap, supported by a central pier. However, as time passed the prospects of it being rebuilt receded. Whilst Pier 17 had been knocked down, Pier 16 had also been damaged and was listing, so required taking down and rebuilding too. The total cost of the repair work at this stage was estimated at £188,000 but the bridge now seemed to come under attack from the fates. Following an underwater survey in December 1961, a contract was awarded to erect a trestle under the bridge next to Pier 16. The contractors brought a twin hulled floating crane, *Tweedledum & Tweedledee*, down from Liverpool but, before it could get to work, the bridge was struck again in an echo of the first disaster. On 17th February 1962, the tanker *BP Explorer* capsized in the river whilst inbound to Sharpness, with a load of petroleum from Swansea for Gloucester and Worcester. At the subsequent Court of Inquiry, it was held that the vessel must have touched ground whilst crossing the river above Beachley and been forced over by the tide. The upturned ship floated past Lydney pier, where it was seen by a witness. However, having cleared the bridge on its way upstream, the vessel struck it when coming back with the ebbing tide, causing further damage estimated at close to £13,000. Tragically, all five of the crew were lost.

Two months later, on 14th April, *Tweedledum & Tweedledee*, the floating crane which the contractors had been using to erect the supporting trestle, broke from its mooring on a flood tide and drifted upstream. Despite the efforts of men aboard the MV *Magpie*, which

had set out from Sharpness to try and take the crane in tow, they were unsuccessful and the vessel drifted back downstream from Awre, to strike the underside of the bridge with its jib whilst also hitting Pier 20. *Tweedledum & Tweedledee* finally grounded near Lydney but had caused another £6,000 worth of damage to the bridge. Another blow came when BR was granted a mere £5,000 in compensation by the High

An interior detail view through the high girders of the 312ft spans towards Sharpness in July 1959. The gas main to the Forest of Dean is on the left and note, too, the pier number, 21, painted inside the cowling in the left foreground; the 7.56 date is believed to refer to the repainting of the bridge. T.B. OWEN

Court, which was nowhere near enough to fund the cost of repairs. By April 1962, these were being estimated at £300,000, although BR still maintained publicly that no decision had been taken and that they were still looking at the possibility of reconstruction.

Also now looming on the horizon was the Beeching report, *The Reshaping of British Railways*. Whilst this was not published until March 1963, the planning for it undoubtedly started at least a couple of years earlier. The railways lost £68 million in 1960, rising to £104 million in 1962, with the inevitable result that the Government of the day were looking for radical cuts in the network and how it was operated. The disaster could not have happened at a worse time for the bridge. Railways were rapidly becoming yesterday's news and the motor car, lorries and buses, as well as motorways, were the way forward. In 1961, construction had begun of a new Severn Bridge, a suspension bridge carrying the M4 into South Wales, which was opened in 1966.

The Sharpness-Lydney school trains were withdrawn at the end of the summer 1962 term and the Berkeley Loop was closed in January 1963. As this carried no regular passenger service, BR did not need to go through any formal closure procedure. Clearly, now, there was little prospect in high places for plans for the repair of the bridge being approved. Accordingly, BR began negotiations with the Central Electricity Generating Board in early 1963, for them to take on the bridge and use it as a transmission line. Perhaps realising what a liability it could be, the final nail in the bridge's coffin came when the CEGB pulled out of the deal in December of that year. Its fate was sealed; demolition was now the only prospect left.

It had been appreciated from the moment the bridge was damaged that demolishing it was by no means the easy option and would be extremely costly. The prospect of the Army using it as a demolition exercise was explored in 1965 but even they balked at all the difficulties

involved, so tenders were sent out to numerous demolition contractors. To give an idea of how difficult a task this was going to be, of the twenty-four firms invited to tender, only four were prepared to do so once the magnitude of the job had been explained and, in the event, none of those were successful. The job eventually went to the Nordman Construction Company of Gloucester, whose contract price for the work was £250,000. The contract stipulated that the bridge had to be removed down to river bed level, leaving no obstructions in the river. The thirteen-arch stone viaduct on the Lydney side also had to be raised to the ground, along with the swing span pier and abutments at the Sharpness end. In the event, these last two were not proceeded with, due to fears that the banks of the Gloucester & Sharpness Canal might be damaged in the process. They remain today as mute testimony to the bridge's existence.

Early in 1967, Nordman Construction announced via the press that demolition of the Severn Bridge was due to start later that year. However, the bridge was to prove as difficult to knock down as it had been to build. The company came up with a detailed plan of how it was to proceed and, at a cost of £1,050 per day, hired a large floating crane, the *Magnus II*, from Hamburg in Germany, which was brought over the North Sea, round the English Channel and up the Bristol Channel by tug. The crane was self propelling, with four motors, one at each corner, making it fully manoueverable. A team of sixty skilled steel erectors would be working on site and it was predicted that the work would take five months to complete. However, the Nordman Company was only six years old and their experience was in road construction, not demolition work of this magnitude. Further, for various reasons, instead of the spring 1965 commencement that had been planned, it was not until late August that work began; a whole summer of likely good weather had been lost.

This corresponding view is looking back towards Severn Bridge station. The rails were laid directly on to substantial timber baulks, which were supported on wooden blocks and braced about every 6 feet. The check rails ran right the way across the bridge. T.B. Owen

Nordmans biggest error was undoubtedly in hiring such an expensive piece of kit as *Magnus II* to work on a tidal river without fully understanding the possible consequences. They had hoped to complete the work for which it was required in nine days but, in the event, it took three weeks. *Magnus II* was scheduled to work round the clock on the twice daily tides but the company failed to maintain this. The method they employed was to lift out the individual spans and then use a wrecking ball to smash holes in the piers prior to pulling them over. Little of this went smoothly, whilst the contract called for the piers to be reduced to the level of the river bed, which this method did not achieve. It was also doubted that the crane could get close enough to the swing span to lift it out, as the jib needed to be near vertical when doing so. *Magnus II* began work on 23rd August and finished on 10th September, leaving for Hamburg the next day and Nordmans with a bill for £21,000. Twenty-one piers were still standing, three spans were still in place and the swing bridge also still remained. Ten of the lifted spans had been dumped on the foreshore on the Sharpness side, with the permission of the Severn River Authority, where they would be cut up, a plan to sell them for possible re-use in South America having come to nothing. In addition, the masonry approach arches had not been touched and the railway remained to be lifted.

A new plan was drawn up, with BR demanding in particular that the masonry arches on the Lydney side should be brought down by 31st December at the latest, as otherwise a planned series of closures of the Severn Tunnel between 1st January 1968 and Easter would be interfered with; it was intended to divert trains via Gloucester and BR did not want the blowing up of the viaduct, which straddled the main line at Purton, to cause any additional hold ups, although the irony of this being due to the demolition of what had been the diversionary route previously seems to have been lost on them. This

was sub-contracted to Swinnerton & Miller of Willenhall, Staffordshire, which was BR's choice not Nordmans. The inspection of the viaduct was completed on 11th December but from this it became clear that so many holes required to be drilled in the stonework to take the explosive charges that there was no chance of bringing it down before 31st December. BR were not impressed.

The blowing up of the viaduct was finally set for 10th March 1968 but all concerned did their best to keep it secret. The location was not ideal for large numbers of people to come and watch and it was likely to be dangerous. The actual blast occurred at around 7.30am but only brought down just over half of it, one of the contractors remarking that "*This is a stubborn old bridge*". Griffith Griffiths had built it well. Six arches remained standing although badly damaged and liable to fall at any moment. The main line was cleared of rubble and ready for traffic again by 10.00pm that night, a process that was partly facilitated by the ballast having been dragged away from the track prior to the blasting so as not to contaminate it and the rails protected with old sleepers. Another contractor, Devenish of Wells in Somerset, was brought in to complete the demolition. As the remaining arches were clear of the track, a second set of blasts took place between trains on 15th March but still one of the piers refused to fall; it later had to be pulled over using a winch.

BR now started pushing even harder for Nordmans to complete the contract but, in the first sign of financial problems, the company requested a £30,000 interim payment against work completed so far. This was outside the terms of the contract and BR refused. The news then emerged that the German owners of *Magnus II* had filed for non-payment of their bill, although Nordmans were counter-claiming, whilst Swinnerton & Miller had also not been paid; Nordmans claimed that they were BR's sub-contractor. Realising that the contract was in danger of failing, BR reluctantly agreed to the interim payment. The

ABOVE: Looking directly across the bridge from the end of the masonry approach viaduct on 12th September 1962. Note the gradient post on the left and also how the gas main was taken up on to the parapet. BILL POTTER/KRM

LEFT: This group of students were brought to see the bridge by their lecturer, John Strange, in February 1967. It was a timely last chance to see it; demolition began six months later. JOHN STRANGE/NPC

OPPOSITE PAGE TOP: No. 1 Pier and the bridge, viewed from the cabin on the swing bridge in July 1959. The pipework on the left is the Sharpness to the Forest of Dean gas main, which was brought under the canal and then up on to the bridge. T.B. OWEN

OPPOSITE PAGE INSET: Notes regarding engines on the bridge from the *General Appendix to the Working Time Table*, October 1960. NPC

OPPOSITE PAGE BOTTOM: No. 1426 rumbles under the cabin and over the swing section with a Berkeley Road to Lydney auto on 10th July 1959. T.B. OWEN

company now bought the old Beachley-Aust ferry *Severn King*, made redundant by the opening of the Severn Road Bridge, and converted it for use in the remaining work on the river. The ferry came equipped with a turntable, which had been used for directing cars into position around its deck, so a mobile crane was now used on it to assist in dismantling the remaining piers and spans. Cutting up of the spans on the river bank was also progressing, although was harder than anticipated, as it was discovered that the ironwork of the bridge had been fabricated in layers. Nothing seemed to want to go to plan.

In what, with hindsight, was clearly a last desperate attempt to rescue their investment in the contract, Nordmans put forward a plan to leave the undemolished portion of the bridge and use it as a stone unloading jetty, bringing craft laden with stone over from quarries on the River Wye. A grab crane would be used to unload it into waiting lorries and Nordmans would save the charges of using the Gloucester & Sharpness Canal. This was outside the terms of the demolition contract and the request was turned down. On 20th November 1968, Nordman Construction went into receivership.

An offer by Nordmans to continue the work under the receiver was stymied when the receiver put the company into liquidation. An offer by the father of Nordman's owner to take over the rest of the contract was also refused and BR decided to undertake the completion of the task themselves, although sub-contracting the destruction of the pier stumps to Swinnerton & Miller again. In January 1969, explosives were used to take down the three remaining spans, whilst work proceeded on removing the remains of the piers. Much of the scrap was removed using a crane positioned on the swing section. The *Severn King* was employed in this work but, on 4th July, at the top of a high tide it broke its bow mooring and swung by the stern on to one of the pier stumps. As the tide ebbed, the vessel was trapped on the pier, eventually coming to rest at an angle of 45 degrees. Local riverman Bill Hardy, who had assisted Nordmans when the *Magnus II* was on site, was brought in again to help with the recovery operation, which took place over the two days of 27th-29th July in appalling weather conditions. Holed amidships, *Severn King* was dumped on the bank near the entrance to Sharpness Docks. Beyond repair, the vessel's engines were removed for salvage

but it was to be over twenty years before the hull was finally cut up.

In September 1969, over two years after demolition had started, the remaining pier stumps were removed with explosives. All that now remained was the swing bridge and pier No. 1, built of stone and double the width of the bridge. It had been decided that the safest way to demolish the swing bridge span was to cut it up *in situ*, a bit at a time from each end so that it remained in balance, after first taking down the signal cabin on top, the engine house and removing the steam engines. This work was undertaken by Underwater Welders Ltd of Cardiff, ironically the company that Nordmans had wanted to use nearly two years earlier to drop the thirteen-arch viaduct on the Lydney side. To add further insult, this stage of the demolition took only a few weeks, Underwater Welders carrying out the operation with a smoothness that belied all the previous problems. The work was completed on 25th January 1970. The final task was the demolition of pier one. Drilling the masonry for the explosive charges commenced in March and, on 13th May, the pier was brought down, the final act in the dismantling of the Severn Bridge. It had taken just under three years and caused the demise of the company contracted to demolish it. Following the demolition of Lydbrook Viaduct in 1965, G.W. Keelings two great engineering masterpieces had now gone.

All that remains to mark its existence is the circular stone pier which carried the swing bridge and the attendant masonry abutment on the Sharpness side of the canal. Whilst they are fitting monuments, with the passage of time the destruction of the Severn Bridge now looks very much like one of those hugely short-sighted decisions of the 1960s which would not be taken today. The removal of such a valuable piece

WORKING OF ENGINES OVER THE SEVERN BRIDGE

Trains running over the Severn Bridge must not be worked by more than one engine in front. Two engines coupled together must not, under any circumstances, be run over the Bridge.

In the event of the failure of an engine at either end of the Bridge and it is necessary for such engine to be taken to the opposite end, or if an engine fails on the Bridge, arrangements must be made for the engine to be worked specially, and four wagons must be placed between the assisting engine and the disabled engine. A competent man must in all cases ride upon the disabled engine.

of infrastructure, which provided an important link over a difficult section of river, has been regretted ever since and there are regular calls to reinstate it. A proposal for a new bridge was put forward by Lydney Town Council as a Millenium project but failed to get off the ground, as support was not sought in the right places. At the time of writing, in 2015, there is a proposal for a hovercraft link between the docks at Lydney and Sharpness. The £6 million scheme would see a £3.5 million hovercraft operating from new transport hubs at each end, crossing the river in ten minutes and carrying up to fifty passengers each time. The impetus behind the project has been generated by the building of a new science and technology campus at Berkeley by South

Gloucestershire & Stroud College. Meanwhile, the idea of a new bridge has been resurrected by the MP for Stroud, as part of wide ranging proposals for economic regeneration in South Gloucestershire but if £6 million buys you a hovercraft service, what price a new bridge?

British Railways was caught between the proverbial rock and a hard place in the early 1960s and, across the country, considerably more was lost that just the Severn Railway Bridge, so the finger of blame should not be pointed too accusingly in their direction for its loss. Rather we should examine the roles of those in power, too short-sighted to see more than five minutes into the future and damn them for so carelessly throwing away the legacy that our Victorian ancestors bequeathed to

us. Although another road bridge, the Second Severn Crossing, opened in 1996 (carrying a new section of the M4, the older route over the Severn Road Bridge being redesignated as the M48), there is still a thirty mile gap between Gloucester and Chepstow where the river cannot be crossed. As you study the pictures that accompany this, despair at the foolishness that allowed such a solid and well built asset as the Severn Railway Bridge to be destroyed.

LEFT: A late afternoon view from the swing span cabin, with the bridge reflected on the water below. The signal visible above and to the left of the carriages indicates that this is a Lydney Town to Berkeley Road auto coming across. T.B. OWEN

BELOW: The swing section from just inside the first river span, showing the change in width from double track to single. T.B. OWEN

looking along the length of the bridge from the swing section cabin in July 1959; the shoreline on the far side is level, so the apparent lean on the bridge to the right is an optical illusion. An ex-GWR 'Mogul' heads south along the main line with a Gloucester to Cardiff 'stopper'. Note the gas main could not be taken over the swing section, so burrows down through the deck of the last span to connect with the pipework seen in the picture on page 301. Trevor Owen took these pictures during a group visit to the Severn Bridge, during which participants were apparently allowed to roam all over it but nothing has so far been discovered about who organised it. T.B. OWEN

Looking north along the canal from the swing section cabin, with some of the vessels hulked on the river bank at Purton visible in the left middle distance. T.B. OWEN

OPPOSITE PAGE TOP: The first of three views no longer possible today, except by using a radio controlled drone. This is looking north up the River Severn. The hamlet of Purton is in the centre, where river and canal turn to the right; confusingly, there is a Purton on each side of the Severn at this point. In the left distance is the Awre peninsula. T.B. OWEN

RIGHT: Maximum speeds on the S&W&SBR section of BR(WR), from the *Working Time Table*, September 1955, including the note that trains were not to cross the iron portion of the Severn Bridge in less than three minutes. NPC

BERKELEY ROAD, LYDNEY TOWN AND SPEECH HOUSE ROAD—COLEFORD BRANCH
(Severn and Wye Line)

Berkeley Road Junction	Junction from Double to Single Line ..	15
Berkeley Road to Sharpness	All Up and Down Trains	40
Sharpness—Over the Junction at South Signal Box ..	All Up and Down Trains	20
Sharpness—Goods Yard and Station Box ..	Drivers of Up Goods trains approaching Station Box must reduce speed to 4 miles per hour when passing through goods yard and must exercise great care when working over goods line, and be prepared to stop at any point.	4
Sharpness	South Docks Junction to and from Passenger Station	20
Sharpness	North Dock Branch	6
Severn Bridge	No engine or train must cross the iron portion of the Severn Bridge in less than 3 minutes. Drivers to keep a sharp look-out when passing over Sharpness South Junction	
Severn Bridge to Otters Pool Junction ..	All Up and Down Trains	15
Lydney Junction	Otters Pool Junction .. .. .. Lydney Junction Station	25
	Otters Pool Junction .. .. .. South Wales Main Line	10
Lydney Town to Tufts Junction	All Up and Down Trains	10
Coleford Branch	Coleford Junction .. .. .. Coleford (Whitecliff) ..	20
Coleford Branch	Coleford (Whitecliff) .. .. .. Coleford Junction	15
Parkend, 12m. 20ch. to 12m. 60ch. ..	All Up and Down Trains	10§
Coleford Junction	Double to Single Line	10
Speech House Road :		15
South End, 14m. 57ch. to 14m. 65ch. ..	All Up and Down Trains	15
North End, 14m. 70ch. to 14m. 77ch. ..	All Up and Down Trains	15

The speed of trains between **Tufts Junction** and **Speech House Road** must not exceed 25 m.p.h. and must be further restricted to lower speeds as shewn.
§—For Passenger trains between Coleford and Coleford Junction, a maximum speed of 15 m.p.h. applies.

The swing section in its normal position, ready for trains to cross, in July 1959. It was swung open when vessels needed to pass through on the canal. T.B. OWEN

A selection of detail views of the Severn Bridge swing span and operating gear all taken by Trevor Owen on 10th July 1959. The first picture, ABOVE LEFT, shows the sets of gears at cabin and base level, as well as the two connecting shafts between them, along with the wheels on which the span rested and rotated on top of the masonry tower. The second view, ABOVE RIGHT, is a close up of the gears at the top, at cabin level.

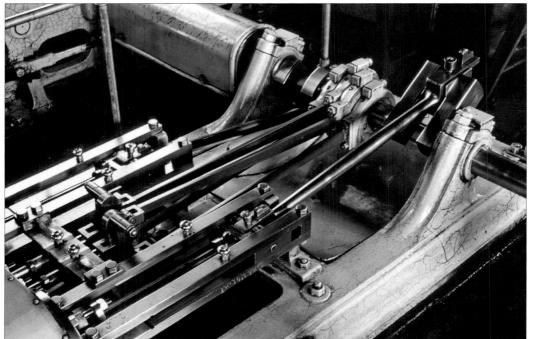

ABOVE: A close up of one of the two horizontal steam engines; their use was alternated, with the one not working acting as a reserve, so a failure would not render the bridge stuck in one position. NPC

OPPOSITE PAGE TOP LEFT: Looking from the first of the iron spans, with members of the visiting party watching the swing bridge in operation. Above right is the Home signal for the swing span.

OPPOSITE PAGE TOP RIGHT: A deck level view of the swing section in place for a vessel to pass through on the canal below. The signal on top of the span was for ships not rail traffic.

OPPOSITE PAGE BOTTOM: One of the swing bridge horizontal steam engines, showing the connecting rods driving a crank shaft, which in turn operated the gear wheels outside. These rotated the outside connecting shafts, which then turned the gear wheels at the base that caused the span to swing. The Hamiltons Windsor Iron Company of Birkenhead, the main contractors for the construction of the bridge, supplied and erected all of the ironwork for it, including the steam engines. Operation of the swing bridge required an engineman and a signalman but at quiet times this was not practical, so each had to be fully competent in the duties of the other, in order to be able carry out single man working when required. ALL T.B. OWEN

A lovely view showing almost the full extent of the bridge in July 1959, from the Sharpness side of the river. Although from less than 100 yards away, the bridge looks frail and graceful and has nothing of the solidity it seemed to display in the close ups of the spans; little wonder than Keeling called it his 'Iron String'. T.B. OWEN

RIGHT: A close-up of the top of Pier No. 19, the first of the double piers (counting from the Sharpness side), with a 174ft span on the left and one of the two 312ft spans on the right. The two outer double piers (No's 19 and 21) displayed white navigation lights either side, lit from dusk until dawn, one of which is clearly seen here. The centre double pier, No. 20, displayed red lights and these had all been converted from oil burning to electric in 1959. R.H. MARROWS

BELOW: After the accident, showing the gap left by the loss of Pier No. 17 and the two spans. Clearly visible is the support trestling put in place as a result of Pier No. 16 being knocked out of alignment. Erected by Peter Lind & Co. in February 1961, it was considered at the time to be stage one of rebuilding the bridge. T.B. OWEN

RIGHT: The gap, looking towards Sharpness from the end of span eighteen. Surprisingly, the Lydney end of the bridge was not fenced off for some time afterwards, so it was still possible to venture out onto the iron spans, although this view may have been taken on an officially organised visit. T.B. OWEN

BELOW: A view south in 1967, taken from the strip of land between the river and the canal, looking towards Sharpness Docks in the background. Note the geese taking off above the swing span. IAN POPE COLLECTION

BOTTOM: Looking north towards the swing bridge, which is seen in the open position again in 1967. The footpath alongside the canal is today promoted as the Severn Way. The gas main connections by Pier No. 1 taking the pipe underground are just in view. IAN POPE COLLECTION

ABOVE: The swing span from the end of the short two-arch masonry approach viaduct on the Sharpness side, on 5th August 1964. Note that this viaduct was built to double track width. BILL POTTER/KRM

LEFT: The decision to construct the swing span and approach viaduct to double track width was taken in February 1877. It was estimated that it would cost up to £10,000 to add this to the contract and the proposal formed part of an additional powers Bill applied for later that year. The worry seems to have been the blockages to traffic on the canal that would have occurred if the bridge required widening at a later date but it looks an odd decision now, given that the rest of the bridge and the thirteen masonry arches at the Lydney end were all built for single track. This view along the deck of the swing span was taken in January 1967. JOHN STRANGE/NPC

BELOW: Two of the three locking keys kept in the cabin, which were provided to lock the clutch gear wheel when maintenance was required to be carried out on the swing span mechanism, thus preventing the bridge from being moved. To be used only on the signalman's authority, the removal of one from its case had also to be reported to the Sharpness stationmaster and the Bridge Inspector. JOHN STRANGE/NPC

RIGHT: The cabin from the deck of the swing span in January 1967, showing the Sharpness Swing Bridge Signal Box nameplate bolted to the supporting girder. As the picture bottom left on the previous page shows, there was a second plate on the other side, which was hidden somewhat by a ledge above it. Both had been painted the same grey colour as the girders by the bridge painters, rather than being picked out as white letters on a black background as was usually done with signal box nameplates by the GWR and their Western Region successors. Both plates still survive, one in the NRM collection at York, whilst the other sold at a railwayana auction in May 2013 for £4,200, where it was described in '*as removed condition*' but had in fact been repainted black and white, which as these pictures show, must have been carried out after removal. JOHN STRANGE/NPC

LEFT AND BELOW: Two views of the semaphore signal positioned on the swing span to give an indication to vessels wishing to pass on the canal. The bridge was required to be swung for any vessel whose masts were higher than the masonry pier supporting the swing span. Although these pictures were taken when the span was open, this was the normal position for the semaphore arm. Any approaching vessel had to give three blasts on the ship's hooter at least 400 yards before the bridge. The signalman would only lower the arm if it was safe to open the bridge, that is if no train was due to cross. On lowering the arm, swinging of the span commenced, with the signalman giving three blasts on a whistle mounted on top of the cabin once it was fully open and safe to pass. At night, red and green lights provided these indications instead, whilst white lights at each end of the span showed that it was open. The signalman also had to keep a watch for craft that could not give an audible warning of their approach. JOHN STRANGE/NPC

Looking west along the expanse of the bridge from the swing section cabin in January 1967. Such was its slender nature that it apparently had a disconcerting tendency to sway perceptibly in strong winds. On the far right shore is the hamlet and former harbour inlet of Purton, to which the Purton Steam Carriage Road of 1830 was bound. The incline to the harbour would have come down the slope on the right edge of the picture. JOHN STRANGE/NPC

ABOVE: The overgrown rails on the approach to the bridge from Sharpness. Note the lever for locking the span in position on the left and the pw hut for the maintenance crew covering the bridge. JOHN STRANGE/NPC

ABOVE RIGHT: A similar view but with a building featuring on the left, the purpose of which is currently unknown. It is not shown on an OS map of 1902 but is there on the 1921 survey. Its position suggests it was provided for observation purposes but any further information would be welcome. It is no longer there today. JOHN STRANGE/NPC

RIGHT: The approach to the bridge from inside the cutting. The signal carried the Home arm for the bridge and the Distant for Severn Bridge station. TREVOR OWEN

BELOW: A view of the cutting curving round to Sharpness station, looking through the broken spectacle glass of the Distant signal in March 1964. DAVID BICK

LEFT: The British Waterways notice on the Sharpness Docks side of the swing span, stating that approaching vessels were required to give three long blasts to warn the signalman of their approach. JOHN STRANGE/NPC

BELOW: The attractive Dutch motor coaster *Tasmanie*, registered at Delfzijl, passing through the swing section in October 1964, bound for Gloucester with a cargo of timber. Powered by a vertical 6-cylinder 396hp engine, with an overall length of 169ft and built by Bodewes Volharding of Foxhol in 1956, the ship traded around northern Europe calling regularly at British ports. In 1970, the vessel was re-registered in the Netherlands Antillies and was then taken on by the Irish company Vartry Shipping of Dublin in 1974. Sold to new Lebanese owners in 1977, she was renamed *Abou El Molouk*. A further move to Greek owners in 1980 brought another name change, to *Vasilas V*, then to *Syra II* in 1984 and finally *Hermes* in 1991. She sank in Piraeus Harbour whilst loading in 1994 but was raised and carried on trading until circa 2005, when her status was changed to '*Continued Existence In Doubt*'. DEREK CHAPLIN

Reflecting the canal's main purpose today, a small pleasure cruiser heads north on 5th August 1967, under the watchful gaze of the photographer's wife Joan. Commercial traffic on the canal is now virtually non-existent, the last regular cargoes being petroleum to Quedgeley (ceased 1985) and the grain traffic to Healing's Mill at Tewkesbury, which had gone over to road transport in the mid 1980s but which enjoyed a brief revival between 1993 and 1998. Note the slight widening in the canal bank that was required to accommodate the pier holding the swing bridge. BILL POTTER/KRM

Bill made a second visit a few weeks later, on 13th September, to record the disappearing bridge, during which he photographed the diminutive and historic coaster *Kyles* heading towards Sharpness Docks. Built on the Clyde by John Fullerton & Co. of Paisley and launched on 12th March 1872, her first owner used her as a tender for fishing fleets, bringing the catch from trawlers back to port. She then moved into general cargo carrying, her registry being changed from Glasgow to Hull in 1900. In 1921, she was converted for use as a sand dredger in the Bristol Channel. Out of service by the outbreak of war in 1939, she was laid up on the Glamorganshire Canal in Cardiff but was sold to salvage contractor, ship owner and repairer Ivor P. Langford of Gloucester in 1944. He removed the sand dredging equipment, re-registered her at Gloucester and returned her to cargo carrying. She was converted from steam to diesel in 1953 and was converted for use as a sludge tanker in 1960, dumping industrial waste in the Bristol Channel, in which role she is seen here heading out fully laden and low in the water. She then became a storage hulk but, on retirement in 1974, the Langford family wanted to see her preserved; she had been a favourite of Ivor Langford, who had resisted the urge to rename her out of respect for her long history under the one name. She was bought by Captain Peter Herbert, a Cornishman and noted sailor and sail boat owner, who traded with her around the Bude area for a few years. She was finally sold by Peter to the embryonic Scottish Maritime Museum (her 24th owner) in 1984 who, 112 years after she had been built, re-registered her in Glasgow. *Kyles* was fully restored in the late 1990s, taking her appearance back to how she had looked when first converted to diesel power in 1953. Based at the SMM's Irvine Harbour site, she is now on the National Historic Ships Committee's 'Designated Vessels' list and is the oldest Clyde-built ship still afloat, although it is only her iron and steel hull that is still (in large part) in original condition. BILL POTTER/KRM

A close-up study of the masonry Pier No. 1, taken from the canal path on 5th August 1967, shortly before the floating crane arrived to begin dismantling the spans. This was the last part of the bridge to be demolished, brought down by explosives on 13th May 1970. BILL POTTER/KRM

The underside of the swing span, showing its construction. Access to the cabin was via an internal staircase from a doorway facing onto the canal. The pier had two windows, one facing down the canal and one across the river, providing natural light to the inside but they were blocked off in later years. BILL POTTER/KRM

The swing span was always turned in an anti-clockwise direction, although it was apparently not equipped with a locking mechanism to prevent it being swung the opposite way. This 1964 view shows the signal in the lowered position, the swing span still being operational at this time. It would appear that it was only taken out of use when the bridge was officially closed and demolition decided upon, after which it was left open to canal traffic. The iron balcony on the pier was where the internal staircase came out, a ladder then leading up to the swing span deck, which was only meant to be climbed when the bridge was closed across the canal. T.B. OWEN

BELOW: *Magnus II* is recorded in the diary entries in Ron Huxley's book as lifting the spans from piers No's 5 and 6, and 4 and 5 on 10th September, and then leaving for Hamburg on the following day. Those spans have clearly been removed here but the photographer gave the date as 8th September. Further, as we shall see, this was not to be the end of the crane's work, which calls some of the diary entries into question. BILL POTTER/KRM

RIGHT: The other casualty of the Severn Road Bridge, seen here in the left background, was the Beachley-Aust car ferry. The ferry ceased operating when the bridge opened on 8th September 1966 and this view shows cars waiting to cross at Beachley Pier on one of the last days. NPC

BOLT FROM SEVERN RAILWAY BRIDGE WHERE SPAN WAS FIXED TO TOP OF COLUMN. BRIDGE TAKEN DOWN IN 1967.

A.W.T. SEPT. 1967.

ABOVE: Clearly taken on the same day as the view overleaf, the last three spans to be lifted await removal from the sandbanks to the shore. However, this was not done before the crane departed, although quite why is not clear, as several spans had already been dumped on the river bank on the Sharpness side. It may have been deemed cheaper, given the hire cost of the crane, to leave them where they were. BILL POTTER/KRM

LEFT: The head of a bolt from the Severn Bridge, which was given to the noted Dean archaeologist A.W. Trotter by the demolition crew in September 1967 and is now in the author's collection. NPC

BELOW: A view of the remains of the bridge from the river bank alongside the old dock, again taken on 8th September. BILL POTTER/KRM

LEFT: Three more views taken on Bill's visit on 8th September. This first picture is interesting because it shows the swing span was still in operation, here closed across the canal and with smoke rising from one of the cabin chimneys. Some of the scrap was removed via the bridge, which is why the swing span remained in use. No record has been found to date as to when it was swung for the last time. Dismantling of the steam engines, signal cabin and span began in late 1969, with the bridge in the open position, so it is likely to have been just prior to then. BILL POTTER/KRM

ABOVE AND RIGHT: At least six of the recovered spans were dumped on the eastern bank close to the swing bridge. As these pictures show, they were lifted from the piers complete with sections of track still in place, the cutting crew having simply sliced through the rails with their acetylene torches. Lengths of gas pipe can also be seen inside some of the spans. Nordmans had hoped to sell the spans for re-use elsewhere, it is believed in South America. At least one report states that a road bridge was built in Chile utilising some of the spans from the Severn Bridge but there is no record of any sale being completed and those that were lifted off intact are believed to have all been cut up here during 1968 by Swinnerton & Miller Ltd, who took over the contract after Nordmans went bankrupt. BILL POTTER/KRM

A distant view of *Magnus II*, which Bill recorded was taken on 13th September 1967, two days after the diary entries in Ron Huxley's book notes the crane as having departed for Hamburg. In the five days since the previous pictures were taken, several more of the piers had been brought down, whilst the crane is seen here lifting the remains of the large spans, which had broken up as they fell into the river, forming a potential underwater hazard in the navigable channel. BILL POTTER/KRM

Moving further south along the river bank, photographer John Strange took several more pictures and, whilst assembling these pages, it was realised that these two joined almost perfectly to give a rather spectacular panorama of the Severn and the remains of the bridge. On the left edge of the picture, a crane can be seen at work on the masonry viaduct on the Lydney side of the river. A diary entry noted this as having been moved in to place on 20th September. Explosives were used to demolish the remaining piers and the last bit of the trestle, the pier stumps then being drilled to a depth of 12ft and more dynamite placed inside to destroy them as completely as possible. Explosives were also used to bring down the last three spans, although it was not until January 1969 that these were tackled. JOHN STRANGE/NPC

The part demolished bridge seen from the junction between the old and new arms of the canal on 2nd October 1967. Nearly three weeks after the departure of the floating crane, the three spans still sit in the river. On the right, the canal heads towards Sharpness New Dock, completed in 1874, whilst the arm on the left leads to the old dock and the S&WR wooden coal tip; the lock from this dock out into the river was finally closed as a cost cutting exercise in 1908 and the arm is today used as a marina. On the right is one of the gas holders of Sharpness Gasworks and a crane can just be made out positioned on the masonry viaduct in the right distance. JOHN STRANGE/NPC

Looking over the stacks of timber later on the same day, with the late afternoon sun painting the scene in rich autumnal hues. JOHN STRANGE/NPC

ABOVE: Sharpness Docks will be covered in detail in the next volume, *Gloucester Midland Lines*, but there are a couple of aspects of it which are relevant to this one. This view of the Old Dock was taken in January 1967 and shows the disused ex-S&WR wooden coal tip, with a couple of lighters moored in front loaded with timber for Gloucester; they will taken up the canal by tug. The white painted ship's bow just glimpsed in the right background belongs to the Training Ship *Vindicatrix*, which we shall also look at more closely in the next volume. JOHN STRANGE/THE TOWY COLLECTION

LEFT: A closer study of the coal tip from the opposite side in August 1965. Working on the counter balance principal, it was provided in 1880 shortly after the bridge opened and, despite being superceded by a larger tip in the main dock in 1908, continued to be used, tipping Forest coal brought across the Severn Bridge and then along the North Dock Branch. Much of this coal went into barges for delivery to the Cadbury factory alongside the canal at Frampton. After the bridge was damaged, the coal trains ran via Gloucester and Berkeley Road to reach the tip, which was used for the last time in 1965 and was demolished circa 1971. JOHN STRANGE/THE TOWY COLLECTION

ABOVE: The coal tip in early October 1967, with the remaining spans of the bridge in the background. The photograph is taken from the grounds of the Sharpness Hotel, built circa 1899 to replace premises originally used by the navvies building the new dock; it is now the Sharpness Dockers Club. JOHN STRANGE/NPC

An overall view of the New Dock looking north in June 1966, included here primarily because the barges in the foreground are laden with hardwood logs for the Pine End Works factory alongside Lydney Docks. The grey painted craft on the right is a floating pneumatic grain elevator, used for discharging grain direct from the hold of a ship into a waiting barge or the silos on the dockside (the concrete rendered buildings behind). The multi-storyed brick warehouse behind is today the last remaining of several similar buildings which used to stand on this side of the dock. NPC

A Sharpness-Berkeley Road auto on a layover between services on 17th October 1964, alongside the fixed Up Distant signal for Sharpness South, installed in 1956 when the layout at the station was altered significantly. This was a favoured point for train crews to wait for their next run up to Berkeley Road and was also the limit of operation after the closure of the bridge. The view is included here as a representation of a train arriving from the Lydney direction. Coming in from the left is the North Dock Branch, which was the direct route to the coal tips followed by Forest of Dean coal trains up until the mid 1950s. BILL POTTER/KRM

ABOVE: During the final four years of its life, when it played host to the auto-worked trains to and from Berkeley Road, Sharpness station enjoyed the attentions of numerous railway photographers. Prior to that, when it was on the through route from the Severn Bridge, it had slumbered in relative anonymity, so this circa 1957 colour view is rare indeed. The signal box, provided in 1903 as a replacement for the two original boxes sited to the north and south of the station, was equipped with a 33 lever frame and was to a standard GWR design in red and blue brick with a hipped slated roof. Uniquely, however, it also boasted a brick waiting shelter built as an extension to its front. The box was closed on 27th October 1957 and removed soon afterwards, and this is the only colour view seen to date which shows it. The station closed on 2nd November 1964 with the withdrawal of the passenger service but the single line running through was retained as a siding whilst the Severn bridge was dismantled; it was finally taken up in 1969. Nothing remains of the station today but the road bridge behind still stands, whilst top right there is just a glimpse of the Severn Bridge & Railway Hotel, which still remains although it is no longer in use as a hotel. NPC

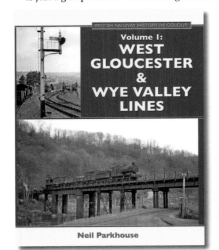

VOL. 1: WEST GLOUCESTER & WYE VALLEY LINES
280 pages. ISBN: 9781899889 76 1
Price: £24.99 plus £5.00 p&p
www.lightmoor.co.uk

The Severn Bridge from the Down platform at Sharpness in July 1959. The station and the branch to Berkeley Road will be covered extensively in the next volume. The signal in the background is on the North Dock Branch. T.B. OWEN

COLOUR IMAGES WANTED FOR THIS SERIES

There are still locations that I have little or nothing of for the planned further volumes in this series, whilst I am always interested in finding images for my collection from anywhere in the county. Anyone with colour slides or photographs of Gloucestershire railways that they would like to share with a wider audience and that I could possibly use in future volumes is invited to contact me directly at: The Bucklands, 80 Tutnalls Street, Lydney, Gloucestershire, GL15 5PQ (neil@lightmoor.co.uk)